FOREVER AGELESS

Your Personal Plan To:

Feel Sexier

Think Smarter

Have More Energy

By

Ron Rothenberg, MD
And
Kathleen Becker, MA, RN

Ron Rothenberg, MD
Kathleen Becker, MA, RN
California HealthSpan Institute
320 Santa Fe Drive, Suite 301
Encinitas, CA 92024
1-800-943-3331
1-760-635-1996
1-760-635-1994 (fax)
E-mail: info@ehealthspan.com

FOREVER AGELESS

The information contained in this book is based on scientific research and the professional experiences of the authors. The information is not intended to be a substitute for consulting with your physician or other health care providers. The publisher and the authors are not responsible for any possible adverse effects resulting from the suggestions contained in this book. All matters pertaining to your health, physical, mental or otherwise, should be supervised by a qualified health care professional.

Published by:
California HealthSpan Institute
320 Santa Fe Drive, Suite 301
Encinitas, CA 92024
(800) 943-3331

Book Producer:
Wilcox Literary Agency
1155 Camino Del Mar, Suite 173
Del Mar, CA 92014
(619) 230-7145

Book Design and Jacket Cover Design:
Thomas Hemann/DreamSchool
(917) 586-6434

Printed in the United States of America

ISBN 1-893436-19-5

Your CHI Internet Book Club site access code number is 7254512849
Visit the CHI website at **www.ehealthspan.com** and enter your
CHI Book Club access code.

ISBN 1-893436-19-5

51995

DEDICATION

To our families whose love and support enriches us daily

To all of the scientists, physicians and other professionals whose daily work in the field of anti-aging medicine offers humanity the tools to combat the disease of aging

and

To our patients whose belief in what we do has afforded us the opportunity to continue to help more and more people improve the quantity and quality of their lives

AUTHORS' NOTE

<u>FOREVER AGELESS</u> was written to educate you about the field of anti-aging medicine and also to be a reference and a companion guide as you embark on your personal anti-aging program. We realize that there is a large amount of information to absorb in this book and we tried to make the scientific information interesting.

We hope that you will read the book in its entirety and incorporate many of the suggestions into your daily life for improved health and well-being. The chapter summaries are to be used as a review or if you do not wish to read each chapter completely, you may refer to the chapter summaries, which highlight the important points in each chapter.

If you want to get started on your own anti-aging program immediately, begin by reading Part Two of the book first. At CHI, we believe that knowledge empowers people to make informed decisions. With that in mind, we hope <u>FOREVER AGELESS</u> empowers you to make informed decisions about your health and your health care options.

CONTENTS

ACKNOWLEDGMENTS

No project is ever done in a vacuum and so it is with this book. Three years ago, California HealthSpan Institute arose out of a need to medically address and treat the signs and symptoms of aging in a scientifically based manner. The Institute has grown over the years due to the hard work of an extremely dedicated staff and the more than satisfactory results our patients have experienced with their anti-aging medical programs.

Over the years, patients and colleagues requested a guidebook that was simple, straightforward and easy to follow, which spelled out just what we did at California HealthSpan Institute. In response to those requests, we created this book. We hope that <u>Forever Ageless</u> will help everyone who reads it have a more robust and healthy life.

We would like to thank Barry Sears, Ph.D., friend and colleague, for his incredible scientific contribution in the field of nutrition and health. The Zone diet is not another quick-fix, fad diet but the diet human beings need to eat to stay healthy and hormonally balanced. We also want to thank our wonderful nutritionist, Coreen Reinhart, who counsels our patients on eating a hormonally correct diet. Coreen is an integral member of our team and continually strives to help all of our patients reach their dietary goals.

Since our beginning, we have had a number of personal trainers on our staff and we thank them all for their contributions to our successful comprehensive anti-aging program. We thank Mike and Tami LeBoss, Tom Serrato and a special thanks to Jacob Harry, whose expertise in exercise physiology and application made the chapter on exercise informative and easy to follow for anyone wishing to begin an effective exercise program.

We want to give special thanks to Jerry Greene, Pharm.D. and his colleagues at University Compounding Pharmacy who work with us daily to meet the needs of our patients. We also want to thank Medquest Pharmacy for their incredible service and commitment to providing cutting-edge technology in many areas of anti-aging medicine.

We could not do our job without reliable and timely laboratory services. Special thanks goes to Claudia Scott, our Lab Corp representative in the San Diego region, who ensures that our laboratory needs are met. We also want to thank the staff at Pinnacle Labs for their diligence in making sure all of our customers throughout the country obtain accurate laboratory services in their local areas.

Finally, we want to thank our office manager, Kris Rosinski and our administrative staff, especially Linda Miller, who kept the home fires burning when we had deadlines to meet in regards to this book.

We are forever grateful to our team at California HealthSpan Institute and to our patients who make our professional lives very rewarding and give us the impetus to continue to forge ahead in this wonderful field of preventive medicine.

FOREWORD

Reversing the aging process has been the goal of mankind since the beginning of recorded history. Now, for the first time, it may be possible to retard that seemingly immutable process. Obviously, no one is going to live forever but it is reasonable to expect to live longer and better. In my opinion, what this means is that you can reasonably expect to have a biological age that is 15 to 20 years less than your chronological age. To achieve that goal, you are going to have to maintain the fidelity of transferring biological information between your 60 trillion cells for as long as possible. When this cellular fidelity fails, your metabolic processes begin to break down and we experience the process of aging.

What ultimately controls this information flow in your body are hormones. Therefore, retarding or even reversing the aging process means controlling your hormones. It is true that as we age, many hormones decrease. Today, however, knowledgeable physicians can effectively replace declining hormone levels. What is not well recognized is that many hormones actually increase as we age and elevated levels of these hormones can only be reduced by diet and lifestyle changes.

Hormonal replacement without treating diet and lifestyle, as if they were drugs to be taken at the right time and with the right dosage, means it will be unlikely that you will ever achieve the maximum extent of anti-aging potential regardless of any amount of hormone replacement therapy.

FOREVER AGELESS presents a comprehensive overview of how hormonal replacement, diet and lifestyle require an integrated approach if you want to retard or reverse the aging process. This book gives you the necessary information to improve your quality of life but it is up to you to incorporate the advice into your every day life.

I have known Ron Rothenberg, M.D., for a number of years and I can guarantee that he is a person who practices the diet and lifestyle he shares with you in this book. The diet and lifestyle changes addressed in this book will always be the foundation upon which any additional hormone replacement therapy should be based since no two people are alike. FOREVER AGELESS is based on years of clinical observations on how individualized hormone replacement programs should be constructed.

As you read the book, I hope you will begin to understand that reversing the aging process is primarily in your hands and, with the advice and support of a qualified physician, reversing the aging process can be taken to an even higher level. If living longer and better is your goal, then reading this book is an excellent starting point.

Barry Sears, Ph.D.

PART ONE

OVERVIEW OF ANTI-AGING MEDICINE

AND

THE MENO AND ANDRO "PAUSE" IN YOUR LIFE

WHAT IS ANTI-AGING MEDICINE

MALE MENOPAUSE, FEMALE MENOPAUSE

CHAPTER ONE

WHAT IS ANTI-AGING MEDICINE

The world is changing and so is the way we view our health and well being as we age. We no longer have to accept the relentless mental and physical declines associated with aging. When we throw away old concepts and look at the something quite differently, it is called a paradigm shift. Looking at aging as a disease that can be treated, may be the biggest paradigm shift in human history. Anti-aging medical interventions, under the supervision of a trained and board certified anti-aging physician, can change your life right now. In the near future, with the advances in medical technology, including human gene research, your life and society will change in previously unimaginable ways. This book will start you on your journey towards improved health and well being. It will teach you the science (anyone can learn it) and help you create a practical and personal anti-aging plan.

This paradigm shift is not based on dreams or science fiction; it is firmly documented in medical and scientific literature. Ownership of this book entitles you to access the latest updates in anti-aging medicine, available on our website. Since anti-aging medicine is changing so rapidly, a book alone without updates would be stuck with yesterday's information and scientific references. For example, when new information is available on the material on page "X", download the update and you have the most current anti-aging information at your fingertips. Also, if you wish to read the abstract of the study referenced, just click on it and voila... We want to interact with you and answer your questions because we want you to have a healthier lifestyle. When you own this book, you can be a member of the California HealthSpan Institute Internet book club. You are in with the "anti-aging in-crowd."

This book is your guide to your personal anti-aging program. We will give you recommendations as to diet, exercise, vitamins, neutraceuticals and hormone replacement therapy. We do not want you to rely on the teenage clerk in a vitamin store (although he or she may be knowledgeable) or your friend who sells vitamins through a multi-level marketing program. It is our goal to provide you with the same information we give our patients. State of the art information changes from day to day and we will keep you current with quarterly updates on our website. Our medical practice provides cutting edge anti-aging medical care. Our goal is good health and a better quality of life by slowing and even reversing the degenerative effects of aging, for our patients and for all who read this book. It is not our primary business to sell vitamins or supplements and we have no vested interest in any particular company that does. Because we are able to remain objective, we can be your advocate. We want to empower you with the scientific knowledge that is the foundation of health and medicine. What you are about to read are not just directions for you to follow about how much of this or that vitamin; they are guidelines based on fact and proven clinically to be successful in slowing and preventing the disease of aging.

These ideas may seem "crazy" to you now but we encourage you to keep an open mind. Continue reading and the data will be presented.

Paradigm shifts:
• There is no biological reason why animals (including humans) have to age

• Immortality is possible (Not in a spiritual sense but in this body, in this life. In a certain sense there are immortal animals)

•Our hormones do not decline because we age, we age because our hormones decline

• There is no reason why humans cannot live to what is considered the maximum lifespan (125 years of age) with full mental and physical function. Of course, no one wants to merely accumulate more years if there is disability or poor quality of life. The goal is to increase "healthspan" not just lifespan

• The maximum lifespan of humans will constantly increase and may even double within a generation

• Wouldn't it be a shame if you were the last person to die from aging?

Anti-Aging Medicine:

There is a new field of medicine, which has examined the research of what causes illness, what causes aging, what causes the decline in physical and mental function. This field is called anti-aging medicine. Physicians practicing anti-aging medicine have begun to offer their patients individualized plans to slow and even reverse aging. Modern medicine will keep many of us alive until we are 100-plus but no one wants to get older with more disabilities. A longer lifespan would be desirable if we are strong and healthy. Approximately 50% of the population, over 80 years of age, have Alzheimer's disease, and large percentages of the older population have type II diabetes, arthritis, osteoporosis and cardiovascular disease. Living longer with these types of disorders does not sound too appealing. We do not want you to be one of the people whose quality of life decreases because you are getting older. We now know, through the practices of anti-aging medicine, that we can alter these dire predictions. What is the difference between traditional medicine and anti-aging medicine? Traditional medicine focuses on treating the effects of the aging process while anti-aging medicine focuses on treating or preventing the causes of aging. Traditional medicine predominately treats external symptoms, which primarily have internal causes. In traditional medicine there is some mention of prevention, some advice about diet but little discussion as to the most hormonally correct type of diet for the human species. There is also some discussion about exercise but what kind of exercise and how much is rarely discussed. Traditional medicine does make an effort towards controlling some risk factors for cardiovascular disease such as cholesterol, although there are more important risk factors that need to be evaluated. Unfortunately, more times than not, traditional medicine reacts to losses and crises in health. If you have a heart attack, use clot busters or surgical procedures. If you develop Alzheimer's or senile dementia, try this medicine or that, even though it probably will not do anything. Anti-aging medicine, on the other hand, works to change the process of aging itself.

Is anti-aging medicine alternative medicine or integrative medicine? No! Anti-aging medicine is "medicine" which combines traditional principles with current medical and technological advances. Is anti-aging medicine the same as geriatric medicine? In a way, it is the opposite. Geriatric medicine helps people cope with the losses of aging, anti-aging medicine seeks to prevent and reverse the losses associated with aging.

This new specialty of medicine, created in 1993 by a small group of forward-thinking physicians, formed The American Academy of Anti-Aging Medicine (A4M). The Academy now has more than 10,000 physician and scientific members, and is the fastest growing scientific society in the world today.

Is anti-aging just an expression of vanity; does it just mean looking younger? No. Anti-aging is the ultimate expression of preventive medicine. We want to maintain function on the highest level, prevent disease and maintain health. A side effect of anti-aging is that you will look younger with improved body composition (muscle to fat ratio) improved skin appearance and even possible reversal of hair loss and graying. The primary goal, however, is improved health and well being! The only way to slow or reverse aging is to slow, prevent or reverse the diseases of aging.

Is anti-aging medicine just part of the current obsession with the physical and does it neglect the spiritual? No. With good health and clear mental-functioning a person can pursue his or her spiritual path with strength and clarity; free from the distractions of illness. The wisdom of age can be communicated clearly to younger generations by the smart, strong and vigorous. It has long been known that spiritual beliefs and practices are effective components of preventive medicine, which help diminish disease and improve outcomes of illnesses.

What about sex?

I thought you would never ask! Anti-aging medicine can restore sexual function to younger levels and it can actually increase sexual function to levels greater than a person had in his or her twenties. For example, women may experience more frequent and intense orgasms, greater nipple and clitoral sensitivity, greater energy and improved body image. For men: even if a 40 something, 50 something or 60 something man thinks his sexual function is okay; if you ask the man about erectile tension (firmness and angle of erections) he might say, "Well, it's not the same as when I was 20." We tell them, "It can be." Add to this a prolonged duration of firm erections, a quicker recovery time between ejaculations and the experience of years of having sex, and wow! Watch out! The improved body image with more lean muscle mass and less fat also helps. Let's not neglect the emotional and intimacy aspects of sex because sex is not just a mechanical act. With improved physical and mental functions, emotional intimacy can also be enhanced. An enhanced sex life helps a person's self-image, confidence and sense of well-being and of course, quality of life.

Society and Anti-Aging:

What about the effects on society of anti-aging medicine? Will all of these old people be a burden to society? Quite the opposite. A vigorous, healthy older population will benefit society in many ways. Many will choose to continue working, contributing and paying taxes instead of retiring. Delaying the degenerative diseases of aging will save society billions. For each year Alzheimer's dementia can be delayed it would save the U.S. economy 6 billion dollars. Won't this money just be spent later if disease is just delayed, but you would get it anyway? No. Since the goal of anti-aging medicine is to rectangularize the functionality curve. That is, to maintain all functions, heart, brain, muscle, lungs etc. at a high level to the end and then fall apart quickly all at once. Isn't that what everyone wants?

What Is Aging?

What is aging and where did it come from? Why do we age? Is there a useful function that it serves such as "kill off the old to make room for the young?" Is it inevitable that things including our bodies and our minds just break down like an aging car?

Aging is the progressive failure of metabolic processes. Each kind of cell in our body has a function to perform. Heart muscle cells have to function for our heart to beat; the nerve cells in our brain have to function so we can think. If the chemical processes in these cells fail then we will have aging of that type of cell and deterioration of the entire organism. We could look at aging as a progressive chance of dying with each advancing year. For example, a person who is 70 years of age has a greater chance of dying in the next year than a person who is 30 years of age.

The Theories of Aging:

There are many theories of what causes aging. We will discuss the major ones and no doubt, there is a combination of causes. From each theory we will explore common themes and what can we learn from each theory and what we can apply today, to advance our own anti-aging program.

To put aging into perspective, we have to think about natural selection. As you know, Darwin came up with this theory to explain the variation of plants and animals on this earth. The principle as most people know it is "Survival of the fittest." Genes are the blueprints of how to make an animal (or person). There is some variation of genes due to combining the genes of the two parents and to random mutations in the genes. If an animal is more "successful" he or she has more offspring and the particular genes are passed on to a greater number of descendents. Therefore, their genes become more frequent in the population. So, our genes have to keep us alive until reproductive age and they keep us alive until we can raise our offspring until they are old enough, strong enough and wise enough to have successful offspring of their own. Could aging have some benefit to society or to an individual? Incorrect arguments could be made: Could it be helpful to get rid of the old? Could aging help an individual? For example, could the decline in hormones protect against cancer?

Let's think about this in terms of natural selection. Changes that take place after reproduction cannot be passed on to the next generation. Assume that there were two animals in a population. A gene mutation occurred to make one run faster. This might help the animal escape predators or catch more food. The odds are that the animal that had this gene would be more successful. He or she would survive to have more offspring and this gene would be seen more and more in the population. To continue this thought experiment, let's say a gene appeared that would cause aging: the decline of physical and mental function after a certain age. Would this gene cause the animal to be more successful and have more offspring? How could it? First of all, it would make its appearance known after reproduction, and secondly, how would it help the animal in the first place?

From this analysis we can see that aging cannot be programmed into our genes to confer some benefit on the species. Aging is obviously in our genes, but maybe it got there by accident and it offers no advantage to an individual or a species.

Another way of looking at this situation is that animals (and humans) don't age in the wild. The lifespan of humans in the Paleolithic era was about 18 years old. Humans died from starvation, trauma (fighting, accidents) infectious disease, etc. Zoo animals age like humans but animals in the wild do not. As you can see, natural selection had no reason to increase human lifespan since those changes would not really alter things and would not increase offspring because life was hard and humans died young. Okay, enough about evolution. Why do we age and what can we do about it? Again, aging is probably a combination of causes, but we want you to be an expert on the leading causes of aging. Each of these causes will suggest an approach to reversing or halting the deterioration of aging. So lets learn a little more science and get ready to take action!

Free Radical Theory:

In 1954, Denham Harman came up with the free radical theory to explain why we age at the cellular level. If cells age, then the entire body ages because we are made up of cells.

During the process of metabolism (burning food to produce energy for our cells) free radicals are a byproduct, analogous to toxic fumes produced by a factory or an automobile. We are also attacked by free radicals from the external environment, from radiation and from toxins.

The definition of a free radical is a molecule with an unpaired electron in its outermost ring. This is an unstable molecule, which tries to latch on to another molecule and get that missing electron, so it will have an even pair. This pairing process destroys the other molecule and "Cellular World War III" results. If the DNA is damaged when the cell divides to make new cells, the copies will be wrong and whatever function that cell performs will not be done correctly. Most of this free radical action takes place in the mitochondria. The mitochondria are the energy power plants of the cells. Without energy the cell cannot do whatever it is supposed to do and this results in a loss of physical, immune or mental function.

Did you know that we have two sets of DNA? One is the "nuclear dna" which we inherit from our parents. This "nuclear dna" contains the entire blueprint of how to build a "you" and also provides instructions for the operation of all the activities of our cells. The other DNA is a simpler set of genes in the mitochondria. We inherit this DNA from our mothers. If this DNA is damaged our cellular power plants, the mitochondria, shut down.

Since we are burning our fuel in the mitochondria, that is where most of our free radicals are produced. Fortunately, we have built-in antioxidants in the human body, especially the antioxidant, Coenzyme Q10 in the mitochondria and others, SOD (Superoxide dismutase) GTH (glutathione) and CAT (catalase). These powerful built-in antioxidants keep us alive through the reproductive age. However, after our 30's these built-in antioxidants cannot keep up with the cellular damage that has been produced by free radicals.
It is interesting to note that the lifespan of a species is proportional to the number of built-in antioxidants it has. Great apes, such as chimps and gorillas, have 98% of the same DNA as humans but their lifespan is only half that of humans. One of the reasons for this is that they have only half the amount of the built-in antioxidants as humans. To better understand this theory, let's go back to what we discussed about evolution. A gorilla child does not need as long a period of education to survive as a human so the species does not have to live as long for successful reproduction and helping the next generation become independent.

Since free radicals are a problem, what is the solution? You guessed it. Let's blot up those free radicals with antioxidants. We have our built-in ones but let's maximize the ones we consume. In the Paleolithic era, our ancestors did not have agriculture and hence, all of the carbohydrates they consumed were fresh fruits and vegetables. Fruits and vegetables are our primary source of antioxidants. Vitamins and other nutraceuticals take us beyond the level of food, but food is the foundation for obtaining necessary antioxidants. Please remember this fact when we talk about the Zone diet and eliminating or limiting the "bad" carbohydrates. We do not get a significant amount of anti-oxidants from "bad" carbohydrates like breads, pasta, desserts, etc.

Since our ancestors evolved with fruits and vegetables as their only source of antioxidants why would we need to take all those pills and capsules? Why can't we just eat a "balanced diet"? As you will learn, there are many different ideas on what a balanced diet is but there is only one way to eat a hormonally correct diet. Further, modern fruits and vegetables, grown industrially, are grown in soil that is often depleted and does not contain adequate amounts of vitamins, minerals and other necessary elements.

Evolution only gets us through reproductive age. We need antioxidant protection for perhaps a hundred years more. The doses of vitamins that we take are often "pharmacological" doses. This means that we are taking them for an effect that is beyond what we could get from food. For example, a dose of Vitamin C that is beneficial for most people is 2 grams (2000 mg) a day. An orange has about 50 mg of vitamin C. So, it would be a busy day of orange eating to get that much Vitamin C. The same goes for vitamin E, etc.

Of all the anti-aging interventions in animal studies, calorie restriction with adequate nutrition has the strongest supporting data. Starvation is definitely not a healthy intervention. However, consuming about 40% less calories but with plenty of protein, good fats and vitamins reduces the diseases of aging and can increase longevity by 50%. This is a rather extreme lifestyle for most people (us included) and I am not recommending that you follow this. We can learn from this information, however. Why does calorie restriction work? Perhaps if we are eating fewer calories, we burn less glucose in our mitochondria and produce less free radicals.

The Neuroendocrine Theory
or "Hormones-R-Us:"

We age because our hormones decline, our hormones do not decline because we age. This paradigm shift could be expanded to add that we age because some of our hormones undesirably increase as we age as well. This is one of the paradigm shifts that anti-aging medicine explores, analyzes, and acts upon with balanced hormone replacement therapy. An important concept is what is a "normal" hormone level and what is a desirable or ideal hormone level. We will discard the old concept that "normal for age" is fine. For example, if a 75-year-old woman's estrogen level is zero, this might be "normal for age". But this absence of estrogen, which her body needs to function properly, may have grave consequences by causing decline in brain, bone, cardiovascular and sexual function. A 50-year old man or woman's testosterone can be "normal for age." Again, restoring the level to a youthful range can have powerful preventive medicine and anti-aging effects.

Welcome to world of hormones, the chemical messengers made in one area of the body, which travel to other areas of the body to regulate all of the body's functions. We now know that hormones have multiple roles that are just being discovered and the old idea of a limited and specific role for most hormones is obsolete. For example, you will learn that testosterone is more than a male hormone and more than a sex hormone. Women need testosterone too. Every cell in our body has receptor sites for testosterone to plug-in and exercise its effects. The same can be said for estrogen. Actually, there is no such thing as estrogen, there are three different estrogens in humans, but we are getting ahead of ourselves.

One of the most exciting aspects of the neuroendocrine theory of aging and hormones is that we can treat the loss of our hormones with balanced natural or bio-identical hormone replacement therapy. We can be proactive and take control. We can measure hormonal blood levels and replace the lacking hormones to maintain the 20-something level indefinitely. Yes, for the duration. Didn't most of us feel our strongest and healthiest in our twenties? In our twenties, there is the least incidence of cancer, virtually no cardiovascular disease and usually no type II diabetes. Will keeping our hormones at the 20-year old level make us 20 years old again? Of course not. We have a lot more experience in life and hopefully better judgement. There is a chance to even be better than we were at twenty.

Hormone replacement therapy has been studied in depth and data is present in the medical literature for the benefits of natural hormone (bio-identical) replacement therapy. In general, the benefits are overwhelming, although there are some concerns and certainly a need for sound medical judgement. Many excellent physicians are not aware of the current data supporting this medical intervention and the "paradigm shift" that is the foundation of anti-aging medicine. Physicians who have studied the anti-aging literature are educated about this current knowledge. Since this area is so controversial and emotional there is an extensive reference list to back up what you read in this book and in our updates. As you already know, you will be able to regularly download current references if you wish to explore the medical literature and read the evidence to support what we are saying.

What hormones do we control in our anti-aging program? Who manages this? Although an educated consumer can begin his or her anti-aging hormone program and certainly control insulin levels through diet, a qualified physician is needed for medical supervision. Some hormones can be bought over the counter in the United States, where the same hormones are prescription drugs in other countries. We carefully study and control most of the hormones in the human body, because hormones work together for optimal function. That's why we call this "balanced hormone replacement therapy." All patients may not need intervention with every hormone; every patient has different needs and every patient is unique. The following is the list of hormones we evaluate with all of our patients. You will learn more about the specifics of each hormone in later chapters.

- Insulin
- Cortisol
- DHEA (dehydroepiandrosterone)
- Pregnenolone
- Testosterone
- DHT (dihydrotestosterone)
- Estrogens (Estrone, Estradiol, Estriol)
- Progesterone
- Thyroid (T3,T4)

Telomere Theory of Aging:

Telomeres are the end segments of our DNA. Every time a cell divides, the two strands (the double helix) of DNA uncoil and each strand gets copied so the two new cells each have a new DNA double helix. Each time a cell divides, it looses a piece of the telomere and when enough is lost the cell cannot reproduce. When cells cannot reproduce, a given tissue cannot be replenished and this causes aging of our tissues and our entire body. Running out of telomeres is then one of the causes of aging.

Now for some scientific background: It was once thought that if a scientist grew cells in vitro (that means outside of the body) in a tissue culture, the cells would divide indefinitely if good scientific techniques were followed. Leonard Hayflick showed that each cell type has a limited number of times it could divide; this became known as the Hayflick limit. What caused this limit? Where was the counter in the cell that kept track of the number of divisions? Now you know the answer - the telomere. Telomeres are sequences of 6 DNA bases; TTAGGG (Thymine, Thymine, Adenine, Guanine, Guanine, and Guanine). Each time the DNA divides, one of these sequences is lost. The telomere functions as a type of plastic shoelace cap that holds the DNA together. When this is lost, the "shoelace" fragments.

Certain cells produce an enzyme called teleomerase. An enzyme is an organic substance that causes a chemical reaction in the body. Every type of enzyme in the body has a specific action. The telomerase enzyme rebuilds the telomere and makes the cell "immortal."Of course, not really immortal since the cell can be killed or crushed but it will not slow down and die from "aging." You may be surprised that these immortal cells are quite common. One example is the spermatogonia cell in the male. Females are born with all their egg cells but males continuously make sperm cells. These germ cells of life have changed and mutated through the eons but the cell line has never died. If it did there would not be any life. How about a lowly bacterium like E. coli? It's immortal. Again, that doesn't mean that you can't kill it but since it reproduces by dividing in two, the original one doesn't actually die. The germ cell line and the E Coli "express" telomerase.

There are even more complex "immortal" organisms like sea anemones or hydras that reproduce by budding instead of sexual reproduction. Sexually reproducing animals express telomerase in the germ cells but do not in the rest of the body. You could look at a sexually reproducing animal (like us) as a DNA replicating machine with a disposable body. But we have a sentimental attachment to this disposable item since it is our mind and body. Animals that reproduce a-sexually are immortal. Therefore, we could say, scientifically that "the penalty for sex is death." What a thought!

Now, the bad news about telomerase. Cancer cells express telomerase. That is the problem with cancer cells. They just keep dividing and making new ones and these cells damage our bodies and can kill us. There is hope, however, in terms of eventually eliminating cancer. Lets look to the near future. If we could control telomerase, we would have a powerful tool that would stop cancer and would make our cells immortal.

Recently, experiments have been done which take old cells without any telomeres left and reverse the loss of telomeres by transferring the cell into an egg cell that has its nucleus removed. Will control of telomerase be an anti-aging treatment in the near future? Stay tuned and we will keep you informed in our updates.

Other Theories of Aging:

Glycation: glucose that accumulates in our tissues causes cross-links in proteins, enzymes and cell membranes. This leads to loss of function of our cells. This may be why patients with diabetes tragically experience the complications of aging at younger ages. Recently, an amino acid supplement known as Carnosine has been shown to slow glycation. We have even started taking the supplement ourselves and recommend it to our patients. Less glycation may be another reason that calorie restriction (mentioned previously in the free radical section) is an effective anti-aging treatment. We can limit glycation in the same we can limit free radical damage; eat what we need, which is not typical of the high-gylcemic-index-carbohydrate American diet. We can control tissue glucose levels by eating hormonally correctly, which combines favorable carbohydrates, favorable proteins and favorable fats. (You'll hear this mantra over and over in this book).

Future anti-aging treatments:

The near future (within 5 years) has exciting potential. The theories of aging discussed above suggest some of these. Since genes for endogenous (built-in) antioxidants are so important for the lifespan of a species, how about increasing the genes in humans that produce the key endogenous anti-oxidants, SOD (super-oxide dismutase) GTH (glutathione) and CAT (catalase)?

Once we improve our genes, how about manipulating the genes that cause aging? Because aging serves no useful purpose and got into our genome accidentally, it has been speculated that there are only a handful of genes that cause aging and the degenerative diseases of aging. Lets get rid of them!

Embryonic stem cell research holds great potential for the treatment and prevention of human disease including the "disease" of aging. Embryonic stems cells (ESC's) are the inner cell mass of the developing embryo (called pre-embryo by some). These cells are totipotent, which means they have the potential to form any cell in the body and in fact, they do form all the cells of the body. Stem cell transplants have been used in medicine for some time in patients whose bone marrow has been destroyed by cancer chemotherapy. The stem cells can produce the needed blood cells that the marrow usually produces. What if we could grow stem cells out of our own DNA? Michael West of Advanced Cell Technology has done this. What if we could take our "old" cells and grow ESC's with young telomeres? The potential is limitless. Could we grow new organs to replace our failing ones? The new organs would not be rejected by the immune system since they would be made of your own DNA. Could we inject the ESC's intravenously or into the brain? Would the ESC's know where to go and what to do to create youthful cells in our minds and bodies? As Michael Fossel, MD, points out, aging is a tug of war that we can win. If the rate of repair to our DNA, cells, tissues, organs and bodies is equal to the rate of damage. The future potential is limitless!

Now that you know some of the theories of aging, we will take you on an educational journey that can change your life by improving your health and sense of well-being. Let the journey begin.

REMEMBER THIS

- Anti-aging medical interventions, under the supervision of a trained and board certified anti-aging physician, can change your life right now

- Our hormones do not decline because we age, we age because our hormones decline

- Wouldn't it be a shame if you were the last person to die from aging

- Currently, about 50% of the population, over 80 years of age, have Alzheimer's disease, and large percentages of the older population have type II diabetes, arthritis, osteoporosis and cardiovascular disease

- Traditional medicine focuses on treating the effects of the aging process while anti-aging medicine focuses on treating or preventing the causes of aging

- Traditional medicine predominately treats external symptoms, which primarily have internal causes

- Anti-aging medicine is "medicine" which combines traditional principles with current medical and technological advances

- Anti-aging medicine can restore sexual function to younger levels and it can actually increase sexual function to levels greater than a person had in his or her twenties

- An enhanced sex life helps a person's self-image, confidence, sense of well-being and quality of life

- The benefits of aging include increased levels of knowledge, wisdom and experience

- The only way to slow or reverse aging is to slow, prevent or reverse the diseases of aging

- For each year Alzheimer's dementia can be delayed it would save the U.S. economy 6 billion dollars

- Aging is the progressive failure of metabolic processes

- Aging is obviously in our genes, but maybe it got there by accident and it offers no advantage to an individual or a species

- Aging is probably a combination of causes

- If cells age, then the entire body ages because we are made-up of cells

- During the process of metabolism (burning food to produce energy for our cells) free radicals are a byproduct

- A free radical is a molecule with an unpaired electron in its outer shell

- Free radicals looking for a partner, destroy cells

- Since free radicals are a problem, let's blot up free radicals with antioxidants

- Fruits and vegetables are our primary source of antioxidants

- Vitamins and other nutraceuticals take us beyond the level of food and provide additional free radical protection with their antioxidant properties

- A dose of Vitamin C that is beneficial for most people is 2 grams (2000 mg) a day

- By eating fewer calories, we burn less glucose in our mitochondria and produce less free radicals

- Hormones are the chemical messengers made in one area of the body, which travel to other areas of the body to regulate all of the body's functions

- We can treat the loss of our hormones with balanced natural (bio-identical) hormone replacement therapy

- Restoring hormone levels to a youthful range can have powerful preventive medicine and anti-aging effects

- Hormones work together for optimal function in the body

- Insulin, Cortisol, DHEA (dehydroepiandrosterone), Pregnenolone, Testosterone, DHT (dihydrotestosterone), Estrogens (Estrone, Estradiol, Estriol), Progesterone, Thyroid (T3,T4) are all major hormones in the body that will be discussed in this book

- Telomeres are the end segments of our DNA

- Each cell type has a limited number of times it can divide and this is known as the Hayflick limit

- Each time a cell divides, it looses a piece of the telomere and when enough is lost the cell cannot reproduce

- When cells cannot reproduce, a given tissue cannot be replenished and this causes aging of our tissues and our entire body

- Running out of telomeres is one of the causes of aging

- Glycation: glucose that accumulates in our tissues causes cross-links in proteins, enzymes and cell membranes, which leads to loss of function of our cells

- We can control tissue glucose levels by eating hormonally correctly, which includes eating favorable carbohydrates, favorable proteins and favorable fats

- Future anti-aging treatments may include gene manipulation, stem cell replacement and an array of exciting new technologies and trends

CHAPTER TWO

MENOPAUSE

Before we discuss male and female menopause separately, we thought it would be interesting to list the similarities between male and female menopause. Male menopause, which usually occurs gradually over a thirty- (30) year period is the result of declining testosterone levels while female menopause, which usually transpires over a five- (5) to ten- (10) year period is the result of declining estrogen, progesterone and testosterone levels.

MALE MENOPAUSE	FEMALE MENOPAUSE
• Decreased testosterone levels	• Decreased estrogen, progesterone and testosterone levels
• Increased body fat	• Increased body fat
• Decreased sense of well-being	• Decreased sense of well-being
• Decreased sexual function	• Decreased sexual function
• Increased incidence of cardiovascular disease	• Increased incidence of cardiovascular disease
• Increased incidence of osteoporosis	• Increased incidence of osteoporosis
• Increased incidence of prostate cancer	• Increased incidence of breast cancer

Since the signs and symptoms of male menopause are currently less
widely recognized as the signs and symptoms of female
menopause, the following test will help men determine if they are
experiencing male menopause.

Male Menopause Test

For each symptom answer 0 to 4 with (1) = No (2) = Rarely (3) =
Usually (4) = Yes

SYMPTOM	SCORE
1. Fatigue, tiredness or loss of energy	
2. Depression, low or negative mood	
3. Irritability, anger or bad temper	
4. Anxiety or nervousness	
5. Loss of memory or concentration	
6. Relationship problems with partner	
7. Loss of sex drive or libido	
8. Erection problems during sex	
9. Loss of morning erections	
10. Decreased intensity of orgasms	
11. Backache, joint pains or stiffness	
12. Heavy drinking past or present	
13. Loss of physical fitness	
14. Feelings of being over-stressed	
TOTAL	

SCORING:

0 - 9	Male menopause unlikely
10 - 19	Male menopause possible
20 - 29	Male menopause probable
30 - 39	Male menopause definite
40 - 56	Male menopause advanced stages

Male Menopause

Testosterone is an essential hormone in men and women. Every cell in the body has receptor sites for testosterone. It is a total body hormone, not just a sex hormone. Natural testosterone replacement therapy has dramatic benefits on health, mood, well-being and sexuality. Let's talk about testosterone and men first.

Every hormone has a "pause." Menopause, which we will discuss later, is defined as the cessation of production of estrogens and progesterone by the ovaries in women. Although women experience a peri-menopausal period prior to actual menopause, generally speaking, a woman undergoes a rather sudden change in hormone levels at around the age of 50. "Andropause" or "male menopause" is defined as the decline in testosterone production by the testicles in men. Male menopause can be a gradual process and varies from one man to the next, but andropause, just like female menopause can have severe health consequences in the long-term. Male menopause symptoms may be subtle, with a gradual decline in function or it may be obvious. Some of the following symptoms may be a result of male menopause:

- Fatigue
- Depression
- Irritability "Grumpy old men" syndrome
- Reduced libido and sexual potency
- Decreased sexual desire and decreased sexual fantasies
- Decreased morning erections "When the only thing stiff in the morning is your back"
- Decreased firmness of erections
- Longer recovery time between orgasms
- Loss of drive and competitive edge
- Stiffness and pain in muscles and joints
- Decreased effectiveness of exercise workouts

More serious medical problems are associated with male menopause that affects the heart and the brain. There is increased aging of the heart and circulation which can lead to the increased incidence of heart attacks and strokes. Brain aging can cause decreased memory, decreased intelligence and the increased rate of dementia such as Alzheimer's dementia.

There is a strong association between decreased testosterone levels and type II diabetes (adult onset diabetes) in men. Type II diabetes can sometimes be "cured" or reversed with testosterone replacement therapy and eating a hormonally correct diet.

Decreased testosterone in men is also associated with elevated LDL (bad) cholesterol, osteoporosis, arthritis and depression.

The cause of male menopause is decreased bio-available (the testosterone that is available for the body to use) testosterone. Added factors that contribute to male menopause include stress, alcohol, increased fat (especially abdominal fat) and lack of exercise.

If low testosterone causes all these problems, from erectile dysfunction to heart attacks to depression, to diabetes; why isn't every older man (over the age of 50 or even younger) receiving testosterone replacement therapy? First, testosterone deficiency is often an unrecognized syndrome. Since it develops slowly, it may not seem to be a dramatic change to an individual man or to his doctor.

More importantly, it's all about paradigm shifts. The approach of medicine has been, "Oh well, that's just normal aging." However, since a major cause of the degeneration of aging is a decline in key hormone levels, lets keep the hormones youthful to prevent these changes. That is what we do in the practice of anti-aging medicine. What about the downside of testosterone replacement? What are the concerns and what is the information in the medical literature? In the past, the concerns about testosterone have been heart function and prostate problems. Considering the heart, the reasoning went like this: Men have more heart attacks than pre-menopausal women do. What is the difference between men and women? Testosterone. So, it must be the testosterone that is causing the heart disease. We now know this is a false assumption. Also, men who abused anabolic steroids had an increased incidence of heart problems. So it must be the testosterone.

What is the actual information in the medical literature and what are possible explanations of the increase in heart disease in men compared to women besides differences in testosterone?

In the last few years there have been a number of studies reported in major medical journals that conclude that testosterone dilates coronary arteries (heart arteries) bringing more blood flow to the heart. In men with angina (heart pain due to decreased blood flow to the heart muscle and may be a warning sign of a heart attack possibly about to happen) testosterone replacement by skin cream improves the symptoms and allows the patient to exercise without angina pain. Did you know that men with heart attacks have lower levels of testosterone and higher levels of estrogen in their bodies? There is no medical evidence which shows that testosterone causes heart disease. Further, it now appears that testosterone may be a potential treatment for heart attacks in men.

Why do pre-menopausal women have fewer heart attacks then men? An explanation may be the decreased iron levels in women. A certain amount of iron is necessary to make red blood cells but increased iron acts as a pro-oxidant. This is the opposite of an anti-oxidant such as vitamin E, vitamin C, beta-carotene etc. "Iron makes you rust" Pre-menopausal women are loosing blood from their menstrual periods and do not have the iron overload found in most men.

When a woman's menstrual periods stop, she has the same incidence of heart attack as a man. Another factor for the decreased incidence of heart attacks in women may be estrogen. Just as testosterone protects the heart in men, estrogen protects the heart in women. Men and women are just different animals. Haven't we known that for years?

It is important to stress that correct testosterone replacement therapy brings the level of testosterone in a man (or woman) to the youthful testosterone range. It is not appropriate to replace testosterone in a man in his 20's who has youthful testosterone levels. Also, as with other hormone replacement therapy, bio-identical hormones are preferred. Bio-identical hormones have the exact molecular structure as the hormones that appear in the human body naturally.

Anabolic steroid use and abuse is not the same as testosterone replacement therapy. These testosterone-like drugs are abused by some bodybuilders and some athletes and can have serious side effects. The testosterone-like drugs just mentioned are never used in anti-aging medicine.

What about the prostate? This male exocrine gland (a gland that secretes hormones externally) is usually described as being the size and shape of a walnut. This little walnut can cause great joy and great heartache in a man's life and it's proper functioning must be monitored throughout a man's lifespan. The prostate gland is located in front of the rectum and below the bladder and surrounds the urethra (the tube that carries urine from the bladder through the penis to urinate). The fluid that the prostate gland produces forms part of the semen, the fluid that carries sperm during orgasm. The medical problems related to the prostate include prostatitis (infection), BPH or benign prostatic hyperplasia (enlargement of the prostate which can interfere with urination) or prostate cancer. After skin cancer, prostate cancer is the most common cancer in men.

The concerns about testosterone replacement therapy are: Does testosterone replacement therapy cause prostate cancer or BPH? There is nothing in the medical literature to suggest that testosterone replacement therapy causes prostate cancer. Dr. John Morley states in the January 2000 issue of Mayo Clinic Proceedings, "There is no clinical evidence that the risk of either prostate cancer or BPH increases with testosterone replacement therapy."

If prostate cancer is present and has spread outside the prostate then testosterone can accelerate its growth. In fact, testosterone blockers are used in that situation.

Thinking about testosterone and prostate cancer, we pose this question, "Do 20-year-old men with sky-high testosterone levels develop prostate cancer or do 80-year-old men with low testosterone levels develop prostate cancer? You know the answer. Multiple studies in the medical literature conclude that testosterone replacement therapy for low testosterone levels does not increase the risk of prostate cancer.

Of course, since prostate cancer is so common, we are very vigilant in screening for prostate cancer. We recommend PSA tests and digital rectal exams every six- (6) months. Actually, we evaluate PSA levels on all of our male patients every three months.

Another dramatic benefit of testosterone replacement therapy is reversing depression, irritability and moodiness; the "grumpy old men" syndrome. In our anti-aging practice, we have consistently seen this effect and there is considerable information in the medical literature to document this action. Many men who are taking SSRI (Specific Serotonin Reuptake Inhibitors) antidepressants like Prozac, Zoloft, Paxil or other prescription medications in the same SSRI family will be able to discontinue them because of bio-identical testosterone replacement therapy. A comment that we often hear from our male patients, after testosterone replacement therapy has been initiated is, "I've never felt better in my life."

The effects of testosterone replacement on body composition are well documented. More muscle, more effective exercise workouts, less fat. Also, there is an increase in bone density and less risk for osteoporosis (men can get this as well as women) and fractures such as hip fracture.

Now, how about sex? Youthful testosterone levels increase libido. Of course this is the part of sex that takes place in your mind, not the physical act of what you do sexually. You will have an increased desire for sex and you may have more sexual fantasies. Remember your sexual appetite when you were younger? Testosterone replacement increases enjoyment and satisfaction from sex and increases erectile function (erection hardness and duration). Some early research studies on testosterone replacement did not find any increase in erectile function, but these studies only lasted a few months. The effect of better sexual function can be gradual; taking about 6 months to a year for actual results to become apparent.

Remember, you did not lose your sexual drive overnight, it took years and in comparison, waiting six months to one year, to gain what you have lost, is a very short period of time.

How do we replace testosterone in men? What are the possible side effects? First we need to establish that there is a need for testosterone replacement therapy. A man may have all of the symptoms of male menopause or he may have more subtle symptoms like a decrease in energy, a decrease in mental focus or a decrease in his libido. Baseline blood tests are drawn (along with other blood tests that are required as part of a comprehensive anti-aging preventive medicine evaluation) and levels of testosterone are determined. The testosterone tests that we examine include the total testosterone, free testosterone and the sex hormone binding globulin.

To understand the significance of the results of your testosterone blood tests, you need to understand the concept of "free" testosterone. Most of the testosterone in the blood is "bound" to sex hormone binding globulin (SHBG). This portion of the testosterone is not available to the tissues of the body. The "free" testosterone is the active portion of testosterone. To explain further, two men could have the same total testosterone in the blood but if one has a higher SHBG he will have less available testosterone for the body to use. When we determine whether a man could benefit from testosterone replacement therapy, we check his free testosterone level. If the free testosterone level is below the youthful range, he is eligible for testosterone replacement with all the potential benefits listed previously.

As mentioned earlier, testosterone replacement therapy (TRT) does not cause prostate cancer but it can accelerate existing prostate cancer and screening tests are necessary. A PSA (Prostate Specific Antigen) test and a digital rectal exam are mandatory prostate cancer screening tests. The PSA is a blood test that can help in determining the possibility of prostate cancer. It is not an absolute yes or no answer, but if a man's PSA is high or rising consistently, as reflected by follow-up PSA tests, urology evaluation is absolutely necessary. A digital rectal exam is essential at least once a year (we encourage our patient's to have a digital rectal exam every six months) to detect any abnormalities in the way the prostate feels on exam. If abnormalities are present, a urology evaluation is necessary. To stress what we just said, please remember this: there is no evidence that testosterone replacement causes prostate cancer, but since prostate cancer is so common in men, ongoing vigilance with the necessary screening tests and consultations is necessary.

Are there any side effects of testosterone replacement that are of concern? The only significant side effect that occasionally occurs is increase in the red blood cells. However, if there were insufficient red blood cells present initially, this effect could be helpful. It is our experience that this side effect is actually uncommon. The production of too many red blood cells seems a more common side effect when testosterone shots are used for testosterone replacement. If a man's red blood cell count increases to a level where the blood is potentially too thick, the patient can donate blood once or twice a year. This action normalizes the red blood cell count.

What about behavior? Does testosterone replacement make men mean, angry or overly aggressive? The answer is "No." This question has been researched and it was found that low testosterone levels are associated with irritability and grouchiness in men. Testosterone replacement makes men more sociable and gregarious. They are more self-confident and assertive and yes, usually they have an increased sex drive.

What forms of testosterone are available and what are the advantages and disadvantages of each? The oral (pill) form of testosterone that is available in the USA (methyltestosterone) is not safe because of possible liver damage. There is another form of oral testosterone (undecanoate), which apparently is safe orally but is not available in the United States.

Testosterone can be given in the form of injections of altered molecules of testosterone (esters), and the effects of the testosterone injections lasts about two weeks. This is a reasonable method of administration but there are some problems with injectable testosterone. First, weekly or every other week injections are required. Secondly, there is a "roller-coaster" effect with the injections. Right after the injection there is a very high blood level of testosterone producing an elevated sense of well-being, lots of energy and lots of libido. As the level declines over the next week or two, these effects wear off possibly producing lethargy and decreased libido. Also, the high testosterone levels can cause a man's body to produce too much estrogen. This conversion of testosterone to estrogen is called aromatiazation. More on this later.

The preferred method of testosterone replacement therapy for most men is by transdermal (through the skin) cream. There are several commercial products but we prefer a skin cream custom-made by a compounding pharmacist. A measured amount of transdermal testosterone cream is applied to the skin daily. Follow-up blood testing (usually six to nine weeks after the testosterone cream has been prescribed and every three months thereafter) will confirm that the cream is being absorbed and that the testosterone blood level is in the youthful male range. The dose and concentration of the testosterone cream can be adjusted up or down as needed, according to lab test results.

Commercial transdermal products include patches that are worn on the scrotum or the body and a skin cream in prepackaged envelopes that is to be used daily.

What about nutrition and supplements? If testosterone levels are low, the only reliable way to raise the levels is by testosterone replacement. However, there are nutritional measures that are important adjuncts to testosterone replacement.

Because testosterone replacement therapy has the potential to increase a man's estrogen level by aromatiazation (the conversion of testosterone into estrogen) other medications or nutritional supplements may be added to a man's testosterone replacement therapy to minimize the potential for increased estrogen levels.

The conversion of testosterone into estrogen (aromatiazation) takes place in the fat cells of the body; especially abdominal fat cells. Keeping body fat in the desirable range limits aromatiazation. Alcohol increases aromatiazation and consuming more than a glass or two of wine per day will produce more estrogen. Zinc deficiency can increase aromatiazation. To keep zinc levels within a therapeutic range, 50 mg per day of zinc is recommended. Chrysin, a plant extract flavinoid is claimed to reduce aromatiazation. There is not a lot research to support the use of chrysin, but it may be useful. We recommend 500 mg of Chrysin daily.

What about DHEA (dihydroepiandosterone) and Androstenedione? These hormones can be purchased without a prescription in the United States. Both are precursors to testosterone in the pathway that the body uses to make testosterone. Adding a precursor does not necessarily increase the hormone "downstream." Both do not significantly raise testosterone in men in most studies.

DHEA raises testosterone in women, and is useful for treating low testosterone levels in women. DHEA has many other health benefits and needs to be replaced when levels are below the youthful range, but its primary purpose is not to raise testosterone levels in men.

Androstenedione (andro) was made famous several years ago when home-run champion Mark McGuire stated that he used it as a supplement. Once again, most studies show that "andro" does not significantly raise testosterone levels. It can, however, raise estrogen levels in men (not a good thing) and decrease HDL cholesterol (the good cholesterol).

Since we are discussing men's supplements, we should mention supplements from plants that are preventive medicine for men's prostate health. Saw palmetto is a plant that has been shown to decrease BPH (enlargement of the prostate) and increase urine flow. The dose we recommend for saw palmetto is 160 mg two times per day. It is often combined with pygeum (50 mg two times per day) and urtica (120 mg two times per day) two other herbal medicines that have complimentary effects on the prostate. Occasionally, some of our male patients may also need the prescription drug Proscar, which is effective at shrinking prostate size and lowering levels of dihydrotestosterone (DHT) which when levels are elevated, may cause prostate enlargement. Proscar, however, is not as effective as the plant extracts just mentioned for relieving the symptoms associated with BPH.

Even though there is no clinical evidence that testosterone replacement causes BPH we know that prostate enlargement is the rule rather than the exception as men get older, therefore, we start our patients on a saw palmetto combination when they begin testosterone replacement. Lycopene, the red pigment in tomatoes is a flavinoid that is associated with decreased levels of prostate cancer. As part of our men's health preventive medicine program, 10 mg of lycopene should be taken per day. Another nutritional supplement we recommend to our male patients on testosterone replacement is Indole 3 Carbinol, which is a combination of cruciferous vegetables such as broccoli and cauliflower; known for their anti-cancer properties, estrogen protection and environmental toxin protection. A dose of 200 mg two times per day (for patients 120 pounds or less) 200 mg three times per day (for patients between 120 and 180 pounds) and a dose of 200 mg four times per day (for patients 180 pounds or greater) of Indole 3 Carbinol daily is recommended.

In summary, men need testosterone to be healthy and treat the signs and symptoms of male menopause. Testosterone replacement can result in a healthier brain, a healthier heart, increased muscle mass, greater bone density, improved mood, improved sense of well-being and an improved sexual life. Replacing lowered testosterone levels as we age is a powerful anti-aging and preventive medicine treatment.

REMEMBER THIS

• Testosterone is an essential hormone in men and women

• Every cell in the body has receptor sites for testosterone

• Testosterone is a total body hormone, not just a sex hormone

• Natural testosterone replacement therapy has dramatic benefits on health, mood, well-being and sexuality

• Every hormone has a "pause"

• Andropause or "male menopause" is defined as the decline in testosterone production by the testicles in men

• Male menopause can be a gradual process and varies from one man to the next, but andropause, just like female menopause can have severe health consequences in the long-term

• Some of the following symptoms may be a result of male menopause:
  • Fatigue
  • Depression
  • Irritability "Grumpy old men" syndrome
  • Reduced libido and sexual potency
  • Decreased sexual desire and decreased sexual fantasies
  • Decreased morning erections "When the only thing stiff in the morning is your back"
  • Decreased firmness of erections
  • Longer recovery time between orgasms
  • Loss of drive and competitive edge
  • Stiffness and pain in muscles and joints
  • Decreased effectiveness of exercise workouts
  • Serious medical problems associated with male menopause are:
    • Increased aging of the heart and circulation
    • Increased incidence of heart attacks and strokes
    • Brain aging

- Decreased memory
- Decreased intelligence
- Increased rate of dementia such as Alzheimer's dementia
- There is a strong association between decreased testosterone levels and type II diabetes (adult onset diabetes) in men
- Type II diabetes can sometimes be "cured" or reversed with a hormonally correct diet and testosterone replacement therapy
- The cause of male menopause is decreased bio-available testosterone
- Other factors that contribute to male menopause include:
- Stress
- Alcohol
- Increased fat (especially abdominal fat)
- Lack of exercise
- Decreased testosterone in men is also associated with:
- Increased estrogen levels
- Elevated LDL (bad) cholesterol
- Osteoporosis
- Arthritis
- Depression

- Testosterone dilates coronary arteries (heart arteries) bringing more blood flow to the heart

- Men with heart attacks have lower levels of testosterone and higher levels of estrogen in their bodies

- There is no medical evidence which shows that testosterone causes heart disease

- Testosterone may be a potential treatment for heart attacks in men

- Iron overload found in many men may be a primary reason why men have more heart attacks than pre-menopausal women

- Testosterone replacement therapy for low testosterone levels does not increase the risk of prostate cancer

- Anabolic steroid use and abuse is not the same as testosterone replacement therapy

- Because prostate cancer is so common, routine screening for prostate cancer is important for every man. We recommend PSA tests and digital rectal exams every six (6) months

- Youthful testosterone levels increase libido

- The "free" testosterone is the active portion of testosterone

- The only significant side effect that occasionally occurs with testosterone replacement therapy is an increase in the red blood cells, which can be corrected by donating one or two units of blood every year

- Testosterone replacement makes men more sociable, gregarious, self-confident, assertive and increases sexual drive

- Oral forms of testosterone found in the United States can cause liver damage

- Testosterone injections can cause a "roller-coaster" effect. Right after the injection there is a very high blood level of testosterone producing an elevated sense of well-being, lots of energy and lots of libido. As the level declines over the next week or two, these effects wear off possibly producing lethargy and decreased libido

- High testosterone levels can cause a man's body to produce too much estrogen

- The conversion of testosterone to estrogen is called aromatiazation

- The preferred method of testosterone replacement therapy for most men is by transdermal (through the skin) cream made by a compounding pharmacist

- Medications or nutritional supplements may be added to a man's testosterone replacement therapy to minimize the potential for increased estrogen levels sometimes associated with testosterone replacement therapy

- The conversion of testosterone into estrogen (aromatiazation) takes place in the fat cells of the body; especially abdominal fat cells

- Keeping body fat in the desirable range limits aromatiazation

- Alcohol increases aromatiazation

- Zinc deficiency can increase aromatiazation. To keep zinc levels within a therapeutic range, 50 mg per day of zinc is recommended

- Chrysin, a plant extract flavinoid is claimed to reduce aromatiazation. We recommend 500 mg of Chrysin daily

- DHEA (dihydroepiandosterone) and Androstenedione, both testosterone precursors, can be purchased without a prescription in the United States

- DHEA (dihydroepiandosterone) and Androstenedione do not significantly raise testosterone levels in men in most studies

- DHEA has many other health benefits and needs to be replaced when levels are below the youthful range but its primary purpose is not to raise testosterone in men

- Androstenedione (andro) does not significantly raise testosterone levels. It can raise estrogen levels in men (not a good thing) and decrease HDL cholesterol (the good cholesterol)

- Saw palmetto is a plant that has been shown to decrease BPH (enlargement of the prostate) and increase urine flow. It is often combined with pygeum and urtica, two other herbal medicines that have complimentary effects on the prostate. We recommend 160 mg of saw palmetto two times per day, pygeum 50 mg two times per day and urtica 120 mg two times per day for prostate health

- Lycopene, the red pigment in tomatoes is a flavinoid that is associated with decreased levels of prostate cancer. As part of our men's health preventive medicine program, a dose of 10 mg of lycopene should be taken daily

• Another nutritional supplement we recommend to our male patients on testosterone replacement is Indole 3 Carbinol, which is a combination of cruciferous vegetables such as broccoli and cauliflower; known for their anti-cancer properties, estrogen protection and environmental toxin protection. A dose of 200 mg two times per day (for patients 120 pounds or less) 200 mg three times per day (for patients between 120 and 180 pounds) and a dose of 200 mg four times per day (for patients 180 pounds or greater) of Indole 3 Carbinol daily is recommended.

• Men need testosterone to be healthy

• Testosterone replacement can result in a healthier brain, a healthier heart, increased muscle mass, greater bone density, improved mood, improved sense of well-being and an improved sexual life.

• Replacing lowered testosterone levels as we age is a powerful anti-aging and preventive medicine treatment

Female Menopause

Today there are more than 45 million women in the United States that are in some stage of menopause and close to 4 million more women will begin to experience some of the signs and symptoms of menopause this year. Menopause causes significant hormone imbalances, which can also lead to severe health problems. We now have the scientific knowledge to naturally and safely treat the hormone irregularities commonly associated with menopause. We can help women move through menopause without all of the unwanted signs and symptoms women of previous generations experienced when menopause occurred.

Once again, let us state that every hormone in the body has a "pause." Menopause is defined as the cessation of the production of estrogens and progesterone by the ovaries in women. Estrogen and progesterone levels in the body decrease dramatically after menopause but they do not disappear completely. The decrease in estrogen production is a major cause of aging in women. In addition to the decline of estrogen and progesterone production, testosterone levels and DHEA levels in menopausal women also lessen. Although women experience a peri-menopausal period, usually lasting for about five years, prior to actual menopause, generally speaking, a woman undergoes a rather sudden change in hormone levels at around the age of 50. Every woman is different but if not treated correctly, female menopause can have detrimental health consequences over an extended period of time.

Symptoms of menopause are different for every woman but they may include:
- Anxiety
- Depression
- Night sweats
- Hot flashes
- Dizziness
- Fatigue
- Mood swings and other psychological changes
- Tearfulness
- Decreased libido

- Vaginal dryness
- Vaginal itching
- Urinary frequency, urinary incontinence or other bladder problems
- Headaches
- Burning or discomfort during sexual intercourse
- Dry flaking skin
- Increased wrinkles
- Difficulty sleeping
- Decreased memory
- Decreased attention span
- Shortness of breath
- Heart palpitations
- Breast Tenderness
- Increase in weight, especially in the abdominal and hip areas
- Increased blood pressure
- Increased cholesterol levels

Estrogen, like testosterone is a total body hormone. Some of the hormone receptor cites that need estrogen are found in the bladder, bones, arteries, vagina, heart, liver and the brain. Without adequate levels of estrogen, these organs cannot function properly. As an example, the walls of the vagina become thinner and vaginal secretions decrease because of low estrogen levels. The vagina actually shrinks and becomes less elastic. This may cause a woman to be more susceptible to vaginal infections and to experience discomfort during sexual intercourse. Low estrogen levels cause the bladder to become thinner, less elastic and the neck of the bladder can actually shrink. The result is urinary frequency and/or painful urination. Because low estrogen levels cause the skin to become thinner and dryer, scalp and body hair become brittle and may fall out more easily. Menopause is the time when a woman's menstrual cycle (which includes ovulation) eventually stops, indicating that she is no longer fertile. Menopause is commonly referred to as "the change of life." A change, thank you very much, that may include symptoms that many women would rather avoid.

Estrogen, in females, is made primarily in the ovaries. For approximately thirty-five years of a woman's life, estrogen, progesterone and testosterone usually maintain a healthy equilibrium throughout the reproductive years. During the first half of a woman's menstrual cycle, estradiol levels increase before ovulation. Once ovulation occurs, progesterone levels increase, making the uterus ready for impregnation. If a woman does not become pregnant, progesterone levels decrease and eventually when the woman has her menses or period, the waste products of the menstrual cycle are expelled.

"Estrogens" are the primary female sex hormones. Did you know that there is no such thing as "estrogen?" The three major estrogens found in the female are estradiol, estriol and estrone. Estradiol (E2) is the most active estrogen in the body but may not be well absorbed. Estrone (E1) known to relieve some of the symptoms of menopause has been associated with some forms of cancer and is selectively used in natural (bio-identical) hormone replacement therapy. Estriol (E3) has been shown to have anti-cancer effects and inhibits breast cancers. Huge amounts of estriol are produced during pregnancy. Adequate levels of natural estrogens in women can assist in:

- Preventing heart disease
- Decreasing cholesterol levels
- Controlling carbohydrate metabolism
- Decreasing blood clotting
- Improving memory and overall cognitive function
- Enhancing the immune system
- Increasing muscle tone
- Improving skin thickness, moistness and elasticity
- Enhancing moistness of the body's mucus membranes
- Decreasing the wasting away of bladder, vaginal and other genital tissue
- Improving attention
- Improving mood and overall sense of well-being
- Preventing osteoporosis
- Increasing libido (sexual drive)
- Preventing or decreasing the incidence of Alzheimer's Disease
- Decreasing many of the symptoms associated with menopause
- Preventing strokes
- Decreasing the risk of colon cancer provided a hormonally correct diet is consumed

Almost all postmenopausal women need natural hormone replacement therapy which includes estrogens, progesterone, testosterone, DHEA and thyroid. It is the rare exception that will not need natural hormone replacement therapy. Soy products contain phytoestrogens which are plant produced estrogen-like compounds that may be beneficial for all women because of their anti-cancer effects.

When clinically indicated, we prescribe natural (bio-identical) estrogen transdermal creams for our female patients that are comprised of estradiol and estriol and made by a compounding pharmacist. We combine estriol 80% with estradiol 20%. Since estrone is not needed for treating and preventing menopause symptoms, and may be the more dangerous estrogen, it is not included in our transdermal creams. Because estriol is the most protective estrogen, it is the major ingredient in our "estrogen" transdermal creams. If a female patient has a history of breast cancer, we may prescribe estriol only. Natural plant estrogens have the same molecular structure as the estrogens found in the human female. These natural plant estrogens are altered so that they have the same bio-identical structure as the estrogens found in the human female because even though the plant estrogens have the same molecular structure, they do not have the same bio-identical structure until they are processed.

Unlike many FDA-approved estrogen medications, natural soy estrogens are safe, effective and may have benefits such as:
- Cancer prevention
- Bone formation stimulation
- Inhibiting atherosclerosis
- Inhibiting the free radical damage caused by LDL cholesterol
- Kidney function protection
- Gallbladder protection (decreases the chance of gallstones)

Some of the side effects of natural estrogen replacement therapy may be fluid retention, increased body fat (usually 5-10 pounds) and increased risk of uterine cancer if not given in conjunction with natural progesterone.

We always prescribe natural micronized progesterone for all of our female patients, which is also made from plant sources; more specifically the wild yam. Again, the molecule in the plant is altered to make it bio-identical. We prefer that our female patients take their natural progesterone in the form of a sublingual (under the tongue) lozenge but if this method of administration is not tolerated then a pill form of the micronized natural progesterone is used. The dose for natural progesterone is dependent upon a woman's serum progesterone level.

The dosage for the estrogen cream is dependent upon a woman's serum estradiol level. We do not recommend oral estrogens because they interfere with insulin/glucose metabolism in the body and with human growth hormone metabolism.

We do not recommend any of the synthetic estrogens such as Premarin. Premarin does not contain any estriol, which is the anti-cancer estrogen produced by the body. Did you know that Premarin is made from the urine of pregnant horses? That is how it got its name; PREgnant MARe urINe. We know that the estrogens found in horses do not have the same molecular structure as the estrogens found in human females. There are more than thirty-five (35) "foreign" or xeno estrogens in Premarin that are not found in the human female. The estrogens found in horses were never intended for use in the human body. Given this fact, we are concerned about the long-term health effects for women using Premarin or some other synthetic estrogen medication. If you are currently using Premarin or another synthetic estrogen, we encourage you to do your homework and ask your physician to prescribe a natural (bio-identical) estrogen and to monitor your hormone levels closely.

Side effects from FDA-approved estrogen and progestin drugs may include blood clot formation, weight gain, gallstones, headaches, fibroid tumors, irritability and fluid retention.

We know that in addition to too much estrogen in body, there are other contributing factors to the increased incidence of breast cancer. Some contributing factors include chlorine-based substances, insecticides, manufacturing chemicals, fungicides. These toxic substances accumulate in the body, more specifically in the fat cells of breast tissue. Soy estrogens block the effect of these toxic substances and therefore, further protect a woman from getting breast cancer.

Estrogen replacement therapy assists in protecting menopausal women from coronary artery disease. Estrogen has an antioxidant effect on free radicals, which helps to keep LDL (the bad cholesterol) levels lower. Taking Vitamin E also helps the antioxidant effect of estrogen. We recommend 400 mg of Vitamin E daily.

Because we are always concerned about increased cancer risks when prescribing estrogen, we include Indole 3 Carbinol (I3C) as part of our female hormone replacement therapy program. Indole 3 Carbinol, which is a combination of cruciferous vegetables such as broccoli and cauliflower; are known for their anti-cancer properties, estrogen protection and environmental toxin protection. A dose of 200 mg two times per day (for patients 120 pounds or less) 200 mg three times per day (for patients between 120 and 180 pounds) and a dose of 200 mg four times per day (for patients 180 pounds or greater) of Indole 3 Carbinol daily is recommended.

Progesterone, primarily a female hormone but also found in males in small amounts, is made in the in the ovaries, the adrenal glands and, in pregnancy, it is produced in the placenta. Progesterone helps estrogen levels stay within a therapeutic range and therefore, can protect against endometrial (the lining of the uterus) cancer, which can be caused by too much estrogen in the body. Progesterone also:
- Protects against osteoporosis
- Protects against breast cancer
- Decreases fluid retention
- Normalizes blood clotting
- Helps maintain normal blood sugar levels
- Assists in lowering LDL cholesterol levels
- Improves libido
- Has a sedative effect on the central nervous system
- Increases the production of the anti-cancer estrogen known as estriol
- Protects brain cells
- Increases the sense of well-being
- Stabilizes mood

Like estrogen, progesterone levels decline as we age and it is impor-tant to keep progesterone levels within a youthful therapeutic range. Natural progesterone replacement therapy has many health benefits and should be part of a complete female natural hormone replacement treatment program, when clinically indicated.

Provera is an FDA-approved synthetic progestin. Progestins are not the same as natural progesterone. Synthetic progestins produce unwanted side effects such as fluid retention, weight gain, depression and breast tenderness. Provera has many potential dangers such as possible birth defects, blood clots, acne, rashes, and breast cancer.

Given the potential dangers of drugs like Premarin and Provera, it is not surprising that many women are reluctant to initiate, when needed, hormone replacement therapy. We hope that by reading this book and educating yourself with other resources, you will learn that natural (bio-identical) hormone replacement therapy has many benefits with very few side effects, if you are monitored by a trained and qualified anti-aging physician.

What about women and testosterone? Testosterone is the third female sex hormone. There is estrogen, progesterone and yes, testosterone. Many perimenopausal women, women who have had an oophorectomy (ovaries removed) and/or a hysterectomy (uterus removed) and even women in their 40's have low levels of testosterone. The symptoms include low or no libido, decreased sense of well-being and decreased strength, especially upper body strength. These problems are quickly reversed with careful testosterone replacement. Blood tests are necessary to determine the correct amount of testosterone. The dose of testosterone is much, much lower than the male dose. We recommend testosterone replacement for women in the form of a transdermal cream made by a compounding pharmacist. The testosterone transdermal cream is also made from wild yams, just like natural progesterone. Again, no plant contains the bioidentical human molecule of human testosterone. Bio-identical testosterone molecules are synthetically produced from the natural plant molecules. We monitor testosterone levels closely and any possible side effects. We want to return a woman's testosterone level to the youthful range. If a woman did not have side effects in her twenties, when her testosterone levels were in the youthful range, she should not have them when her testosterone is being replaced by bio-identical testosterone. If a woman's testosterone levels become too high, she may experience oily skin or acne. Acne or oily skin might be a sign to lower testosterone doses. It is also possible that unwanted facial hair could appear, if testosterone levels continued to rise but we try to avoid this by lowering the dose of testosterone to eliminate this side effect.

Another hormone that is part of our female hormone replacement therapy is DHEA (dehydroepiandrosterone). DHEA is a precursor to all of the sex hormones in both males and females. Giving women DHEA will usually assist in raising their serum testosterone levels to a youthful range and may make the need for testosterone replacement unnecessary. DHEA can improve mood, improve cognitive function, improve immune system response, improve bone density, increase energy and improve sense of well-being. DHEA can also increase estrogen levels and should be given with Melatonin, another body hormone that helps protect against breast cancer. DHEA can increase testosterone levels in women and the same side effects that are associated with testosterone replacement can occur with DHEA. Again, if the side effects of oily skin, acne or unwanted facial hair appear, we can solve the problem by lowering the dose of DHEA.

Another supplement that is often used effectively to treat many of the signs and symptoms associated with menopause is the plant black cohosh or more properly named Cimicufuga racemosa. Black cohosh, trademarked as Remifemin, has been used in Europe for years to treat hot flashes, depression, anxiety, vaginal dryness and other menopausal symptoms. Although we do not use this supplement in our practice, there is considerable documentation that it is effective and has few side effects. If a woman does not wish to take bio-identical estrogen, phytoestrogens such as soy extract and black cohosh can be used.

Natural hormone replacement therapy for peri-menopausal and menopausal women has many long-term health benefits. We encourage you to have the necessary baseline laboratory blood tests done, to see if you are a candidate for natural hormone replacement therapy. If you are a candidate, we assure you that the outcomes achieved by balancing your body's hormones will make you wonder why you waited so long to feel so much better.

REMEMBER THIS

• Today there are more than 45 million women in the United States that are in some stage of menopause

• Close to 4 million more women will begin to experience some of the signs and symptoms of menopause this year

• Every hormone in the body has a "pause"

• Menopause is defined as the cessation of production of estrogens and progesterone by the ovaries in women. Although women experience a peri-menopausal period prior to actual menopause, generally speaking, a woman undergoes a rather sudden change in hormone levels at around the age of 50

• We now have the scientific knowledge to naturally and safely treat the hormone irregularities commonly associated with menopause

• The decrease in estrogen production is a major cause of aging in women

• In addition to the decline of estrogen and progesterone production, testosterone levels and DHEA levels in menopausal women also lessen

• Women experience a peri-menopausal period, usually lasting for about five years

• Symptoms of menopause are different for every woman but they may include:
  • Anxiety
  • Depression
  • Night sweats
  • Hot flashes
  • Dizziness
  • Fatigue
  • Mood swings and other psychological changes

- Tearfulness
- Decreased libido
- Vaginal dryness
- Vaginal itching
- Urinary frequency, urinary incontinence or other bladder problems
- Headaches
- Burning or discomfort during sexual intercourse
- Dry flaking skin
- Increased wrinkles
- Difficulty sleeping
- Decreased memory
- Decreased attention span
- Shortness of breath
- Heart palpitations
- Breast Tenderness
- Increase in weight, especially in the abdominal and hip areas
- Increased blood pressure

- Estrogen, like testosterone is a total body hormone

- Some of the hormone receptor cites that need estrogen are found in the bladder, bones, arteries, vagina, heart, liver and the brain

- Inadequate levels of estrogen cause many organs in the body to function improperly

- Low levels of estrogen may cause the walls of the vagina to become thinner and vaginal secretions may decrease. The vagina actually shrinks and becomes less elastic. This may cause a woman to be more susceptible to vaginal infections and to experience discomfort during sexual intercourse

- Low estrogen levels cause the bladder to become thinner, less elastic and the neck of the bladder can actually shrink. The result is urinary frequency and/or painful urination

- Low estrogen levels cause the skin to become thinner and dryer

- Low estrogen levels can cause the scalp and body hair to become brittle and hair may fall out more easily

- Estrogen, in females, is made primarily in the ovaries

- "Estrogens" are the primary female sex hormones

- The three major estrogens found in the female are estradiol, estriol and estrone. Estradiol is the most active estrogen in the body but may not be well absorbed. Estrone known to relieve some of the symptoms of menopause has been associated with some forms of cancer and is selectively used in natural (bio-identical) hormone replacement therapy. Estriol has been shown to have anti-cancer effects and inhibits breast cancers

- Adequate levels of natural estrogens in women can assist in:
  - Preventing heart disease
  - Decreasing cholesterol levels
  - Controlling carbohydrate metabolism
  - Decreasing blood clotting
  - Improving memory and overall cognitive function
  - Enhancing the immune system
  - Increasing muscle tone
  - Improving skin thickness, moistness and elasticity
  - Enhancing moistness of the body's mucus membranes
  - Decreasing the wasting away of bladder, vaginal and other genital tissue
  - Improving attention
  - Improving mood and overall sense of well-being
  - Preventing osteoporosis
  - Increasing libido (sexual drive)
  - Preventing or decreasing the incidence of Alzheimer's Disease
  - Decreasing many of the symptoms associated with menopause
  - Preventing strokes
  - Decreasing the risk of colon cancer provided a hormonally correct diet is consumed

- We prescribe natural (bio-identical) estrogen transdermal creams for our female patients that are comprised of estradiol and estriol and made by a compounding pharmacist

- If a female patient has a history of breast cancer, we may prescribe estriol only

- Bio-identical estrogen cream is made from plant sources (phytoestrogens), primarily soy, which has the same molecular structure as the estrogens found in humans but is synthetically converted to be bio-identical to the estrogens found in the human female

- The dose for natural estrogen is dependent upon a woman's serum estradiol level

- Bio-identical estrogen made from soy is safe, effective and may have numerous benefits such as:
  - Bone formation stimulation
  - Inhibiting atherosclerosis
  - Inhibiting the free radical damage caused by LDL cholesterol
  - Kidney function protection
  - Gallbladder protection (decreases the chance of gallstones)

- Some of the side effects of natural estrogen replacement therapy may be fluid retention, increased body fat (usually 5-10 pounds) and increased risk of uterine cancer if not given in conjunction with natural progesterone

- The dose for natural progesterone is dependent upon a woman's serum progesterone level

- We do not recommend any of the synthetic estrogens such as Premarin

- Premarin does not contain any estriol, which is the anti-cancer estrogen produced by the body

- Premarin is made from the urine of pregnant horses

- We know that the estrogens found in horses do not have the same molecular structure as the estrogens found in human females. The estrogens found in horses were never intended for use in the human body.

- We are concerned about the long-term health effects for women using Premarin or some other synthetic estrogen medication

- Side effects from FDA-approved estrogen and progestin drugs may include blood clot formation, weight gain, gallstones, headaches, fibroid tumors, irritability and fluid retention

- Phytoestrogens (estrogens made from soy) can actually balance estrogen effects on the body, keeping estrogen levels in a more therapeutic range

- Some other contributing factors to breast cancer include chlorine-based substances, insecticides, manufacturing chemicals, fungicides. These toxic substances accumulate in the body, more specifically in the fat cells of breast tissue. Soy estrogens block the effect of these toxic substances and therefore, further protect a woman from getting breast cancer

- Estrogen replacement therapy assists in protecting menopausal women from coronary artery disease

- Estrogen has an antioxidant effect on free radicals, which helps to keep LDL (the bad cholesterol) levels lower

- Taking Vitamin E also helps the antioxidant effect of estrogen. We recommend 400 mg of Vitamin E daily.

- Since we are always concerned about increased cancer risks when prescribing estrogen, we include Indole 3 Carbinol (I3C) as part of our female hormone replacement therapy program. I3C is a compound made from cruciferous vegetables such as broccoli and cauliflower, which may reduce the risk of cancer, especially breast cancer and prostate cancer

- Progesterone, primarily a female hormone but also found in males in small amounts, is made in the in the ovaries, the adrenal glands and, in pregnancy, it is produced in the placenta

- Progesterone helps estrogen levels stay within a therapeutic range

- Progesterone protects against endometrial (the lining of the uterus) cancer, which can be caused by too much estrogen in the body

- Progesterone also:
  - Protects against osteoporosis
  - Protects against breast cancer
  - Decreases fluid retention
  - Normalizes blood clotting
  - Helps maintain normal blood sugar levels
  - Assists in lowering LDL cholesterol levels
  - Improves libido
  - Has a sedative effect on the central nervous system
  - Increases the production of the anti-cancer estrogen known as estriol
  - Protects brain cells
  - Increases the sense of well-being
  - Stabilizes mood

- Provera is an FDA-approved synthetic progestin

- Progestins are not the same as natural progesterone

- Synthetic progestins produce unwanted side effects such as fluid retention, weight gain, depression and breast tenderness. Provera has many potential dangers such as possible birth defects, blood clots, acne, rashes, and breast cancer

- Testosterone is the third female sex hormone

- Symptoms of low testosterone include low or no libido, decreased sense of well-being and decreased strength, especially upper body strength

- Blood tests are necessary to determine the correct amount of testosterone

- The female dose of testosterone is much lower than the male dose of testosterone

- We recommend testosterone replacement for women in the form of a transdermal cream made by a compounding pharmacist

- Testosterone transdermal cream is also made from wild yams, just like natural progesterone

- The only side effects of testosterone replacement therapy in women may be unwanted facial hair and acne. Lowering the dose of testosterone can eliminate these side effects

- DHEA is a precursor to all of the sex hormones in both males and females

- DHEA will usually assist in raising female serum testosterone levels to a youthful range and may make the need for testosterone replacement unnecessary

- DHEA can improve mood, improve cognitive function, improve immune system response, improve bone density, increase energy and improve sense of well-being

- DHEA can increase estrogen levels and should be given with Melatonin, another body hormone that helps protect against breast cancer

- The only side effects from DHEA supplementation in women may be unwanted facial hair and acne. These side effects can be eliminated by lowering the dose of DHEA

- Another supplement that is often used effectively to treat many of the signs and symptoms associated with menopause is the plant black cohosh or more properly named Cimicufuga racemosa

- Black cohosh, trademarked as Remifemin, has been used in Europe for years to treat hot flashes, depression, anxiety, vaginal dryness and other menopausal symptoms. Although we do not use this supplement in our practice, there is considerable documentation that it is effective and has few side effects

- Natural hormone replacement therapy for peri-menopausal and menopausal women has many long-term health benefits. We encourage you to have the necessary baseline laboratory blood tests done, to see if you are a candidate for natural hormone replacement therapy

PART TWO

YOUR PERSONAL "FOREVER AGELESS" PLAN

GETTING STARTED

YOUR EVALUATION DAY

YOUR PERSONAL ANTI-AGING PLAN

FOLLOW-UP

CHAPTER THREE

GETTING STARTED

We hope that you have read the first chapter of this book and now know what anti-aging medicine is and what it is not. Or, maybe you have heard about anti-aging medicine from your friends, attended a lecture or seminar, seen programs on television or read articles in newspapers or magazines. You may have also used the Internet to research anti-aging medicine. Whatever your source of information, the next step to beginning your own personal anti-aging program is getting started. This chapter will discuss what you need to do to get started. If you want to learn more about the science of anti-aging medicine before you get started, please read Part Three of this book and then return to this chapter. If you want to get started on your personal anti-aging program right now and wish to read Part Three later, then we suggest that you keep reading.

At California HealthSpan Institute (CHI) we receive numerous calls daily from potential patients, throughout the country, asking us what anti-aging medicine is, what we do, how we do it and how much does it cost. To be most beneficial in answering these questions and to clearly explain how to get started on your personal anti-aging program, we have provided a question and answer format that will take you step by step through the process of beginning your anti-aging program. Whether you contact CHI or another physician practice that specializes in anti-aging medicine, many of the following questions will help you determine if the anti-aging physician you are thinking of using, is qualified and equipped to provide you with an ongoing, comprehensive, individualized anti-aging program.

STEP ONE: LEARN WHAT ANTI-AGING MEDICINE IS

Question:
What is anti-aging medicine?

Answer:
Anti-aging medicine is a new field of medicine that continually examines the scientific research of what causes illness, what causes aging and what causes the decline in physical and mental function as we age. Anti-aging medicine offers patients individualized plans to slow and even reverse aging. Anti-aging medicine offers patients an improved healthspan, not just a longer lifespan. Anti-aging medicine looks at internal causes for treating or preventing external symptoms. Anti-aging medicine is truly preventive medicine that works to change the process of aging itself. Anti-aging medicine works to prevent many of the mental and physical losses currently associated with aging. Anti-aging medicine helps patients maintain the highest mental and physical function possible for the duration of their lives. The primary goal of anti-aging medicine is improved health and well-being.

Question:
Why do we age?

Answer:
We age because our hormone levels decline, our hormone levels do not decline because we age. We age because of free radical damage that we may not be keeping up with, with our current regime of vitamins, minerals and other supplements, dietary practices and lifestyle behaviors. We age because segments of our DNA cannot reproduce after they have divided a certain number of times. We age because we may have too much insulin and glucose in our bodies due to improper diet or some other reason. Aging is a combination of causes and these are just a few of the causes we know about at this time.

Question:
How can I learn more about anti-aging medicine?

Answer:

You can visit the California HealthSpan Institute (CHI) website at **www.ehealthspan.com** to learn more about anti-aging medicine. You may also visit the American Academy of Anti-Aging Medicine (A4M) website at **www.worldhealth.net** to learn more about anti-aging medicine. Another good resource to learn more about anti-aging medicine is the Life Extension website at **www.LifeExtension.com.** If you do not have Internet access, there are a number of books dedicated to anti-aging medicine. One of the best books, in our opinion, is <u>Brain Longevity</u> by Dharma Singh Khalsa, M.D. Dr. Ronald M. Klatz, president and founder of the American Academy of Anti-Aging Medicine has written several books on anti-aging medicine. Two of his books are <u>Hormones of Youth</u> and <u>Ten Weeks To A Younger You</u>. Another excellent resource is <u>The Anti-Aging Zone</u> by Barry Sears, Ph.D. or visit his website at **www.drsears.com**.

STEP TWO: FIND A QUALIFIED ANTI-AGING PHYSICIAN

Question:
How do I find a qualified anti-aging doctor where I live?

Answer:
Unlike your primary care physician, your anti-aging physician does not need to reside in your hometown. CHI has anti-aging patients throughout the United States. The only visit you need to make to your anti-aging physician is for your Evaluation Day. Follow-up care can be done successfully by telephone. Your anti-aging physician does not take the place of your primary care physician. Your anti-aging physician specializes in your anti-aging medical needs only. If, however, you feel more comfortable having an anti-aging physician in your local area, you can contact the American Academy of Anti-Aging Medicine (A4M) and they will provide you

with a reference list of qualified anti-aging physicians throughout the country. The phone number for the American Academy of Anti Aging Medicine, which is located in Chicago, Illinois, is (773) 528-4333.

STEP THREE: GET YOUR LAB WORK DONE

Question:
What type of lab work needs to be done and why?

Answer:
The baseline laboratory tests that are ordered tell us what your hormone levels are, how your kidneys and liver are functioning, what your fat levels are in your blood, if you have inflammation that may put you at risk for cardiovascular disease, what your blood cell counts are, if you are at risk for osteoporosis and for men, certain blood tests may identify possible problems with the prostate gland.

The specific mandatory baseline tests that we order are:

• Complete Blood Count: Measures blood cell counts; red blood cells, white blood cells, platelet count, hemoglobin, hematocrit, etc.

• Comprehensive Metabolic Panel: Measures glucose, sodium, potassium, chloride, calcium and other electrolytes and minerals, in addition to evaluating kidney and liver function

• Lipid Profile: Measures cholesterol, triglycerides, HDL, LDL and cholesterol/HDL ratio

• Hemoglobin A1C:Measures how many of your oxygen-carrying red blood cells are bound by glucose and is a more direct measure of glucose intolerance than a fasting glucose level

• Fasting Insulin: Measures insulin levels

• Homocysteine: Measures waste products of protein metabolism which can cause your arteries to clog. High homocysteine levels are associated with a greater risk for cardiovascular disease, even if your lipid profile is normal

- Cardio C-Reactive Protein: May be the most accurate measure for evaluating inflammation in the arteries. Elevated C-Reactive Protein levels are associated with greater risk for strokes and heart attacks

- DHEA-Sulfate: Measures DHEA levels, a very important hormone

- F &T Testosterone & SHBG: Measures free and total testosterone levels and sex hormone binding globulin in both males and females

- Estradiol: Measures estradiol levels in both men and women

- Progesterone: Measures progesterone levels in women

- IGF1 (Somatomedin C) Measures growth hormone secretion levels in the body

- LH: Measures leutenizing hormone levels in both men and women. LH stimulates estrogen and progesterone production

- FSH: Measures follicle stimulating hormone levels in both men and women. FSH stimulates estrogen and sperm production

- DHT: Measures dihydrotestosterone levels in men

- TSH: Measures levels of the thyroid-stimulating hormone

- Free T4: Measures free levels of the thyroid hormone thyroxine

- Free T3: Measures free levels of the thyroid hormone triiodothyronine

- PSA: Measures levels of the prostate specific antigen in the male prostate gland

- N-Telopeptides: A urine test that can indicate risk for or evidence of the disease osteoporosis

- Antioxidant Screen: An optional blood test that measures various antioxidant levels in the body including vitamin A, vitamin C, vitamin E, etc.

Question:
Do I need to be fasting for my baseline laboratory tests?
Answer:
Yes, you need to be fasting for your baseline blood work. You may not have anything to eat or drink, except water, after midnight the night before your blood is drawn.

Question:
How much does the lab work cost?

Answer:
Generally speaking, the baseline laboratory tests usually cost about $550.00. Prices may vary, however. If requested, we provide prospective patients with a list of the required baseline laboratory tests and instruct them to take the list to their primary care physician and ask their physician to order the tests. Sometimes insurance will pay for the laboratory tests if they are ordered by a primary care provider. At this time, we do not bill insurance for any of the services we offer because it has been our experience that insurance carriers are not up to speed with the latest trends and technologies of anti-aging medicine and therefore, they do not cover most preventive services. A little editorial comment is appropriate here. We believe that is it much more cost effective to prevent disease and illness rather than pay for the effects of disease and illness later down the road. Someday, we hope, insurance carriers will join in that simple and cost effective wisdom.

Question:
Where do I get my lab work done?

Answer:
If you live in the San Diego, California region, we contract with Lab Corp or Quest Diagnostics laboratories. Both corporations have numerous draw sites throughout San Diego County and are famil-

iar with the specialized tests we order. If you do not live in San Diego County, do not despair. We coordinate with Pinnacle Labs in Salt Lake City, Utah for lab work to be done anywhere in the country. We send Pinnacle Labs a prescription for your blood work and they facilitate with a local lab in your area, to make sure the appropriate lab tests are done and that the lab has the correct test material to collect your blood samples. Pinnacle Labs will contact you to schedule your blood work and you will pay them directly for the tests. Once the lab tests are completed, Pinnacle Labs sends CHI the results. If you live in San Diego, Lab Corp or Quest Diagnostics sends CHI your lab results. If you have your lab work done with CHI and not Pinnacle, you will pay CHI for your lab tests. CHI then pays Lab Corps or Quest Diagnostics for your tests. If you plan on seeing someone other than CHI for your anti-aging medical care, you will need to contact them regarding their procedures for obtaining lab work.

STEP FOUR:
SCHEDULE AN EVALUATION DAY

Question:
What do I do once I have had my lab work done?

Answer:
You will need to check with your anti-aging physician, as to what you do next. If your are going to be a patient of CHI, once you have your lab work done, you need to contact us to schedule an Evaluation Day. It usually takes about ten (10) days to receive all of your lab results. Therefore, you may plan on scheduling an Evaluation Day ten days from the time you have your lab work done.

Question:
What happens once I schedule my Evaluation Day?

Answer:
Once again, we do not know what other anti-aging medical practices do, so you will need to check with them. If, however, you are a

CHI patient, we send you a comprehensive Health Assessment Form that must be completed at least one week prior to your Evaluation Day. The form is then mailed to our office for processing by your anti-aging health care team. You are also sent instructions and a schedule for your Evaluation Day. If you are coming from out of the region, we also send you information about hotel accommodations or any other information that may be appropriate. We inform our patients that they can expect to spend anywhere from four to eight hours with us on Evaluation Day, depending on the number of screening tests and consultations done on Evaluation Day.

Question:
Can I just get my lab work done and not schedule an Evaluation Day?

Answer:

Yes, you can get your lab work done and not schedule an Evaluation Day. You will want to schedule a Lab Interpretation Consultation, however, with your anti-aging physician. This consultation lasts about one hour and may be done at the physician's office or over the phone. If you are going to take the time and spend the money to have your laboratory work done, we think that you at least owe it to yourself, to learn what your results are and what options are available to improve your hormone levels or address any other concerns, that your lab test results might reveal. The cost for a comprehensive lab interpretation consultation varies but will usually range between $150.00 to $250.00.

Question:
What is an Evaluation Day?

Answer:

An Evaluation Day is the time that your anti-aging physician and his/her staff have scheduled to evaluate your mental and physical status through diagnostic testing and consultations. The minimum that we require for our patients on Evaluation Day is a comprehensive history and physical done by an anti-aging physician, a comprehensive lab test consultation, an H Scan, which is a thirty minute computerized test that measures the twelve biomarkers of aging (hearing, vision, lung capacity, reaction time, memory, etc.) to determine your biological age as opposed to your chronological age, a fifteen minute computerized cognitive assessment test to further identify any early warning signs of mental decline, an impedance test which measures body fat and an hour consultation with our nutritionist. The HealthScan, which uses electronic beam tomography to assess cardiac risk, tumor risk and also measures bone density, is an optional screening test that is highly recommended. An hour consultation with one of our qualified exercise trainers is also strongly recommended but is optional. Chapter Four of this book will discuss, in greater detail, a typical Evaluation Day.

Question:
How much does an Evaluation Day cost?

Answer:
The cost for an Evaluation Day varies from one anti-aging medical practice to another. Typically, the cost for an Evaluation Day can range from $1,200 to $2,500 depending on the number of screening tests and consultations that are performed and also, depending on what your anti-aging physician charges for the various consultations and diagnostic tests.

STEP FIVE: OBTAIN ANSWERS TO ANY OTHER QUESTIONS YOU MAY HAVE

Question:
How long do I need to be on an anti-aging program?

Answer:
Currently, the treatment modalities offered by your anti-aging physician which include diet, exercise, natural or bio-identical hormone replacement therapy, vitamin, mineral and other supplementation, brain boosting supplements and medications, brain exercises and stress reduction techniques are the best options we have to prevent the unwanted effects of aging. So, the answer is that you will need to be on an anti-aging program for the rest of your life. If

you are not on an anti-aging program, you can look around and see what aging can do to the body and to the mind. The choice is yours. Further, as we state many times throughout this book, we can recommend the necessary treatments for anti-aging but it is up to you to make some lifestyle changes and to commit, on a daily basis, to improving your health and well-being. We have a partnership with our patients but the only way that partnership is successful is if everyone does his/her part. You will not see the results we know are possible if you do not follow the guidelines we provide. All of the staff at CHI are on their own anti-aging programs, which are based on their individual lab values. We feel that we cannot effectively recommend anti-aging treatment options to our patients if we are not participating in our own anti-aging programs.

Question:
What are some of the benefits of an anti-aging program?

Answer:
Some of the benefits of an anti-aging program include the loss of body fat, skin rejuvenation, improved memory, better concentration, improved reaction time, a better sense of well-being, a stronger immune system, increased physical performance and better sexual functioning.

Question:
Can I just replace my estrogen, progesterone or testosterone? Can I use synthetic medications?

Answer:
You can just replace your estrogen, progesterone or testosterone if your lab results indicate that this is necessary. However, if you were going to tune your piano so that it had the most melodic sound possible, would you just tune one key? The same principle works for hormone replacement. Although it is better to replace some hormones rather than doing nothing at all, it is much more beneficial to return all of your hormone levels to a youthful therapeutic range so that your body will once again work in harmony; just like it did

when you were younger. In regards to using synthetic hormone replacement like Premarin, Provera, etc., it is not healthful in the long term. Replacing hormones with bio-identical hormones, hormones that have the same molecular structures that are found naturally in your body, is much more healthful and there will be little or no unwanted side effects over the course of time.

Question:
If I cannot afford anti-aging treatment, will changing my diet help me?

Answer:
Eating a hormonally correct diet is the most important thing you can do for yourself. If you read Chapter Seven in this book, you will learn why you need to eat hormonally correctly for improved health and well-being. The food you put in your mouth is the foundation for determining your present and future health and well-being.

Question:
Do I have to exercise?

Answer:
Absolutely. The human body needs exercise to thrive. Exercise can greatly improve your chances for increased longevity. Taking a walk every day is not too difficult. You need to exercise to rid your body of toxins and to help new cells grow. Exercising is a critical component to the success of your anti-aging program. Read Chapter Nine in this book to learn why you need to exercise.

STEP SIX: ASK THE COST OF YOUR ANTI-AGING PROGRAM

Question:
How much does an anti-aging program cost?

Answer:
The annual cost of an anti-aging program will usually be between $4,000 and $6,000 annually for hormone balancing without human

growth hormone. Included in these figures are the cost of your pre-scription medications, your quarterly lab test fees, physician charges and the cost of your vitamins, minerals and supplements. If it is clinically indicated that you need human growth hormone, the annual cost of your anti-aging program can range from approximately $8,000 to $25,000 per year, depending on the number of units of human growth hormone you need every week and depending upon the cost of your prescription medications, your physician charges, the cost of your quarterly lab tests and the cost of your vitamins, minerals and supplements. Sometimes, various insurance carriers will pay for certain prescription medications, including estrogen, progesterone and testosterone.

If you have a medical savings account, which some companies now offer instead of the standard commercial insurance health plan, you may have the option to decide how your health care dollars are going to be spent. If not, you will need to look at your budget and determine how you are going to spend your money. You will need to decide if it is more important to budget for preventing disease and illness or if it is more important to budget for a new car every few years. Every person needs to assess his/her priorities and decide what is most important in their lives. We are of the opinion that investing in one's health and wellness is the most important thing a person can do. The choice is yours. Hopefully, someday, insurance carriers will enthusiastically pay for anti-aging medicine, which is truly preventative medicine.

REMEMBER THIS

- If you want to learn more about the science of anti-aging medicine before you get started, please read Part Three of this book and then return to this chapter

- Anti-aging medicine is a new field of medicine that continually examines the scientific research of what causes illness, what causes aging and what causes the decline in physical and mental function as we age

- Anti-aging medicine offers patients individualized plans to slow and even reverse aging

- Anti-aging medicine looks at internal causes for treating or preventing external symptoms

- Anti-aging medicine works to prevent many of the mental and physical losses currently associated with aging

- Anti-aging medicine helps patients maintain the highest mental and physical function possible for the duration of their lives

- The primary goal of anti-aging medicine is improved health and well-being

- We age because our hormone levels decline, our hormone levels do not decline because we age

- To learn more about anti-aging medicine you can visit the California HealthSpan Institute (CHI) website at www.ehealthspan.com, the American Academy of Anti-Aging Medicine (A4M) website at www.worldhealth.net and the Life Extension website at www.LifeExtension.com and Dr. Sears' website at www.drsears.com

- A few books dedicated to anti-aging medicine are Brain Longevity by Dharma Singh Khalsa, M.D., and Hormones of Youth and Ten

Weeks To A Younger You by Dr. Ronald M. Klatz, president and founder of the American Academy of Anti-Aging and The Anti-Aging Zone by Barry Sears, Ph.D.

- Unlike your primary care physician, your anti-aging physician does not need to reside in your hometown. CHI has anti-aging patients throughout the United States. The only visit you need to make to your anti-aging physician is for your Evaluation Day. Follow-up care can be done successfully by telephone

- Your anti-aging physician does not take the place of your primary care physician. Your anti-aging physician specializes in your anti-aging medical needs only. If, however, you feel more comfortable having an anti-aging physician in your local area, you can contact the American Academy of Anti-Aging Medicine (A4M) and they will provide you with a reference list of qualified anti-aging physicians throughout the country. The phone number for the American Academy of Anti Aging Medicine, which is located in Chicago, Illinois, is (773) 528-4333

- The baseline laboratory tests that are ordered tell us what your hormone levels are, how your kidneys and liver are functioning, what your fat levels are in your blood, if you have inflammation that may put you at risk for cardiovascular disease, what your blood cell counts are, if you are at risk for osteoporosis and for men, certain blood tests may identify possible problems with the prostate gland. The specific mandatory baseline tests that we order are:
  - Complete Blood Count: Measures blood cell counts
  - Comp. Metabolic Panel: Measures glucose, sodium, potassium, chloride and other electrolytes and minerals, in addition to evaluating kidney and liver function
  - Lipid Profile: Measures cholesterol, triglycerides, HDL, LDL and cardiac risk factor
  - Hemoglobin A1C: Measures the amount of glucose found in your red blood cells
  - Fasting Insulin: Measures insulin levels
  - Homocysteine: Measures waste products of protein metabolism, which can cause your arteries to clog. High homocysteine

levels are associated with a greater risk for cardiovascular disease, even if your lipid profile is normal

- Cardio C-Reactive Protein: May be the most accurate measure for evaluating inflammation in the arteries. Elevated C-Reactive Protein levels are associated with greater risk for strokes and heart attacks
- DHEA-Sulfate: Measure DHEA levels
- F &T Testosterone — Measures free and total testosterone levels and sex hormone & SHBG: binding globulin in both males and females
- Estradiol: Measures estradiol levels in both men and women
- Progesterone: Measures progesterone levels in women only
- IGF1 (Somatomedin C) Measures growth hormone secretion levels in the body
- LH: Measures leutenizing hormone levels in both men and women
- FSH: Measures follicle stimulating hormone levels in both men and women
- DHT: Measures dihydrotestosterone levels in men only
- TSH: Measures levels of the thyroid stimulating hormone
- Free T4: Measures free levels of the thyroid hormone thyroxine
- Free T3: Measures free levels of the thyroid hormone tri-iodothyronine
- PSA: Measures levels of the prostate specific antigen in the male prostate gland
- N-Telopeptides: A urine test that can indicate risk for or evidence of the disease osteoporosis
- Antioxidant Screen — An optional blood test that measures various antioxidant levels in the body including vitamin A, vitamin C, vitamin E, etc.

- You need to be fasting for your blood work. You may not have anything to eat or drink, except water, after midnight the night before your blood is drawn

- Generally speaking, the baseline laboratory tests usually cost about $550.00. Prices may vary, however. If requested, we provide prospective patients with a list of the required baseline laboratory tests and instruct them to take the list to their primary care physician and ask their physician to order the tests

- Sometimes insurance will pay for the laboratory tests if they are ordered by a primary care provider

- At this time, we do not bill insurance for any of the services we offer because it has been our experience that insurance carriers are not up to speed with the latest trends and technologies of anti-aging medicine and therefore, they do not cover most preventive services

- If you live in the San Diego region, Lab Corp or Quest Diagnostics laboratories will do your lab work. Both corporations have numerous draw sites throughout San Diego County and are familiar with the specialized tests we order

- If you do not live in San Diego County, we coordinate with Pinnacle Labs in Salt Lake City, Utah for lab work to be done any-where in the country. We send Pinnacle Labs a prescription for your blood work and they facilitate with a local lab in your area, to make sure the appropriate lab tests are done and that the lab has the correct test material to collect your blood samples. Pinnacle Labs will contact you to schedule your blood work and you will pay them directly for the tests. Once the lab tests are com-pleted, Pinnacle Labs sends CHI the results

- If you live in San Diego, Lab Corp or Quest Diagnostics sends CHI the lab results. If you have your lab work done with CHI and not Pinnacle, you will pay CHI for your lab tests. CHI then pays Lab Corps or Quest Diagnostics for your tests

- If you plan on seeing someone other than CHI for your anti-aging medical care, you will need to contact them regarding their pro-cedures for obtaining lab work

- After your lab work is done, you will need to check with your anti-aging physician, as to what you do next

- If your are going to be a patient of CHI, once you have your lab work done, you need to contact us to schedule an Evaluation Day. It usually takes about ten (10) days to receive all of your lab results. Therefore, you may plan on scheduling an Evaluation Day ten days from the time you have your lab work done

- We do not know what other anti-aging medical practices do for their Evaluation Day, so you will need to check with them

- If you are a CHI patient, we send you a comprehensive Health Assessment Form that must be completed at least one week prior to your Evaluation Day. The form is then mailed to our office for processing by your anti-aging health care team. You are also sent instructions and a schedule for your Evaluation Day. If you are coming from out of the region, we also send you information about hotel accommodations or any other information that may be appropriate

- We inform our patients that they can expect to spend anywhere from four to eight hours with us on Evaluation Day, depending on the number of screening tests and consultations done on Evaluation Day

- You can get your lab work done and not schedule an Evaluation Day. You will want to schedule a Lab Interpretation Consultation, however, with your anti-aging physician. This consultation lasts about one hour and may be done at the physician's office or over the phone. If you are going to take the time and spend the money to have your laboratory work done, we think that you at least owe it to yourself, to learn what your results are and what options are available to improve your hormone levels or address any other concerns, that your lab test results might reveal

- The cost for a comprehensive lab interpretation consultation varies but will usually range between $150.00 to $250.00

- An Evaluation Day is the time that your anti-aging physician and his staff have scheduled to evaluate your mental and physical status through various diagnostic testing and consultations. The minimum that we require for our patients on Evaluation Day is a comprehensive history and physical done by an anti-aging physician, a comprehensive lab test consultation, an H Scan, which is a

thirty minute computerized test that measures the twelve biomarkers of aging (hearing, vision, lung capacity, reaction time,
memory, etc.) to determine your biological age as opposed to your
chronological age, a fifteen minute computerized cognitive
assessment test to further identify any early warning signs of
mental decline, an impedance test which measures body fat and
an hour consultation with our nutritionist. The HealthScan, which
uses electronic beam tomography to access cardiac risk, tumor
risk and also measures bone density, is an optional screening test
that is highly recommended. An hour consultation with one of
our qualified exercise trainers is also strongly recommended but
is optional

• The cost for an Evaluation Day varies from one anti-aging medical practice to another. Typically, the cost for an Evaluation Day
  can range from $1,200 to $2,500 depending on the number of
  screening tests and consultations that are performed and also,
  depending on what your anti-aging physician charges for the various consultations and diagnostic tests

• Currently, the treatment modalities offered by your anti-aging
  physician which include diet, exercise, natural or bio-identical
  hormone replacement therapy, vitamin, mineral and other supplementation, brain boosting supplements and medications, brain
  exercises and stress reduction techniques are the best options we
  have to prevent the unwanted effects of aging

• You will need to be on an anti-aging program for the rest of your
  life

• If you are not on an anti-aging program, you can look around and
  see what aging can do to the body and to the mind

• We can recommend the necessary treatments for anti-aging but it
  is up to you to make some lifestyle changes and to commit, on a
  daily basis, to improving your health and well-being

• Some of the benefits of an anti-aging program include the loss of
  body fat, skin rejuvenation, improved memory, better concentra-

tion, improved reaction time, a better sense of well-being, a stronger immune system, increased physical performance and better sexual functioning

• You can just replace your estrogen, progesterone or testosterone if your lab results indicate that this is necessary. However, if you were going to tune your piano so that it had the most melodic sound possible, would you just tune one key? The same principle works for hormone replacement. Although it is better to replace some hormones rather than doing nothing at all, it is much more beneficial to return all of your hormone levels to a youthful therapeutic range so that your body will once again work in harmony; just like it did when you were younger

• Using synthetic hormone replacement like Premarin, Provera, etc., it is not healthful in the long term. Replacing hormones with bio-identical hormones, hormones that have the same molecular structures that are found naturally in your body is much more healthful and there will be little or no unwanted side effects over the course of time

• Eating a hormonally correct diet is the most important thing you can do for yourself. The food you put in your mouth is the basis for determining your present and future health and well-being

• The human body needs exercise to thrive. Exercise can greatly improve your chances for greater longevity. Taking a walk every day is not too difficult. You need to exercise to rid your body of toxins and to help new cells grow. Exercising is a critical component to the success of your anti-aging program

• The annual cost of an anti-aging program will usually be between $4,000 and $6,000 annually for hormone balancing without human growth hormone. Included in these figures are the cost of your prescription medications, your quarterly lab test fees, physician charges and the cost of your vitamins, minerals and supplements

• If it is clinically indicated that you need human growth hormone, the annual cost of your anti-aging program can range from approximately $8,000 to $25,000 per year, depending on the number of units of human growth hormone you need every week and depending upon the cost of your prescription medications, your physician charges, the cost of your quarterly lab tests and the cost of your vitamins, minerals and supplements

• Sometimes, various insurance carriers will pay for certain prescription medications, including estrogen, progesterone and testosterone

• You will need to look at your budget and determine how you are going to spend your money. You will need to decide if it is more important to budget for preventing disease and illness or if it is more important to budget for a new car every few years

• Every person needs to assess his/her priorities and decide what is most important in their lives. We are of the opinion that investing in one's health and wellness is the most important thing a person can do. The choice is yours

• Hopefully, someday, insurance carriers will enthusiastically pay for anti-aging medicine, which is truly preventative medicine

YOUR EVALUATION DAY

CHAPTER FOUR

YOUR EVALUATION DAY

It is now time for your Evaluation Day. You have had your baseline laboratory work done at least ten days prior to your Evaluation Day. It takes ten days for all of your baseline laboratory work to be completed. We thought it might be interesting for you to follow a typical couple through their Evaluation Day to give you a better understanding of what to expect. We like to treat couples together for their anti-aging medical needs because it has been our experience that when just one partner begins to feel the benefits of their anti-aging program, the other partner is left behind feeling all of the effects that aging can bring without medical intervention. A comprehensive anti-aging program will:

- Replace hormone levels to those of a 20-30 year old
- Enrich the body with optimum doses of proven antioxidants and nutraceuticals
- Enhance health through eating a hormonally correct diet
- Improve brain function through diet, exercise, hormone replacement and various brain boosting medications and supplements and also, brain exercises
- Improve physical exercise performance, which includes aerobic anaerobic and flexibility training
- Decrease body fat
- Increase muscle fiber
- Make bones stronger
- Improve energy levels and sense of well-being
- Improve skin texture and quality
- Enhance immune system function
- Increase libido and improve sexual performance

Since we cannot take you on your own Evaluation Day journey, because we do not know your lab values and we do not know your medical history, we will take you on an Evaluation Day journey with a middle-aged couple, Meno and Andro Pause.

Meno is a 45-year old female marketing executive who is just beginning to feel some of the effects of pending menopause or as we say in the medical field, Mrs. Pause is peri-menopausal. Meno states that she is "stressed-out" from the demands of being a full-time mother and a successful professional. Meno tells us that she really tries to eat a low fat diet most of the time, but she is still experiencing weight gain, especially around her middle and in her thighs. Meno says that she is not sleeping well these days and does not know why. Meno says that she has very little interest in sex and that she is always tired.

Meno's husband, Andro, is a 52-year old male who owns a chain of successful sporting good stores. Andro states that he has become depressed lately and he has noticed that his sexual performance is not what it used to be. Andro says that he works-out at least four times per week but he is not seeing many results from his vigorous exercise routine. Andro has also had to buy 36-inch waist pants, which troubles him greatly. Andro tells us that he is less patient with his three children, ages 10, 15 and 17 these days and they call him a "grumpy old man."

Prior to their Evaluation Day, Mr. and Mrs. Pause were sent a comprehensive seventeen- page Health and Wellness Assessment form to complete. The form addresses the patient's current and past medical history and the patient's family medical history. There are also numerous pages to complete on the patient's dietary habits and several pages on social and occupational issues. The completed assessment forms are mailed to CHI at least one week prior to the scheduled Evaluation Day. Completed assessment forms are reviewed by the physician, the nursing staff, the nutritionist and the trainer prior to a patient's Evaluation Day in preparation for creating a comprehensive anti-aging program for the patient. The assessment forms of Mr. and Mrs. Pause assist the physician and his staff in outlining initial anti-aging programs for the couple. As stated earlier, CHI recommends that couples be treated concurrently, so they may both experience the benefits of returning their hormone levels to those of a twenty to thirty year old and of the other lifestyle changes that will be recommended on their Evaluation Day.

Anti-aging program costs, program benefits and program components are discussed, via phone, with Mr. and Mrs. Pause prior to their Evaluation Day. These same topics are once again, thoroughly reviewed on Evaluation Day. It is stressed that currently, many anti-aging treatment modalities are not covered by insurance and expenses for Evaluation Day and subsequent anti-aging treatment options will most likely be an out of pocket expense. We feel that an investment in one's health and well-being is money well spent but we realize that not everyone may have that same opinion.

Mr. and Mrs. Pause will have the following procedures or consultations done on their Evaluation Day:

- Comprehensive History and Physical done by a CHI physician

- Comprehensive Lab Interpretation done by a CHI physician

- Body fat analysis done by Impedance testing

- Electronic Beam Computerized Tomography Screening Test

- Comprehensive Nutritional Assessment

- Comprehensive Exercise Assessment

- Cognitive Assessment Testing

- H Scan Testing (tests the 12 biomarkers of aging)

- Comprehensive Nursing Assessment

Mr. and Mrs. Pause begin their anti-aging Evaluation Day at 9:00 a.m. with a visit to Vital Imaging of La Jolla, where they will each have an Electronic Beam Computed Tomography (EBCT) test. The test is a non-invasive radiological procedure that takes about fifteen minutes and has no more exposure to x-ray than a typical chest x-ray. The EBCT scans a patient's torso and is an excellent screening device for coronary artery disease, cancer and also determines bone density, which can be a sign of osteoporosis if results are low. Once the test is completed, Mr. and Mrs. Pause, meet with a staff cardiologist at Vital Imaging of La Jolla to discuss the results of their respective EBCT's. The staff cardiologist then contacts CHI to discuss test results with a CHI physician. The entire process at Vital Imaging of La Jolla takes approximately one and one half-hours. When Mr. and Mrs. Pause finish their respective EBCT's, they drive to CHI for the remainder of the day.

Upon arriving at CHI, Mr. and Mrs. Pause each spend about fifteen minutes completing necessary paperwork, which gives the CHI staff permission to treat them. Once the paperwork is completed, Andro proceeds to the H-Scan testing area with a CHI staff member to complete a supervised 30-minute computerized baseline anti-aging test. The H-Scan tests hearing, vision, lung capacity, memory, reaction time, vibro-tactial sensitivity and coordination. The test measures the patient's results against the results of thousands of similar patients in a database. The purpose of the test is to ascertain a patient's biological age as opposed to his/her chronological age. A patient might be fifty chronologically but forty or sixty biologically, as an example. Once we know Andro's biological age, we can more effectively design his anti-aging program. A repeat H Scan test in one-year, should quantitatively show improved test responses because of the anti-aging interventions recommended by CHI, which has typically been CHI's experience over the last three years of treating hundreds of patients.

While Andro completes his H Scan, Meno is asked to complete a fifteen to twenty-minute computerized cognitive assessment test administered by a CHI staff member. This test measures psychomotor reflexes, delayed memory and working memory. Psychomotor reflex testing measures a person's physical reaction time and delayed memory testing measures a person's recall speed and the capacity and accuracy of their short term memory. Working memory-testing measures how well your right and left brain communicates and is an accurate reflection of cognitive processing speed. Since the results of the cognitive assessment test are so sensitive, they can assist the CHI physician in identifying potential brain functioning problems at an earlier stage. Therefore, preventive and/or corrective treatment can be recommended before symptoms become pronounced. Just as people have their blood pressure monitored, their blood work checked for diabetes or elevated cholesterol levels, they should also begin cognitive check-ups if they are forty years of age or older, have a family history of Alzheimer's Disease, have depression, have Attention Deficit Disorder or think that a particular medication might be impairing their memory.

Meno scored within the normal range on her cognitive assessment tests but computerized brain exercises are recommended and the reasons for these exercises are explained. Just as the rest of Meno's body needs exercise, so does her brain. A series of computerized cognitive enhancement exercises (known as anaerobic brain exercises) are important for all adults to assist in maintaining and enhancing brain function. The CHI physician will discuss the test results in detail with Meno during her history and physical.

When Meno completes her cognitive assessment testing, she proceeds to the H-Scan testing area, to complete her H-Scan. Andro finishes his H-Scan in record time and he then completes his cognitive assessment testing. It is noted that Andro scores out of the normal range on the cognitive assessment test. Other baseline cognitive testing is done to determine the cause for the abnormal test results. Upon further cognitive testing, it is clear that Andro is suffering from depression and Attention Deficit Disorder. The cognitive assessment test results for both Andro and Meno will assist the physician in prescribing effective treatment options to improve brain health. Computerized brain exercises are also recommended for Andro. Both Meno and Andro will be able to use their personal home computer to log-on to their brain exercise programs. Andro and Meno will take home a CD and instructions for installing the software for the interactive brain exercise program called Think Fast! The program is state of the art in cognitive enhancement exercises and was developed by Cognitive Care, Inc. in Irvine, California.

After Andro completes his cognitive assessment testing, he is greet-ed by a CHI anti-aging physician for his two-hour comprehensive history and physical. The physician consults with Andro to learn more about his medical history, his family's medical history, his social history and any other pertinent information. Chatting with Andro reveals that his father died of prostate cancer at age 70 and that his mother has high blood pressure but is otherwise alive and well. Andro has one brother and one sister; both younger and they are alive and well. Andro states that he has always been very active in sports and though he was not good enough for professional base-ball, he did play in the minor leagues for about five years. Andro states that he has worked very hard to be successful in the sporting goods industry but it takes lots of concentration and lots of time away from home. Andro says that he does not seem as sharp men-tally as he was a few years ago and this concerns him greatly. Andro also tells the doctor that he sometimes is not able to get an erection and his wife seems to have little interest in sex these days but his sexual drive isn't all that great either. Andro tells the doctor that he just figures he is aging and he does not like the effects of aging that he is currently feeling.

After listening to the patient for some time, the CHI physician explains what anti-aging medicine is and why it is so effective at delaying, preventing or correcting many of the disease processes and debilitating signs and symptoms associated with aging. After about an hour and one half, the CHI physician asks the nursing staff to obtain a height, weight, body fat percentage, blood pressure, pulse, respiration and temperature on the patient. The nursing staff, at this time, also obtains a nursing history from the patient and offers further anti-aging treatment education. Once the nursing staff has completed this process, pictures are taken of the patient for his chart. The pictures are a reminder of how the patient looked prior to beginning his anti-aging program Follow-up pictures may be taken sometime in the future to compare the noticeable changes that occur when someone is on an anti-aging program for one or more years. After the picture taking, Andro is asked to disrobe and put a patient gown on. When the patient is ready, the CHI physician, completes a physical exam which includes testing reflexes, listening to heart and lungs, listening to the carotid arteries for any abnormalities, palpating for any abdominal masses, checking peripheral pulses for any possible circulatory problems, checking vision, ears, nose and throat and performing a prostate and digital rectal exam. When Andro has completed his physical exam, he is asked to dress and proceed to his consultation with the nutritionist.

When Meno completes her H Scan, she meets with the CHI nutritionist, who has created a tentative nutritional plan for the patient. After an hour-long consultation with the nutritionist, which includes patient teaching on a hormonally correct diet, more specifically teaching about a Zone diet, Meno is given a twenty-page customized nutritional program to assist her in eating a more healthful diet. The nutritionist has calculated Meno's daily protein requirements based on Meno's activity level, her percent body fat and her lean muscle mass. The nutritionist explains to Meno why she is gaining weight on her low-fat diet and why the proper amounts of protein, favorable carbohydrates and favorable fats need to be part of her three meals per day and her two snacks during the day. Eating a hormonally correct diet will help Meno drop the unwanted pounds she has picked up over that last few years and it will also improve her overall health and well-being. The nutritional program created for Meno includes sample menus that can be easily incorporated into Meno's everyday life. Meno learns that the nutritionist is available, at any time, for consultation and that this service is included in the cost of Meno's anti-aging program.

When Meno is finished with the nutritionist, she then meets with one of the CHI certified trainers for an hour consultation. The exercise trainer will discuss Meno's current exercise program. Based on the patient's lifestyle and exercise preferences, the CHI trainer will design a specific and effective exercise program for Meno and will work with her so that she can experience, first-hand, on Evaluation Day, the necessary exercises she needs to do, to maximize her exercise efforts. A CHI trainer is available after Evaluation Day, at an added cost, to assist patients who live locally should the service be requested. For patients living outside of the CHI geographical area, we recommend enlisting the help of a qualified trainer, even for a short time, to get started on a comprehensive and effective exercise program.

While Andro meets with the nutritionist and the trainer, Meno is seen by a CHI physician for her comprehensive lab analysis, history and physical and nursing assessment. The physician learns that Meno's parents are alive and well and she has one sister who is two years older. Meno tells the doctor that she is always tired, has trouble sleeping, has little interest in sex these days and feels very stressed. Meno says she does not like what she sees when she looks in the mirror. She notices more wrinkles on her face and everything seems to be drooping south on her body. After an hour and one half, the physician performs Meno's physical exam, in the presence of a female nursing staff member. The physical exam that is done on female patients by a CHI physician is the same as the male exam except a breast exam is done and a pelvic exam is deferred to the female patient's primary care physician or OB/GYN physician. A digital rectal exam might be done on a female patient if there is an indication that the patient has a history of rectal bleeding or ulcers.

In between all of the tests and consultations that Mr. and Mrs. Pause are having on Evaluation Day, there is still enough time to have a hormonally correct lunch. Mr. and Mrs. Pause are asked to choose from a variety of salads, served with grilled chicken breasts for their lunchtime entrée. The CHI physician dines with Mr. and Mrs. Pause, as this is a time to become better acquainted with the couple.

During their respective time with the CHI physician, laboratory test results are discussed with Andro and Meno. Andro's lab tests revealed that his lipid profile is normal, his blood count is normal, his electrolytes are normal, his liver enzymes are slightly elevated, his homocysteine and cardio-C-Reactive protein (tests for cardiac risk) are normal and his fasting insulin, his hemoglobin A1C and fasting glucose levels are slightly elevated. Andro's total and free testosterone levels (the testosterone that is bio-available) are quite low, his DHEA Sulfate level is low, his free T3 level is low (the thyroid hormone that is bio-available) his IGF1 level is very low (measures how much growth hormone is in the body), his DHT (another testosterone level) is okay, his estrogen level is fine, his PSA level is good and his N-Telopeptides level is borderline (a urine test that screens for osteoporosis). Andro also had an antioxidant screen done and it reveals that his vitamin C, vitamin E, beta-carotene and other antioxidant levels are not within therapeutic range.

Based on Andro's lab results and other test results, including a body fat percentage of 22%, the CHI physician recommends a Zone Diet, an exercise program that includes aerobic, anaerobic and flexibility training and bio-identical hormone replacement therapy. Since Andro's testosterone levels, DHEA Sulfate, thyroid and IGF1 levels are all low, the CHI physician recommends bio-identical hormone replacement therapy with a 20% testosterone transdermal cream to be applied two times per day to return testosterone levels to those of a 20-30 year old. This will also assist in improving Andro's less than satisfying sexual performance and low interest in sex over the last year and Andro will notice definite improvement from his exercise regime. To raise DHEA Sulfate levels, DHEA is suggested to return levels to a youthful range and human growth hormone is prescribed to return IGFI to a youthful range.

Because Andro may be on the verge of osteoporosis, based on his N-Telopedtide results, a daily dose of calcium is prescribed. Further, Andro is asked to decrease his alcohol consumption to only several times per week since his liver enzymes are elevated and his glucose, fasting insulin and hemoglobin A1C are all elevated. Due to Andro's lifestyle and diet, if he does not change his diet and some of his behaviors, he may continue to be at increased risk for adult onset diabetes and possible liver problems in the future.

Andro complained of mild depression and his cognitive assessment test validated that concern, in addition to Attention Deficit Disorder. Andro's thyroid levels were low and this may be a reason for his lack of energy and his mild depression. Armour Desiccated Thyroid taken daily, which replaces both T3 and T4 thyroid hormones, is prescribed for the patient. Other nutraceuticals, including antioxidants are prescribed for the patient and will be discussed in the following chapter. To address his cognitive concerns, it is also recommended that Andro take the nutritional supplement 5-HTP to increase his serotonin levels. To improve his concentration levels, Vinpocetine is recommended, as is Deprenyl.

Meno's lab values revealed that her electrolytes, complete blood count and fasting insulin levels were all fine. However, Meno's estrogen, progesterone, testosterone and thyroid levels were all low, which is most likely why she is feeling tired all of the time and explains her lack of interest in sex. Because she is unable to sleep, it is recommended that Meno begin taking Melatonin, which is a wonderful antioxidant and also induces a better night's sleep. Melatonin is also recommended for Andro. Meno's DHEA Sulfate level was extremely low, as was her IGF1 level. Meno's percentage of body fat was 32% and she has gained about ten pounds in the last few years. Further, Meno is occasionally having hot flashes and night sweats. Meno also thought that her memory was slipping. To return her hormone levels to a youthful range, the CHI physician prescribed natural estrogen cream two times per day, micronized Progesterone Lozenges two times per day, DHEA daily and Armour Desiccated Thyroid daily. If Meno's testosterone level does not increase within the next three months by taking DHEA, the CHI physician will consider adding Testosterone transdermal cream 1% daily to her anti-aging program. Meno was started on human growth hormone (HGH) to improve her IGF1 levels. Meno was also started on various vitamins and nutraceuticals, which will be discussed in the next chapter. To improve her mental capabilities, Meno was started on Deprenyl every other day.

Since Meno was eating lots of unfavorable carbohydrates and not exercising routinely, it was recommended that she begin eating a Zone diet and that she start an exercise program that she would be committed to. Meno agreed to follow the recommendations of the CHI physician because she wanted to feel healthy and full of life once again.

At the end of their 8-hour Evaluation Day, Mr. and Mrs. Pause were a bit overwhelmed but also excited about beginning their anti-aging programs. They were asked to make at least a six-month commitment to improving their health and well-being because it sometimes takes that long to begin to see some of the positive effects an anti-aging program can offer. Mr. and Mrs. Pause agreed to make the commitment because they both wanted to feel better and have a better quality of life.

Mr. and Mrs. Pause each received a CHI Patient Journal at the end of their Evaluation Day. Included in each journal is an overview of

CHI, definitions about various hormones and other nutraceuticals, copies of lab results, copies of their EBCT test, copies of their H Scan test, copies of their cognitive assessment test (with a CD and patient instructions for installing the on-line brain exercise program that had been prescribed for both of them) a medication and supplement listing, instructions on human growth hormone administration, copies of their comprehensive nutritional programs, instructions for their individual exercise programs, copies of anti-aging articles that are informative and copies of the legal consent forms they had signed.

Andro and Meno were instructed on the administration and use of human growth hormone (HGH) and on the administration of various other medications and supplements that had been prescribed by the CHI physician. Husband and wife were encouraged to contact CHI at anytime for any questions or concerns they might have. They were told that they would be required to have follow-up lab testing every three months and baseline testing done annually, which would include lab tests, cognitive assessment testing and H Scan testing. Impedance testing would be done every six months, to measure percent body fat. Mr. and Mrs. Pause were told that if they followed their diet, did their exercise programs at least three to five times per week and took their medications and supplements as the CHI physician prescribed, they could expect to see results in the not too distant future.

Evaluation Days are fun and very informative. We can tell you, after a year on their respective anti-aging programs, Mr. and Mrs. Pause are now Mr. and Mrs. Hormone Happy. Follow-up lab tests reveal youthful hormone levels for both husband and wife. Meno's percent body fat has dropped to 24% and she has shed ten pounds. Andro's body fat percentage has dropped to 18% and he is now sporting a 33-inch waistline and has better biceps and triceps than he did in his late twenties.

Meno's facial skin has a certain glow and her wrinkles appear to be decreasing. Meno also tells us that she no longer has hot flashes, night sweats or vaginal dryness. She also has a renewed interest in sex and she and her husband are enjoying a very satisfying sex life.

Mr. and Mrs. Pause say they have more energy and feel "more alive" these days. Andro does not drink alcohol at all and his liver enzymes look great. He told us that his sexual performance is the best it has ever been and his is very happy and grateful for his good health.

We think about Mr. and Mrs. Pause a year ago and look at them now. We see this same story repeated over and over because anti-aging medicine works. The results are seen in our patients every day. We hope you will get your lab work done and schedule an Evaluation Day with us or a qualified anti-aging physician of your choice. Your good health and well-being is only a few lab tests and an Evaluation Day away. What are you waiting for?

The following two pages are samples of a baseline H Scan test result and a baseline Cognitive Assessment test result that all of our patients take on their Evaluation Day.

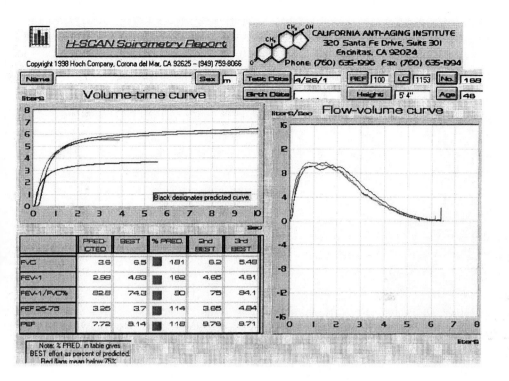

H-SCAN Spirometry Report

Copyright 1998 Hoch Company, Corona del Mar, CA 92625 – (949) 759-8066

CALIFORNIA ANTI-AGING INSTITUTE
320 Santa Fe Drive, Suite 301
Encinitas, CA 92024
Phone: (760) 635-1996 Fax: (760) 635-1994

Name: ____ Sex: m Test Date: 4/26/1 REF 100 LC 1153 No. 168

Birth Date: ____ Height: 5'4" Age: 48

Volume-time curve (liters)

Black designates predicted curve.

Flow-volume curve (liters/sec)

	PRED-CTED	BEST	% PRED	2nd BEST	3rd BEST
FVC	3.6	6.5	181	6.2	5.48
FEV-1	2.98	4.83	162	4.65	4.61
FEV-1/FVC%	82.8	74.3	90	75	84.1
FEF 25-75	3.25	3.7	114	3.85	4.84
PEF	7.72	9.14	118	9.76	9.71

Note: % PRED. in table gives BEST effort as percent of predicted. Red bars mean below 75%

H-SCAN TEST REPORT

Copyright 1998 Hoch Company, Corona del Mar, CA 92625 – (949) 759-8066

CALIFORNIA ANTI-AGING INSTITUTE
320 Santa Fe Drive, Suite 301
Encinitas, CA 92024
Phone: (760) 635-1996 Fax: (760) 635-1994

Name: ____ Sex: m Test Date: 4/26/1 Participant No. 168

The table below shows the score you obtained on each test. The percentiles column, designated "%-ILE", shows how you compare to others of your age and sex on each test, based on tests of 2,462 office workers. For example, a %-ILE of 79 indicates you scored better than 78% of persons of your age and sex, while 50 is average. # indicates that the test was skipped or that the score was outside of acceptable limits and won't count. The percentiles are also plotted on the bar graph, numbered as in the table.

The computer calculates (but does not show) the age of which each test

score is typical. It then produces a weighted average of these "typical" ages, which is listed as your "Test age based on combination of scores" below the graph. Tests marked # are omitted from this average. (Below age 30, the average is less accurate because little aging has taken place. Below age 22, lungs and reactions are not fully developed and these scores are omitted from the average.)

No claims for these tests, such as claims regarding health or aging, are made or are authorized to be made beyond the statements on this chart.

TEST	SCORE	%-ILE
1. Auditory reaction time, sec	.16	34
2. Highest audible pitch, kHz	12.5	67
3. Vibrotactile sensitivity, dB	33	38
4. Visual reaction time, sec	.235	12
5. Muscle movement time, sec	.214	10
6. Lung: forced vital capacity, liters	6.41	99
7. Lung: forced expiratory vol-1 sec, liters	4.83	98
8. Visual react. time with decision, sec	.29	#
9. Muscle move. time with decision, sec	.128	42
10. Memory, length of sequence	7	16
11. Alternate button tapping time, sec	25	11
12. Visual accommodation, diopters	.9	#

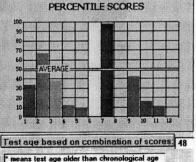

PERCENTILE SCORES

AVERAGE

Test age based on combination of scores: 48

* means test age older than chronological age

For office use: QL -2 AGUGIQLIHTlbd= 46| 31| 48| 163| 7/13/54

Neuro-Cognitive Assessment/Test Report

California Healthspan Institute, A Medical Group
320 Santa Fe Drive
Suite 301
Encinitas, CA, California 92024-5138
United States

Neuro-Cognitive Assessment/Test Report

Report Date: Mar 22, 2001	**Patient:**		
Test Date: Mar 22, 2001	**Gender:**	F	
Test Admin: Kathleen Becker, MA, RN.	**Patient ID:**	555686	
Provider: R Rothenberg, M.D.	**DOB:**		/ Age 45
Dr. Phone: 760-635-1996	**Work Phone:**		
Dr. Fax: 760-635-1994	**Home Fax:**		
Dr. Email: rrothenberg@californiaantiaging.com	**Patient Email:**		

Indication For Test: Neuro-Cognitive Assessment Testing was performed on the patient. The reason for the test was to establish a baseline and to evaluate the following as indicated by office staff prior to the test:

<u>Possible Depression</u> AND <u>Stress or Anxiety</u>

Patient History and Risk Factor Summary:

The neurological history information recorded suggests that the patient is at increased risk of cognitive impairment.

The medication(s) recorded suggest that the patient is at increased risk of cognitive impairment.

Test Results: If you decide to, or already are treating for depression, follow up monitoring using the Neuro-Cognitive Series 1 test is recommened after 90-days of treatment. The results of all tests that were conducted during this session and a summary of their results are as follows:

Series/Test Name	Within Normal Range	Out of Normal Range
Neuro-Cognitive Series 2		
Delayed Memory	X	
Working Memory	X	
Immediate Memory	X	
Psychometric Testing		
GDS Depression Scale		X

Interpretation of Neuro-Cognitive Test Results: One or more of the Patient's neuro-cognitive test results were found to be out of normal range in the direction of poor performance. This represents performance in approximately the bottom 2% of people the same age.

Recommended Action: If you decide to, or already are treating for depression, follow up monitoring using the Neuro-Cognitive Series 1 test is recommended after 90-days of treatment.

REMEMBER THIS

• Get your baseline laboratory work done at least ten days prior to your Evaluation Day

• It takes ten days for all of your baseline laboratory work to be completed

• We prefer to treat couples together for their anti-aging medical needs because it has been our experience that when just one partner begins to feel the benefits of their anti-aging program, the other partner is left behind feeling all of the effects that aging can bring, without medical intervention

• A comprehensive anti-aging program will:
  • Replace hormone levels to those of a 20-30 year old
  • Enrich the body with optimum doses of proven antioxidants and nutraceuticals
  • Enhance health through eating a hormonally correct diet
  • Improve brain function through diet, exercise, hormone replacement and various brain boosting medications and supplements and also, brain exercises
  • Improve physical exercise performance, which includes aerobic anaerobic and flexibility training
  • Decrease body fat
  • Increase muscle fiber
  • Make bones stronger
  • Improve energy levels and sense of well-being
  • Improve skin texture and quality
  • Enhance immune system function
  • Increase libido and improve sexual performance

• At CHI, prior to Evaluation Day you will be sent a comprehensive seventeen- page Health and Wellness Assessment form to complete. The form addresses your current and past medical history and your family medical history. There are also numerous pages to complete on your dietary habits and several pages on social and occupational issues

- At CHI, anti-aging program costs, program benefits and program components are discussed, via phone, with every patient prior to their Evaluation Day. These same topics are once again, thoroughly reviewed on Evaluation Day

- Many anti-aging treatment modalities are not covered by insurance and expenses for Evaluation Day and subsequent anti-aging treatment options will most likely be an out of pocket expense

- At CHI, you will have the following procedures or consultations done on Evaluation Day:
  - Comprehensive History and Physical done by a CHI physician
  - Comprehensive Lab Interpretation done by a CHI physician
  - Body fat analysis done by Impedance testing
  - Electronic Beam Computerized Tomography Screening Test
  - Comprehensive Nutritional Assessment
  - Comprehensive Exercise Assessment
  - Cognitive Assessment Testing
  - H Scan Testing (tests the 12 biomarkers of aging)
  - Comprehensive Nursing Assessment

- At CHI, your anti-aging Evaluation Day will begin at 9:00 a.m. with a visit to Vital Imaging of La Jolla, where you will have an Electronic Beam Computed Tomography test (EBCT). The EBCT scans a patient's torso and is an excellent screening device for coronary artery disease, cancer and also determines bone density, which can be a sign of osteoporosis if results are low

- Upon arriving at CHI you will spend about fifteen minutes completing necessary paperwork, which gives the CHI staff permission to treat you.

- The H-Scan tests hearing, vision, lung capacity, memory, reaction time, vibro-tactial sensitivity and coordination. The test measures the patient's results against the results of thousands of similar patients in a database. The purpose of the test is to ascertain a patient's biological age as opposed to his/her chronological age

- At CHI, you will take a fifteen to twenty-minute computerized cognitive assessment test, which measures psychomotor reflexes, delayed memory and working memory. Psychomotor reflex testing measures a person's physical reaction time and delayed memory testing measures a person's recall speed and the capacity and accuracy of their short term memory. Working memory testing measures how well your right and left brain communicates and is an accurate reflection of cognitive processing speed

- Just as people have their blood pressure monitored, their blood work checked for diabetes or elevated cholesterol levels, they should also begin cognitive check-ups if they are forty years of age or older, have a family history of Alzheimer's Disease, have depression, have Attention Deficit Disorder or think that a particular medication might be impairing their memory

- Cognitive enhancement exercises (known as anaerobic brain exercises) are important for all adults to assist in maintaining and enhancing brain function

- At CHI, you will have a two-hour comprehensive history and physical with a CHI physician

- The CHI physician will explain what anti-aging medicine is and why it is so effective at delaying, preventing or correcting many of the disease processes and debilitating signs and symptoms associated with aging

- The CHI physician will complete a physical exam which includes testing reflexes, listening to heart and lungs, listening to the carotid arteries for any abnormalities, palpating for any abdominal masses, checking peripheral pulses for any possible circulatory problems, checking vision, ears, nose and throat and performing a prostate and digital rectal exam. For female patients, a breast exam is done but a pelvic exam is deferred to the patient's primary care doctor or their OB/GYN physician

- At CHI, you will have an hour-long consultation, with the nutritionist, which includes patient teaching on a hormonally correct diet, more specifically teaching about a Zone diet. You will be given a customized nutritional program to assist you in eating a more healthful diet. The nutritionist will calculate your daily pro-

tein requirements based on your activity level, percent body fat
and lean muscle mass

- At CHI, the nutritionist is available, at any time, for consultation
  and this service is included in the cost of your anti-aging program
  when you are on human growth hormone

- At CHI, you will meet with one of the CHI certified trainers for an
  hour consultation. The exercise trainer will discuss your current
  exercise program. Based on your lifestyle and exercise preferences, the CHI trainer will design a specific and effective exercise
  program for you. The trainer will work with you to show you the
  necessary exercises you need to do, to maximize your exercise
  efforts. A CHI trainer is available after Evaluation Day, at an
  added cost, to assist patients who live locally should the service
  be requested. For patients living outside of the CHI geographical
  area, we recommend enlisting the help of a qualified trainer, even
  for a short time, to get started on a comprehensive and effective
  exercise program

- During your history and physical the CHI physician will discuss
  your laboratory test results

- Based on your lab test results and the results of the other tests you
  completed on your Evaluation Day, the CHI physician will recommend a Zone Diet, an exercise program that includes aerobic,
  anaerobic and flexibility training and bio-identical hormone
  replacement therapy regime. Other nutraceuticals, including
  antioxidants will also be prescribed

- At the end of your 8-hour Evaluation Day, you may feel a bit overwhelmed but also excited about beginning your anti-aging program

- At CHI we ask our patients to make at least a six-month commitment to improving their health and well-being because it sometimes takes that long to begin to see some of the positive effects an
  anti-aging program can offer

- At CHI, you will receive a CHI Patient Journal at the end of your Evaluation Day. Included in your patient journal is an overview of CHI, definitions about various hormones and other nutraceuticals, copies of lab results, copies of your EBCT test, copies of your H Scan test, copies of your cognitive assessment test (with a CD and patient instructions for installing the on-line brain exercise program that may have been prescribed) a medication and supplement listing, instructions on human growth hormone administration, a copy of your comprehensive nutritional program, instructions for your individual exercise program, copies of anti-aging articles that are informative and copies of the legal consent forms you signed

- At CHI, you will be instructed on the administration and use of human growth hormone (HGH) and on the administration of various other medications and supplements that have been prescribed by the CHI physician

- You will be required to have follow-up lab testing every three months and baseline testing done annually, which would include lab tests, cognitive assessment testing and H Scan testing. Impedance testing is done every six months, to measure percent body fat

YOUR PERSONAL ANTI-AGING PLAN

CHAPTER FIVE

YOUR PERSONAL ANTI-AGING PLAN

You have had your lab work done and you have had your Evaluation Day. At the end of your comprehensive Evaluation Day, you will be instructed on your personal anti-aging program. Once again, since we do not know your lab values and the results of your screening tests, which are done on Evaluation Day in our practice, we cannot actually design a customized anti-aging program for you in this book. What we can do, however, is share with you, the anti-aging programs we created for Mr. and Mrs. Pause, whom you became acquainted with in Chapter Four.

Before sharing Mr. and Mrs. Pause's anti-aging programs, we want to emphasize that even if you cannot afford or do not wish to begin an anti-aging program, under the supervision of a trained and qualified anti-aging physician, there are a few things that you can do on your own to improve your health. Doing something is better than doing nothing at all. To begin with, we recommend that you educate yourself on the Zone diet and the best way to do that is to buy the books, Zone-Meals In Minutes and The Soy Zone both by Barry Sears, Ph.D. These books will assist you in successfully changing your dietary habits so that you can enjoy better health. The books also contain some wonderful recipes that are easy to prepare and quite tasty.

The second thing you can do to improve your health is to begin an effective exercise program. Walking is a good form of exercise and it does not cost a thing, except for the time you need to allow in your daily schedule to actually walk. It is preferable that you incorporate flexibility, aerobic and anaerobic training into your exercise program but if you are not willing or unable to do that, then at least walk, run, swim, play basketball or use that treadmill that has been sitting in the corner of your bedroom or some other room. Reading Chapter Nine in this book will also help you with your exercise routine. Start moving and you will see the results of an improved body image and overall improved health.

The third thing you can do to fight the effects of aging is ask your primary care physician to order the necessary lab tests, to see what your key hormone levels are. Give this book to your physician and ask him or her to read it. Ask your physician to become educated in anti-aging medicine, which we believe is the foundation for 21st Century medicine, or find a physician who knows the benefits of the information presented in this book and is trained to meet your anti-aging needs.

You will need to begin to take supplements that will truly help you combat the disease of aging. Not all supplements are created equal and you want to make sure that you are spending your money wisely when you buy dietary supplements. There are some very good supplements on the market and there are some that are not so good. We use a compounding pharmacy for our prescription medications and also, for some of our supplements because we know they use the highest quality ingredients. We use Zone fish oil capsules (Omega 3 oils) because they are molecularly distilled which means that they have removed any contaminants such as PCB's that fish are exposed to. We also purchase a large portion of our supplements from Life Extension Foundation in Florida because they are well known for their continuing commitment to providing some of the highest quality products in the market today. To get most of your vitamin, mineral and other supplement needs met, you need to take a high quality vitamin combination. Life Extension Mix, in powder, capsule or tablet form is a very good vitamin combination. Our favorite vitamin combination, however, is the Supra Pak, made by Supra Health. Each Supra Pak container holds thirty pre-packaged vitamin packets with nine supplements inside of each package. You can learn more about Life Extension products by calling 800-544-4440 or visiting their website at **www.lifeextension.com.** . To learn more about the Supra Pak and Supra Health, you can contact them at 888-716-9186 or you may wish to visit their website at

www.suprahealth.com. In addition to fish oil capsules and an effective vitamin mixture, we also feel that taking the antioxidants, CoEnzyme10 (CoQ10) and Carnosine are essential for all patients.

If your are eating a hormonally correct diet, exercising and taking the necessary vitamins, minerals and other supplements, you are better off than your friend who continues to eat lots of processed foods and continues to be a couch potato. The choice is yours. We also hope that you will take some action to ensure that your hormone levels are returned to youthful levels naturally and safely. Enlisting the expertise of a trained and qualified anti-aging physician can do this. And, finally, learn to manage the stress in your life. We encourage you to read Chapter Fourteen in this book to learn more about stress reduction.

The symptoms associated with aging are caused by a variety of factors and to combat those factors, it takes a commitment on your part to make some necessary lifestyle changes. There is no magic pill or magic solution to youthfulness. To remain youthful from the inside-out takes work, every day. For example, it takes commitment to get out of bed at 5:30 a.m., every morning for a mile swim or a mile jog before work. It takes commitment to do resistance training and flexibility training. It takes commitment to take those twenty, thirty or even forty supplements every day. It takes commitment to have a Caesar salad with a grilled chicken breast instead of the delicious looking pizza that your co-workers are enjoying for lunch. It takes commitment to have your lab tests done every three months and to make sure you are following the directions of your anti-aging physician. It takes commitment to look at your budget and determine whether an investment in your current and future health is more important than buying a new car, buying more clothes or taking that second vacation this year.

We have learned that anything worthwhile in life is never easy and maintaining your anti-aging program takes work and sacrifice but the rewards are immeasurable. When we have our health, we take it for granted, when we do not have our health, all we wish for is to feel good again because nothing else really matters when we are not healthy. We believe that there are no instant cures or quick fixes for anything. It is the little things that you do every day in your life that make dreams become reality. If something sounds to good to be true than it probably is not true. We do not want you to spend your hard-earned money on gimmicks that just take your money and in the long run do not improve your overall health and well-being. So, if you are ready and willing, you can increase your health and well-being by making a daily commitment to do what needs to be done to fight the unwanted effects of aging.

Now it is time to share with you the anti-aging programs we created for Meno and Andro Pause. We will begin with Meno's program. If you remember, when Meno saw us on her Evaluation Day, she complained of being "stressed-out," having little energy, gaining weight, an inability to sleep well and having little or no interest in sex. Meno was also experiencing intermittent hot flashes, night sweats, decreased memory, more wrinkles on her face and she felt everything in her body was drooping southward. Meno's concerns are common for women her age.

Meno's lab test results revealed that her estrogen, testosterone, progesterone, IGF-1 (measures growth hormone) thyroid and DHEA sulfate levels were all low. Additionally, Meno had a body fat percentage of 32% and had gained about ten pounds over the last few years. Meno's cognitive assessment results were within the normal range and she scored okay on her H-Scan. Meno was just beginning to experience many of the signs and symptoms of declining hormone levels and she was also feeling the effects of stress overload.

Since Meno was still menstruating, we prescribed a transdermal (applied to the skin) estrogen cream called Bi-Est, which is made from bio-identical estradiol and estriol, 5 mg/GM 1/4 tsp. two times per day on days one through twenty-four of her menstrual cycle and Progesterone micronized lozenges made from bio-identical progesterone, 100 mg lozenge in the morning and 100 mg lozenge at bedtime, to be dissolved under the tongue, on days fourteen through twenty-four of her menstrual cycle. Progesterone may cause drowsiness and Meno was advised of this possible effect. When a woman is no longer menstruating, the estrogen and progesterone are given daily because cycling these medications is not necessary. Even though Meno's testosterone levels were low, we did not initially prescribe Testosterone transdermal cream 1% 1/8 tsp. daily because we know that many times a woman's testosterone levels will return to a youthful range with DHEA supplementation only. The reason we prescribe transdermal creams and lozenges for estrogen, progesterone and testosterone is that the creams and lozenges have the opportunity to be absorbed by the body before they are absorbed by the digestive tract, which can make the medications less effective.

Meno's thyroid levels were low and she had little energy. To return her thyroid levels to a youthful range, we prescribed Armour Desiccated Thyroid 1-grain daily, to be taken every morning. Armour Desiccated Thyroid replaces both T3 and T4 thyroid hormones.

Meno felt her memory was not as sharp as it once was, so we prescribed Deprenyl 5 mg every other morning. Deprenyl increases libido, improves memory, enhances attention and language abilities and most importantly it increases dopamine levels in the brain. Dopamine is an important neuro transmitter. To further improve Meno's memory, we recommended Acetyl L Carnitine 500 mg every morning. Acetyl L Carnitine is a brain booster and increases the production of the most important neurotransmitter, acetylcholine. Phosphatidyl Serine 100 mg every morning was also recommended to improve Meno's memory and overall brain health because it keeps brain cells functioning correctly and encourages nerve growth of damaged nerve networks. Vinpocetine, a memory enhancer, 60 mg in the morning and 30 mg in the afternoon, was also recommended. Pregnenolone, known as the grandmother hormone in the body, was important for Meno's improved brain functioning and also important because it was a precursor to all of the steroidal hormones in the body. The dose of Pregnenolone for Meno was 100 mg every morning. Initially, we started Meno on Melatonin 500 mcg (1/2 mg) to help her sleep and also because Melatonin is a wonderful antioxidant that improves cellular immunity. Low melatonin levels have been associated with decreased thinking ability. We told Meno to increase her Melatonin dose to 1 mg at bedtime in a few weeks because that is the minimum recommended dose of Melatonin for patients over the age of forty. To further improve her brain health, the proper amount of B vitamins would be included in the vitamin supplement we would recommend for Meno.

DHEA 25 mg every morning, the steroidal mother hormone of the body was prescribed for Meno because her DHEA Sulfate level was low. As mentioned earlier, DHEA replacement in women many times also improves testosterone levels and testosterone supplementation is not needed when this occurs. DHEA has anti-obesity; anti-tumor, anti-aging and anti-cancer properties and it also protects brain cells.

We recommended that Meno start taking the super vitamins made by Supra Health, called the Supra Pak. These vitamins contain a majority of the vitamins, minerals and other supplements and the effective doses required to combat many of the signs and symptoms associated with aging. Meno was told to start with one Supra Pak packet daily for one to two weeks and to eventually increase her dose of these mega vitamins to one packet in the morning with food and one packet later in the day with food. Occasionally, some of our patients have some gastrointestinal upset when they start taking the super vitamins but the upset usually subsides in a few weeks. If the upset continues, patients may be switched to the Life Extension Mix vitamins and they usually do well with this brand.

For breast cancer protection, we recommend that all of our female patients take Indole 3 Carbinol (dose dependent upon patient's weight) which is an extract made from cruciferous vegetables such as broccoli and cauliflower. Indole 3 Carbinol (I3C) 200 mg three times per day was recommended for Meno.

Since most women are at a greater risk for developing osteoporosis than most men, we recommend TriBoron, a calcium, magnesium and boron mixture, for all of our female patients unless it is contraindicated because of some other health condition the patient may have. For Meno, we recommended TriBoron 1500 mg in the morning and 1500-mg in the evening. For the best absorption, it is better to take calcium before eating but if that is not possible, take one dose in the morning and one dose in the evening with your meals. Some patients take all of their calcium at bedtime because they state that it helps them sleep better. Every patient is different.

One of the most important supplements we recommend for all of our patients is CoEnzyme 10 (CoQ10). CoQ10 is an important inherent antioxidant that decreases with age. Because many patients with cardiovascular disease have low levels of CoQ10, we may recommend higher doses of CoQ10 for them. For Meno, we recommended 60 mg of CoQ10 (Solanova brand) one time per day.

Carnosine, like CoQ10 is a very important anti-aging supplement. Carnosine has antioxidant properties and also enhances protein metabolism and the metabolism of our cellular DNA. Meno's dose of Carnosine will be 500 mg three times per day.

Of course, we cannot forget a daily dose of baby Aspirin. We prescribe 81 mg of Aspirin daily to all of our patients unless it is contraindicated for some other health reason. Aspirin has anti-inflammatory properties and it also assists in keeping the blood thinned.

Because Meno's IGF-1 levels are low, human growth hormone (HGH) replacement is indicated. We instructed Meno on the preparation, use and storage of her HGH. Meno will start on 6 IU's of HGH every week, six days per week and one day off, to let her own pituitary gland do its work. After three weeks, Meno's dose of HGH will increase to 9 IU's per week and she will remain on that dose until she has her first set of follow-up lab work. At that time, depending on her lab results her HGH dose will be adjusted accordingly, as will any other hormone medications or supplements.

Meno is instructed on a Zone diet by our nutritionist and given menus that are tailored to her daily protein requirements. We told Meno that she could think about fixing a protein shake for breakfast that also included some fruit and a tablespoon of peanut or almond butter because the protein shake or "Smoothie" helps all those vitamins and others supplements go down the food pipe a little easier and provides her with the proper ratios of protein, carbohydrates and fats.

Meno was also instructed, by one of our trainers, on some basic flex-ibility exercises, aerobic exercises and resistance-type exercises that she could do at home. Meno decided to purchase an ABS Swiss Fitness ball and some exercise bands in preparation for beginning her exercise program.

After meeting with a CHI physician, a CHI nurse, the nutritionist and the exercise trainer, Meno felt she was ready to begin her anti-aging program as soon as she got home. In addition to the anti-aging program we recommended we also felt that Meno would ben-efit greatly by attending a comprehensive stress reduction program. We gave Meno a list of references that she could contact to help her effectively reduce the stress in her life.

Meno's supplement/medication routine and instructions about diet and exercise, that we discussed in the preceding paragraphs, is listed below:
- Bi-Est transdermal cream 1/4 tsp. every morning and 1/4 tsp. every evening (days 1-24 of menstrual cycle)
- Progesterone lozenges 100 mg (sublingually) 1 in the morning and 1 at bedtime (days 14-24 of menstrual cycle)
- Armour Desiccated Thyroid 1 grain 1 tab every morning
- Deprenyl 5 mg 1 cap every other morning
- Acetyl L Carnitine 500 mg 1 cap every morning
- Phosphatidyl Serine 100 mg 1 cap every morning
- Vinpocetine 30 mg 2 caps in the morning and 1 cap in the after-noon
- Pregnenolone 50 mg 2 caps in the morning
- Melatonin 500 mcg 1 cap at bedtime (increase to 2 caps at bed-time in 1-2 weeks)
- Supra Pak vitamins 1 Pak with breakfast (after 1-2 weeks, increase to 2 Paks daily, 1 with breakfast and 1 with dinner)
- DHEA 25 mg 1 cap every morning
- Indole 3 Carbinol 200 mg 1 cap three times per day
- Carnosine 500 mg 1 cap three times per day
- CoQ10 60 mg (Solanova brand) 1 cap every morning
- Aspirin 81 mg 1 tab every morning
- Tri Boron 1500 mg in the morning and 1500 mg in the evening
- HGH 6 IU's per week for 3 weeks, after 3 weeks increase dose

to 9 IU's per week. Take HGH six days per week, one time per day (give dose in the morning within one hour of waking or at bedtime) Do not take any HGH one day per week

- Follow the Zone diet and use the nutrition program designed especially for you
- Follow the exercise program designed especially for you
- Follow the stress reduction techniques we gave you and attend a stress reduction workshop
- Begin at home brain exercises using the ThinkFast! Software
- Call CHI at anytime with any questions or concerns you may have
- CHI will notify you when your next lab tests need to be done and will continually monitor your anti-aging program and your progress

We have not forgotten about Andro and the anti-aging program we recommended for him. The following paragraphs will explain Andro's anti-aging program.

On Andro's Evaluation Day, we learned that he had a high-stress job, was depressed, had poor sexual performance (he could not get an erection sometimes) had a decreased interest in sex, his waist size had increased by three inches, he was not patient with his family or his employees and his kids thought he was just a grumpy old man. Andro thought he was not as sharp as he once was and that his memory was slipping. Even though Andro was going to the gym four times per week and had a good exercise routine for flexibility, aerobic and anaerobic training, his muscles did not seem as firm and as dense as they once were.

Andro's H-Scan results were okay but he scored out of range on his Cognitive Assessment tests, which showed he had Attention Deficit Disorder and that he was depressed. Andro's lipid panel (cholesterol, HDL, LDL, triglycerides) was okay but his liver enzymes were elevated. His fasting insulin, fasting glucose and hemoglobin AIC were all slightly elevated which concerned us. Was Andro at risk for developing Type II diabetes and at further risk for cardiovascular disease in the not too distant future? Andro's free and total testosterone levels were very low, as was his DHEA Sulfate level, his IGF-

1 (growth hormone level) his thyroid hormone levels and his urine N-Telopeptides level, which tests for osteoporosis, was borderline. Also, Andro's antioxidant screen revealed that his vitamin C, vitamin E, beta-carotene and other antioxidant levels were all low. Andro also had a current body fat percentage of 22%.

To address Andro's problems, we prescribed Testosterone transdermal cream 20% 1/4 tsp. two times per day to increase his testosterone levels and Armour Desiccated Thyroid 1 grain every morning to increase his thyroid levels. We also told Andro that taking the Testosterone transdermal cream would most likely resolve his erection problems but if it did not, we could think about adding Viagra to his list of medications. Andro was also aware that testosterone replacement therapy improved sexual drive and satisfaction in both men and women. Andro was looking forward to that benefit of his anti-aging program, and all of the many health benefits of bio-identical testosterone replacement therapy.

We recommended DHEA 50 mg every morning to increase Andro's DHEA levels, which would help with brain health; improved lean muscle mass and overall improved immunity. To address his depression and also his elevated insulin and glucose levels we recommended that Andro decrease his alcohol consumption to one or two glasses of wine per week or to delete alcohol altogether. We also told Andro that it was very important for him to begin to eat a hormonally correct diet.

We recommended that Andro take 5-HTP 50 mg 1-2 caps at bedtime to help his depression. 5-HTP, a precursor to tryptophan, increases serotonin levels in the brain. Serotonin is an important neurotransmitter that induces sleep; controls pain and is also known as the "feel good" neurotransmitter.

To improve his memory and his attention span, we prescribed Deprenyl 5-mg daily. Deprenyl increases libido, improves memory, enhances attention and language skills and increases the levels of dopamine in the brain. Because of his low Vitamin E levels, we also prescribed additional vitamin E (there is already vitamin E in the supra vitamins we recommend) in the amount of 400 mg daily to improve Andro's brain health. As with Meno, Andro was instructed to begin using the ThinkFast! software as part of his brain exercise program. Other brain boosting supplements that we recommended for Andro were Acetyl L Carnitine 500 mg daily, Phosphatidyl Serine 100 mg daily, Vinpocetine 30 mg, two caps in the morning and one in the afternoon, Pregnenolone 100 mg daily and Melatonin 500 mcg, one at bedtime, because Melatonin helps a person sleep but it is also a powerful antioxidant and good for brain health.

Andro was suffering from stress but not as much as his wife was. We told Andro that he should think about attending a stress reduction workshop with his wife. At the very least, Andro needed to routinely practice the stress reduction techniques CHI recommended.

Like his wife, Andro was started on the super vitamin, mineral and other supplement mixture known as the Supra Pak from Supra Health. Andro was instructed to take one Supra Pak daily for one or two weeks and then to increase his dose to two packets per day.

For prostate health, we recommend that all of our male patients take Indole 3 Carbinol (dose dependent upon patient's weight) which is an extract made from cruciferous vegetables such as broccoli and cauliflower. Indole 3 Carbinol (I3C) 200 mg four times per day was recommended for Andro. We also recommend that our male patients take a combination of saw palmetto, lycopene, urtica and pygeum to protect their prostate from enlargement and possible cancer. We use Life Extension's Natural Prostate formula for our male patients. We told Andro to take two caps of the Natural Prostate formula daily.

Andro was at risk for developing osteoporosis because his urine N-Telopeptides test was borderline. We recommended TriBoron, a calcium, magnesium and boron mixture, 1500-mg in the morning for Andro.

As we stated with Meno, one of the most important supplements we recommend for all of our patients is CoEnzyme 10 (CoQ10). CoQ10 is an important inherent antioxidant that decreases with age. For Andro, we recommended 60 mg of CoQ10 (Solanova brand) one time per day.

Carnosine, like CoQ10, is a very important anti-aging supplement. Carnosine has antioxidant properties and also enhances protein metabolism and the metabolism of our cellular DNA. Andro's dose of Carnosine will be 500 mg three times per day.

We prescribed 81 mg of Aspirin daily for Andro because of Aspirin's anti-inflammatory properties and its blood thinning capabilities.

Because Andro's IGF-1 levels are low, human growth hormone (HGH) replacement is indicated. We instructed Andro on the preparation, use and storage of his HGH. Andro will start on 6 IU's of HGH every week, six days per week and one day off, to let his own pituitary gland do its work. After three weeks, Andro's dose of HGH will increase to 9 IU's per week and he will remain on that dose until he has his first set of follow-up lab work. At that time, depending on his lab results his HGH dose will be adjusted accordingly, as will his other hormone medications and supplements.

Andro was given detailed instructions on the Zone diet by our nutritionist and he was also given menus that were tailored to his daily protein requirements. Andro was very knowledgeable about his exercise routine but he listened to the advice of the CHI trainer and stated he would incorporate some of the suggestions into his exercise routine.

After meeting with a CHI physician, a CHI nurse, the nutritionist and the exercise trainer, Andro was excited about beginning his anti-aging program.

Andro's supplement/medication routine and instructions about diet and exercise, that we discussed in the preceding paragraphs, is listed below:
- Testosterone transdermal cream 20% 1/4 tsp. every morning and every evening
- Armour Desiccated Thyroid 1 grain 1 tab every morning
- Deprenyl 5 mg 1 cap every morning
- Acetyl L Carnitine 500 mg 1 cap every morning
- Phosphatidyl Serine 100 mg 1 cap every morning
- Vinpocetine 30 mg 2 caps in the morning and 1 cap in the afternoon

- Pregnenolone 50 mg 2 caps in the morning
- Melatonin 500 mcg 1 cap at bedtime (increase to 2 caps at bedtime in 1-2 weeks)
- Supra Pak vitamins 1 Pak with breakfast (after 1-2 weeks, increase to 2 Paks daily, 1 with breakfast and 1 with dinner)
- Vitamin E 400 mg 1 cap every morning
- DHEA 25 mg 2 caps every morning
- 5-HTP 50 mg 1-2 caps at bedtime
- Natural Prostate Formula 2 caps daily
- Indole 3 Carbinol 200 mg 1 cap four times per day
- Carnosine 500 mg 1 cap three times per day
- CoQ10 60 mg (Solanova brand) 1 cap every morning
- Aspirin 81 mg 1 tab every morning
- Tri Boron 1500 mg in the morning
- HGH 6 IU's per week for 3 weeks, after 3 weeks increase dose to 9 IU's per week. Take HGH six days per week, one time per day (give dose in the morning within one hour of waking or at bedtime) Do not take any HGH one day per week
- Follow the Zone diet and use the nutrition program designed especially for you
- Incorporate the suggestions from our trainer into your current exercise program
- Follow the stress reduction techniques we gave you
- Begin at home brain exercises using the ThinkFast! Software
- Call CHI at anytime with any questions or concerns you may have
- CHI will notify you when your next lab tests need to be done and will continually monitor your anti-aging program and your progress

We hope that by sharing Andro and Meno's anti-aging program, that you have a better idea why we do what we do, how we do it and what is required by the patient to ensure that optimal outcomes will be obtained that will improve health and well-being. Every patient is an individual and every anti-aging program we create is unique, based on the patient's needs. Our goal at CHI is to prevent illness and disease through anti-aging medical intervention.

REMEMBER THIS

• We cannot actually design a customized anti-aging program for you in this book but we can share with you, the anti-aging programs we created for Mr. and Mrs. Pause, whom you became acquainted with in Chapter Four

• If you cannot afford or do not wish to begin an anti-aging program, under the supervision of a trained and qualified anti-aging physician, there are a few things that you can do on your own to improve your health

• We recommend that you educate yourself on the Zone diet and the best way to do that is to buy the books, Zone Meals In Minutes and The Soy Zone both by Barry Sears, Ph.D.

• Begin an effective exercise program

• Start moving and you will see the results of an improved body image and overall improved health

• Ask your primary care physician to order the necessary lab tests, to see what your key hormone levels are

• Give this book to your physician and ask him or her to read it

• Ask your physician to become educated in anti-aging medicine, which we believe is the foundation for 21st Century medicine, or find a physician who knows the benefits of the information presented in this book and is trained to meet your anti-aging needs

• You will need to begin to take supplements that will truly help you combat the disease of aging

• Not all supplements are created equal

• We use a compounding pharmacy for our prescription medications and also, for some of our supplements because we know they use the highest quality ingredients

- We use Zone fish oil capsules (Omega 3 oils) because they are molecularly distilled which means that they have removed any contaminants such as PCB's that fish are exposed to

- We purchase a large portion of our supplements from Life Extension Foundation in Florida because they are well known for their continuing commitment to providing some of the highest quality products in the market today

- To get most of your vitamin, mineral and other supplement needs met, you need to take a high quality vitamin combination

- Life Extension Mix, in powder, capsule or tablet form is a very good vitamin combination

- Our favorite vitamin combination is the Supra Pak, made by Supra Health. Each Supra Pak container holds thirty pre-packaged vitamin packets with nine supplements inside of each package

- You can learn more about Life Extension products by calling 800-544-4440 or visiting their website at **www.lifeextension.com**

- To learn more about the Supra Pak and Supra Health, you can contact them at 888-716-9186 or you may wish to visit their website at **www.suprahealth.com**

- Taking the antioxidants, CoEnzyme10 (CoQ10) and Carnosine are essential for all patients

- If your are eating a hormonally correct diet, exercising and taking the necessary vitamins, minerals and other supplements, you are better off than doing nothing at all

- There is no magic pill or magic solution to youthfulness

- To remain youthful from the inside-out takes work, every day

- Anything worthwhile in life is never easy and maintaining your anti-aging program takes work and sacrifice but the rewards are immeasurable

- When we have our health, we take it for granted, when we do not have our health, all we wish for is to feel good again because nothing else really matters when we are not healthy

- There are no instant cures or quick fixes for anything. It is the little things that you do every day in your life that make dreams become reality

- Based on all of Meno's test results and consultations, we created the following anti-aging program for Meno, a 45-year old married, female marketing professional:
  - Bi-Est transdermal cream 1/4 tsp. every morning and 1/4 tsp. every evening (days 1-24 of menstrual cycle)
  - Progesterone lozenges 100 mg (sublingually) 1 in the morning and 1 at bedtime (days 14-24 of menstrual cycle)
  - Armour Desiccated Thyroid 1 grain 1 tab every morning
  - Deprenyl 5 mg 1 cap every other morning
  - Acetyl L Carnitine 500 mg 1 cap every morning
  - Phosphatidyl Serine 100 mg 1 cap every morning
  - Vinpocetine 30 mg 2 caps in the morning and 1 cap in the afternoon
  - Pregnenolone 50 mg 2 caps in the morning
  - Melatonin 500 mcg 1 cap at bedtime (increase to 2 caps at bedtime in 1-2 weeks)
  - Supra Pak vitamins 1 Pak with breakfast (after 1-2 weeks, increase to 2 Paks daily, 1 with breakfast and 1 with dinner)
  - DHEA 25 mg 1 cap every morning
  - Indole 3 Carbinol 200 mg 1 cap three times per day
  - Carnosine 500 mg 1 cap three times per day
  - CoQ10 60 mg (Solanova brand) 1 cap every morning
  - Aspirin 81 mg 1 tab every morning
  - Tri Boron 1500 mg in the morning and 1500 mg in the evening
  - HGH 6 IU's per week for 3 weeks, after 3 weeks increase dose to 9 IU's per week. Take HGH six days per week, one time per day (give dose in the morning within one hour of waking or at bedtime) Do not take any HGH one day per week
  - Follow the Zone diet and use the nutrition program designed especially for you
  - Follow the exercise program designed especially for you
  - Follow the stress reduction techniques we gave you and attend a stress reduction workshop

- Begin at home brain exercises using the ThinkFast! Software
- Call CHI at anytime with any questions or concerns you may have
- CHI will notify you when your next lab tests need to be done and will continually monitor your anti-aging program and your progress

- Andro is a 52-year old male who is a successful, married businessperson with three children. Based on all of Andro's test results and consultations, we created the following anti-aging program for him:
  - Testosterone transdermal cream 20% 1/4 tsp. every morning and every evening
  - Armour Desiccated Thyroid 1 grain 1 tab every morning
  - Deprenyl 5 mg 1 cap every morning
  - Acetyl L Carnitine 500 mg 1 cap every morning
  - Phosphatidyl Serine 100 mg 1 cap every morning
  - Vinpocetine 30 mg 2 caps in the morning and 1 cap in the afternoon
  - Pregnenolone 50 mg 2 caps in the morning
  - Melatonin 500 mcg 1 cap at bedtime (increase to 2 caps at bedtime in 1-2 weeks)
  - Supra Pak vitamins 1 Pak with breakfast (after 1-2 weeks, increase to 2 Paks daily, 1 with breakfast and 1 with dinner)
  - Vitamin E 400 mg 1 cap every morning
  - DHEA 25 mg 2 caps every morning
  - 5-HTP 50 mg 1-2 caps at bedtime
  - Natural Prostate Formula 2 caps daily
  - Indole 3 Carbinol 200 mg 1 cap four times per day
  - Carnosine 500 mg 1 cap three times per day
  - CoQ10 60 mg (Solanova brand) 1 cap every morning
  - Aspirin 81 mg 1 tab every morning
  - Tri Boron 1500 mg in the morning
  - HGH 6 IU's per week for 3 weeks, after 3 weeks increase dose to 9 IU's per week. Take HGH six days per week, one time per day (give dose in the morning within one hour of waking or at bedtime) Do not take any HGH one day per week
  - Follow the Zone diet and use the nutrition program designed especially for you

- Incorporate the suggestions from our trainer into your current exercise program
- Follow the stress reduction techniques we gave you
- Begin at home brain exercises using the ThinkFast! Software
- Call CHI at anytime with any questions or concerns you may have
- CHI will notify you when your next lab tests need to be done and will continually monitor your anti-aging program and your progress

CHAPTER SIX

FOLLOW-UP

Follow-up care varies from one physician anti-aging practice to another. We thought, however, that you might find it useful to learn what we do at CHI in regards to follow-up care.

Assuming you are a CHI patient, you have had your lab work done, you have had your Evaluation Day and now, you have been on your personal anti-aging program for about three months. During the last three months, if you are a CHI patient, you have been contacted monthly, to check on your progress and you may have also been working with our nutritionist and one of our trainers on an individual basis.

Approximately, nine weeks from beginning your anti-aging program, you are required to have follow-up lab work. If you live in the San Diego region, you will be sent a lab requisition and you will be requested to have your lab work done as soon as possible. If you live outside of the San Diego region, and you are a CHI patient, you will be contacted by Pinnacle Labs to have your lab work done in your area. Pinnacle will schedule the time and date for your lab work.

It usually takes about ten days to receive all of your lab work. As soon as CHI receives the results of your lab tests, you will be contacted to schedule a follow-up office visit or you will be contacted to schedule a phone consultation with a CHI physician. For your anti-aging program to be the most effective, it is important that you have your lab work done when requested. Depending on your lab values, your hormone medications and supplement doses will be adjusted appropriately. The goal is to return your hormone levels to those of a twenty to thirty-year old. In regards to hormone levels, some people respond more quickly and some people take more fine-tuning to return their hormone levels to a youthful range. Once again, every patient is different and that is why every anti-aging program may be different, depending on what each individual patient needs.

With our patients, we emphasize that lab values are just a snapshot in time. We look at our patients, first and foremost, and assess how they are feeling and how they are responding to treatment. If a lab value seems to be inconsistent with how the patient is feeling or if the lab value is way out of range, we may request repeat lab work. We try not to let our patients become fixated on "numbers" where their lab values are concerned. The important thing is that hormone levels do not become too high. Lab tests help guide us in returning hormone levels to a youthful range. Lab values are a valuable tool in medicine but most important is the experience and expertise of your anti-aging physician and your continuing ownership of your own health and well-being. Your anti-aging physician can only be your guide because it is up to you to take the journey towards improved health and well-being.

Your first follow-up lab panel will include a DHEA Sulfate level, an IGF-1 level, a free and total testosterone level, including sex hormone binding globulin (SHBG) a PSA level for men only, a DHT level for men only, a serum estradiol level for both men and women, a TSH level, a free T3 level and a free T4 level and a progesterone level for women only. We also include a hemoglobin and hematocrit as part of our male follow-up lab panel because if a man is on testosterone, he could begin to have too many red blood cells circulating in the body and monitoring the hemoglobin and hematocrit will alert the physician if that happens. To correct the condition of too many red blood cells, a patient might be asked to donate a unit of blood if his hemoglobin and hematocrit become too high. This will also help eliminate the possibility of iron levels getting too high. Women do not usually have this problem because they menstruate monthly and that keeps the red blood cell count lowered. Speaking of menstruation, if a woman is still menstruating, we prefer that she have her lab work done between her nineteenth and twenty-first day of her menstrual cycle to give us the most accurate accounting of her hormone levels. If a woman is no longer menstruating, she can have her lab work done anytime.

Follow-up lab tests are done every three months at CHI, which include all of the major hormone levels mentioned previously. Annually, a baseline lab panel is done to check metabolic function, liver function, lipid levels, insulin and glucose levels and cardiac risk factors such as homocysteine and cardio C-reactive protein. If a patient has any disease process such as diabetes, cardiovascular disease, cancer, or some other concerns, additional lab work may be done as often as is necessary, to monitor the patient effectively. Once again, your anti-aging physician does not take the place of your primary care physician or any other physician specialist. Your anti-aging physician specializes in anti-aging medicine.

To summarize, you will need the following lab tests done every three months (you do not need to fast for the following tests and the lab tests should be done about five hours after your last hormone dose, i.e., if you applied your testosterone at 7:00 a.m., you should have your labs done at around noon):
- DHEA Sulfate
- Free and Total Testosterone, including SHBG
- IGF-1 (Somatomedin C)
- Estradiol (men and women)
- Progesterone (women only)
- PSA (men only)
- DHT (men only)
- TSH
- Free T3
- Free T4
- Other lab tests as indicated for the individual patient

You will need the following lab tests done annually (you will need to fast for your annual baseline lab tests):
- Complete Blood Count
- Comprehensive Metabolic Panel
- Lipid Profile (fasting)
- Homocysteine (fasting)
- Cardio C-Reactive Protein (fasting)
- Fasting Insulin
- Hemoglobin A1C
- TSH

- Free T3
- Free T4
- Free and Total Testosterone, including SHBG
- DHEA Sulfate
- IGF-1 (Somatomedin C)
- Estradiol (men and women)
- Progesterone (women only)
- FSH (men and women)
- LH (men and women)
- PSA (men only)
- DHT (men only)
- Urine N-Telopeptides
- Pantox Lipid and/or Vitamin Screen (optional)
- Other lab tests as indicated for the individual patient

In addition to follow-up lab work, you are encouraged to contact your anti-aging physician with any questions you may have. Your anti-aging physician will keep you abreast of the latest trends and technologies in anti-aging medicine, as they become available. At CHI, our research is ongoing. If there are effective new treatment modalities that have been tested, we may incorporate the new interventions into our patients' anti-aging programs as appropriate.

On your Evaluation Day at CHI your body fat is calculated. For patients that live locally, we calculate body fat every six months, and if a patient is following his/her anti-aging program, we see some significant decreases in body fat. This is one of the things that anti-aging medicine can do for you; decrease body fat.

On Evaluation Day at CHI, a patient has a baseline H-Scan, which tests the twelve biomarkers of aging. The test determines biological age as opposed to chronological age. We ask patients to repeat this test annually to determine the biological age after anti-aging interventions.

The Cognitive Assessment test is also done on Evaluation Day to test working memory, delayed memory and psychomotor reflexes. We ask patients to repeat this test annually to assess cognitive improvement as a result of their anti-aging program.

Another test performed on Evaluation Day for many of our patients is the electronic beam computed tomography (EBCT). Unless results are abnormal, we recommend that patients have this screening test every two years.

If a patient is at high risk for osteoporosis or has osteoporosis, we may request that the patient have a Dexascan and total body analysis done, to further assess bone loss. Although the EBCT assesses bone density, the Dexascan is still the gold standard for determining bone density in the entire body.

During Evaluation Day, male patients are given a prostate exam and a digital rectal exam. As part of our follow-up with our male patients, we encourage them to have a prostate and digital rectal exam every six months. We also monitor PSA levels every three months. If a PSA level rises more than 0.7 in a year or 0.35 within six months, we immediately refer our male patients to a urologist for consultation.

For our female patients, we encourage them to have an annual Pap smear and pelvic examination and a breast examination done by their primary care physician or their OB/GYN physician. Although a Pap smear cannot be counted upon to detect uterine cancer, it is important that all women have this test done annually. Some of our female patients ask why we do not include the cancer screening blood work CA-125 (ovarian cancer marker) and CA-15-3 (breast cancer marker) as part of our baseline laboratory tests. The reason is that both tests are not sensitive or specific enough to completely rule out the presence of cancer and we do not want our patients to experience a false sense of security from negative test results. We will order the tests, however, if there is a hereditary risk for either types of cancer or if the patient requests the test. A female patient is referred to their OB/GYN physician for follow-up if a breast, uterine, ovarian or cervical cancer risk is suspected.

We perform breast examinations on Evaluation Day for all female patients unless the patient prefers to always have this done by their primary care physician or their OB/GYN physician. If a patient is at risk for breast cancer because of family history, we encourage annual mammograms or more frequently, if necessary. If a female patient is less than fifty years of age and does not have a hereditary risk of breast cancer, we encourage mammograms every two years if they are not on hormone replacement therapy. If a female patient is on hormone replacement therapy and/or is fifty years of age or older, we encourage annual mammograms.

We also encourage all of our female patients to do monthly breast exams. Most women are familiar with how to check their breasts for lumps or any other unusual signs, such as swelling, discharge from the nipple, a change in size of the breast, a change in appearance of the breast or a change in color of the breast, areola or nipple. Breast exams should be done standing up and lying down. With the second, third and fourth fingers of either the right or the left hand, a circular, then vertical motion should be used with the three fingers to check each breast for any abnormalities. If a woman is checking her left breast, she should use her right hand and if she is checking her right breast, she should use her left hand. Monthly self-breast examinations should always be done and are a personal health responsibility for every woman. If any lumps or other abnormalities are noted during the self-breast examination, the patient's primary care physician should be notified immediately.

Improving your lifestyle can reduce the incidence of colon cancer and rectal cancer. Lifestyle improvements include eating a hormonally correct diet, which includes adequate amounts of fiber, exercising, reducing the stress in your life, stopping smoking, decreasing or eliminating alcohol consumption and keeping your hormone levels in a youthful therapeutic range. If there is a family history of colon cancer or if you have colorectal polyps, it is important that you have a rectal exam and have your stool tested for blood annually. It is also important to have these simple tests done every year even if you do not have a family history of colon cancer. If a patient, male or female is fifty years of age or older, we strongly encourage them to have a colonoscopy or flexible sigmoidoscopy to screen for colon cancer every three to five years. Today, there is an alternative to the invasive conventional colonoscopy and it is called the virtual colonoscopy. A patient's colon is gently inflated with air and high speed Electron Beam Tomography scans the abdomen. The entire radiological procedure takes about twenty seconds, while a patient holds his/her breath. Once the colon is scanned, the computer reconstructs the images into a three-dimensional image and the entire colon can be viewed from all angles to look for any polyps or other abnormalities.

The CHI nutritionist sees all CHI patients on Evaluation Day. The nutritionist is available for individual consultations, at any time, with all of our patients. The cost of follow-up nutritional counseling is included in the program costs for all of our patients on human growth hormone and is an additional charge of $60.00 per hour for all other patients. Since eating a hormonally correct diet is the foundation to improved health and well-being, we encourage our patients to meet with the nutritionist as often as is needed to assist them is successfully achieving and maintaining their dietary goals.

Our trainers are always available for exercise consultations and many of our patients have enlisted their expertise on an on-going basis. The cost for a personal trainer can range from $60.00 per hour to $100.00 per hour. Performing the right type of exercise will help you achieve your exercise goals and our trainers are dedicated to seeing you succeed.

Stress reduction techniques discussed in Chapter Fourteen of this book will help you, on an ongoing basis, to reduce the stress in your life. If you need to attend a stress reduction workshop or wish individual counseling in stress reduction, we can provide you with a list of resources.

If some of your medications and/or supplements are not agreeing with you, all you need to do is pick up the phone and we will adjust your medication/supplement regime to be more user-friendly. A few patients tell us that they just cannot take so many supplements and medications. Our first response is, "If you were told that you had a terminal disease and the only way you could stay alive was to take all of these medications/supplements, would you do it?" The answer we usually receive is, "Yes, of course I would take all of the medications and supplements." We then reply, "Well, you do have a terminal disease and it is called aging and right now, this is the best alternative we have to combat the signs and symptoms of aging." If, however, the patient just will not take what is needed, we work with the patient to decide what supplements/medications he or she will take because, once again, doing something is better than doing nothing at all.

Anti-aging medicine is a dynamic and exciting process with the medical staff and the patient together, working constantly towards maintaining and gaining vitality. This is a stark comparison to what we normally see, which is the physician and the patient constantly coping with the loss of this function or that function. Anti-aging medicine is a wonderful paradigm shift for all of us. We think we are fortunate to live in an era where science has provided us with the opportunity to stay as young and as healthy as we can for the duration of our lives. It is much easier to fix something before it is broken or to maintain something before it can no longer be maintained.

Your follow-up care is important in determining the degree of success you will experience with your anti-aging program. We work very hard to provide the most comprehensive anti-aging programs possible. We will give you the tools to become more healthy and vibrant, we will be there to guide you but the success of your anti-aging program is up to you. It is what you do every day that matters. Will you take your supplements and medications? Will you exercise? Will you eat a hormonally correct diet? Will you work on reducing the stress in your life? Will you exercise your brain and will you take the necessary brain boosters? Will you get your lab work done every three months? Will you consult with the physician, the nursing staff, the nutritionist and the trainer if you need help? Will you have the necessary screening tests done on a routine basis to prevent disease and illness or to detect a problem early on? Will you take as good care of yourself as you do your car? The human engine needs constant tuning and upkeep just like that nice car in your garage. We hope that you will work with us or the anti-aging physician of your choice to be all that you can be now and in the future.

REMEMBER THIS

- Follow-up care varies from one physician anti-aging practice to another

- At CHI, approximately, nine weeks from beginning your anti-aging program, you are required to have follow-up lab work. If you live in the San Diego region, you will be sent a lab requisition and you will be requested to have your lab work done as soon as possible. If you live outside of the San Diego region, and you are a CHI patient, you will be contacted by Pinnacle Labs to have your lab work done in your area. Pinnacle will schedule the time and date for your lab work

- It usually takes about ten days to receive all of your lab work. As soon as CHI receives the results of your lab tests, you will be contacted to schedule a follow-up office visit or you will be contacted to schedule a phone consultation with a CHI physician

- For your anti-aging program to be the most effective, it is important that you have your lab work done when requested

- Depending on your lab values, your hormone medications and supplement doses will be adjusted appropriately

- In regards to your hormone levels, the goal is to return your hormone levels to those of a twenty to thirty-year old

- Some people respond more quickly and some people take more fine-tuning to return their hormone levels to a youthful range

- Lab values are just a snapshot in time. If a lab value seems to be inconsistent with how the patient is feeling or if the lab value is way out of range, we may request repeat lab work. We try not to let our patients become fixated on "numbers" where their lab values are concerned. The important thing is that hormone levels do not become too high

- Lab tests help guide us in returning hormone levels to a youthful range

- Your first follow-up lab panel will include a DHEA Sulfate level, an IGF-1 level, a free and total testosterone level, including sex hormone binding globulin (SHBG) a PSA level for men only, a DHT level for men only, a serum estradiol level for both men and women, a TSH level, a free T3 level and a free T4 level and a progesterone level (for women only). We also include a hemoglobin and hematocrit as part of our male follow-up lab panel

- If a woman is still menstruating, we prefer that she have her lab work done between her nineteenth and twenty-first day of her menstrual cycle to give us the most accurate accounting of her hormone levels. If a woman is no longer menstruating, she can have her lab work done anytime

- Follow-up lab tests are done every three months at CHI, which include all of the major hormone levels

- Annually, a baseline lab panel is done to check metabolic function, liver function, lipid levels, insulin and glucose levels and cardiac risk factors such as homocysteine and cardio C-reactive protein

- Additional lab work may be done as often as is necessary, to monitor the patient effectively

- Your anti-aging physician does not take the place of your primary care physician or any other physician specialist

- You will need the following lab tests done every three months (you do not need to fast for the following tests and the lab tests should be done about five hours after your last hormone dose, i.e., if you applied your testosterone at 7:00 a.m., you should have your labs done at around noon):
  - DHEA Sulfate
  - Free and Total Testosterone, including SHBG
  - IGF-1 (Somatomedin C)
  - Estradiol (men and women)
  - Progesterone (women only)
  - PSA (men only)
  - DHT (men only)

- TSH
- Free T3
- Free T4
- Other lab tests as indicated for the individual patient

- You will need the following lab tests done annually (you will need to fast for your annual baseline lab tests):
  - Complete Blood Count
  - Comprehensive Metabolic Panel
  - Lipid Profile (fasting)
  - Homocysteine (fasting)
  - Cardio C-Reactive Protein (fasting)
  - Fasting Insulin
  - Hemoglobin A1C
  - TSH
  - Free T3
  - Free T4
  - Free and Total Testosterone, including SHBG
  - DHEA Sulfate
  - IGF-1 (Somatomedin C)
  - Estradiol (men and women)
  - Progesterone (women only)
  - FSH (men and women)
  - LH (men and women)
  - PSA (men only)
  - DHT (men only)
  - Urine N-Telopeptides
  - Pantox Lipid and/or Vitamin Screen (optional)
  - Other lab tests as indicated for the individual patient

- Your anti-aging physician will keep you abreast of the latest trends and technologies in anti-aging medicine, as they become available

- On your Evaluation Day at CHI your body fat is calculated. For patients that live locally, we calculate body fat every six months

- If a patient is following his/her anti-aging program, expect to see significant decreases in body fat. This is one of the things that anti-aging medicine can do for you; decrease body fat

- On Evaluation Day at CHI, a patient has a baseline H-Scan, which tests the twelve biomarkers of aging. The test determines biological age as opposed to chronological age. We ask patients to repeat this test annually to determine the biological age after anti-aging interventions

- The Cognitive Assessment test is done on Evaluation Day to test working memory, delayed memory and psychomotor reflexes. We ask patients to repeat this test annually to assess cognitive improvement as a result of their anti-aging program

- Another test performed on Evaluation Day for many of our patients is the electronic beam computed tomography (EBCT). Unless results are abnormal, we recommend that patients have this screening test every two years

- If a patient is at high risk for osteoporosis or has osteoporosis, we may request that the patient have a Dexascan and total body analysis done, to further assess bone loss

- During Evaluation Day, male patients are given a prostate exam and a digital rectal exam. As part of our follow-up with our male patients, we encourage them to have a prostate and digital rectal exam every six months. We also monitor PSA levels every three months

- If a PSA level rises more than 0.7 in a year or 0.35 within six months, we immediately refer our male patients to a urologist for consultation

- For our female patients, we encourage them to have an annual Pap smear and pelvic examination and a breast examination done by their primary care physician or their OB/GYN physician

- Although a Pap smear cannot be counted upon to detect uterine cancer, it is important that all women have this test done annually

- We perform breast examinations on Evaluation Day for all female patients unless the patient prefers to always have this done by their primary care physician or their OB/GYN physician

- If a patient is at risk for breast cancer because of family history, we encourage annual mammograms or more frequently, if necessary. If a female patient is less than fifty years of age and does not have a hereditary risk of breast cancer, we encourage mammograms every two years if they are not on hormone replacement therapy. If a female patient is on hormone replacement therapy and/or is fifty years of age or older, we encourage annual mammograms

- We encourage all of our female patients to do monthly breast exams

- Monthly self-breast examinations should always be done and are a personal health responsibility for every woman. If any lumps or other abnormalities are noted during the self-breast examination, the patient's primary care physician should be notified immediately

- Improving your lifestyle can reduce the incidence of colon cancer and rectal cancer

- Lifestyle improvements include eating a hormonally correct diet, which includes adequate amounts of fiber, exercising, reducing the stress in your life, stopping smoking, decreasing or eliminating alcohol consumption and keeping your hormone levels in a youthful therapeutic range

- If there is a family history of colon cancer or if you have colorectal polyps, it is important that you have a rectal exam and have your stool tested for blood annually. It is also important to have these simple tests done every year even if you do not have a family history of colon cancer

- If a patient, male or female is fifty years of age or older, we strongly encourage them to have a colonoscopy or flexible sigmoidoscopy to screen for colon cancer every three to five years

- Today, there is an alternative to the invasive conventional colonoscopy and it is called the virtual colonoscopy. A patient's colon is gently inflated with air and high speed Electron Beam

Tomography scans the abdomen. The entire radiological procedure takes about twenty seconds, while a patient holds his/her breath. Once the colon is scanned, the computer reconstructs the images into a three-dimensional image and the entire colon can be viewed from all angles to look for any polyps or other abnormalities

- The CHI nutritionist sees all CHI patients on Evaluation Day. The nutritionist is available for individual consultations, at any time, with all of our patients

- Since eating a hormonally correct diet is the foundation to improved health and well-being, we encourage our patients to meet with the nutritionist as often as is needed to assist them is successfully achieving and maintaining their dietary goals

- Performing the right type of exercise will help you achieve your exercise goals and our trainers are dedicated to seeing you succeed

- Stress reduction techniques discussed in Chapter Fourteen of this book will help you, on an ongoing basis, to reduce the stress in your life. If you need to attend a stress reduction workshop or wish individual counseling in stress reduction, we can provide you with a list of resources

- If some of your medications and/or supplements are not agreeing with you, we will adjust your medication/supplement regime to be user-friendlier

- Anti-aging medicine is a dynamic and exciting process with the medical staff and the patient together, working constantly towards maintaining and gaining vitality

- Anti-aging medicine is a wonderful paradigm shift for all of us. We think we are fortunate to live in an era where science has provided us with the opportunity to stay as young and as healthy as we can for the duration of our lives. It is much easier to fix something before it is broken or to maintain something before it can no longer be maintained

- Your follow-up care is important in determining the degree of success you will experience with your anti-aging program

- The success of your anti-aging program is up to you

- The human engine needs constant tuning and upkeep just like that nice car in your garage

PART THREE

COMPONENTS OF THE "FOREVER AGELESS" PLAN

A HORMONALLY CORRECT DIET

VITAMINS, MINERALS AND OTHER SUPPLEMENTS

EXERCISE

SUPPLEMENTS FOR ATHLETIC PERFORMANCE
AND BODYBUILDING

HUMAN GROWTH HORMONE

OTHER HORMONES

BRAIN HEALTH

STRESS REDUCTION

CHAPTER SEVEN

A HORMONALLY CORRECT DIET

The cornerstone to improving your health and well being, is good nutrition. Nutrition is defined as the process of being nourished. All living organisms need the proper nourishment to sustain life and to provide the necessary energy to carry out the activities of living. In today's fast paced world and information explosion, it is sometimes difficult to take the time to eat properly or to sort out fact from fiction, with all of the dietary recommendations we are exposed to on a daily basis.

Before discussing basic nutritional facts and what you should eat and when you should eat, it is interesting to note recent health statistics from the World Health Organization and the Center for Disease Control. Did you know that the number one cause of death in the world is from ischaemic heart disease? Ischaemic heart disease is caused by atherosclerosis, which narrows the arteries in the heart. This produces inadequate blood flow and can lead to angina, heart attacks and cardiomyopathy. Further review of these statistics revealed that all the Western industrialized societies and even China, India and other southeastern Asian countries, are experiencing alarming mortality rates due to ischaemic heart disease. Africa was the only reporting country where ischaemic heart disease was not the number one cause of death. In Africa, the leading cause of death was HIV and AIDS. Ischaemic heart disease outranks infectious disease, as a major cause of death in the world. Statistics showed that 21.1% of the world population died from infectious disease, while 28.5% of the world population died from cardiovascular diseases. Cancer was the fourth leading cause of death in the United States and worldwide, accounted for 11.3% of the overall mortality rate.

There will always be microorganisms that will be a threat to mankind. With every new antibiotic that is created, it seems new resistant strains of microorganisms develop. The best way to fight these microorganisms is to keep your body healthy and to maintain your own immune system. Infectious diseases, although a major concern, are not the biggest enemy we must fight today in our quest to maintain health and well being. The biggest enemy today, killing mankind, is ischaemic heart disease. Why is this? Could your diet be killing you? We think so. The biggest threat to your health today is what you put in your mouth. You have the power to improve your health, your quality of life and your longevity by controlling what you eat and when you eat.

MOTHER KNEW BEST:

When your mother told you to eat your fruits and vegetables, she was giving you some excellent advice. To maintain health and well being, human beings need to eat the proper ratios of proteins, carbohydrates and fats, at regular intervals. In addition, human beings are composed of about 70% water and need to keep the radiator full at all times. Drinking at least eight 8-ounce glasses of purified water every day is the minimum daily fluid requirement for an adult. Not drinking enough water may cause dehydration, which can lead to all sorts of health problems. There is no substitute for water; not juice, soda pop, coffee or other types of beverages. We tell our patients to eat their calories and not drink them. Try to have water and tea as the main sources of fluid in your diet.

We ask patients to tell us what their average daily diet consists of. Most of our new patients have a diet that is loaded with lots of unfavorable carbohydrates and unfavorable fats. They wonder why, at age forty, fifty or even younger, they have a spare tire around their middle. We know why; too many unfavorable carbohydrates and many times, the wrong type of fat in their diets. We ask patients what type of fuel they put in their cars. They tell us, "Unleaded of course. If I did not put unleaded fuel in my car, it would not run properly." Well, the same thing applies to the food we eat. Maybe we should call food the fuel you put in your body to make it run. If you put leaded fuel in your human gas tank, so to speak, how can you expect it to run efficiently? We take better care of our car engines than we do our own human engine, the body. No wonder the incidence of heart disease, diabetes, hypertension and obesity is on the rise in the United States. We are consuming the wrong blend of fuel.

Back to what your mother taught you. If your mother was like mine, she made sure you ate enough fruits and vegetables every day, drank lots of water and yes, when you were young, she gave you a dose of cod liver oil. Mother also made sure that you had enough protein in your diet to ensure health and well being.

Even though I did not want to eat breakfast, my mother insisted. She told me that it was the most important meal of the day. She was right. Remembering my childhood, I ate three "square" meals per day and I also had a snack or two, consisting of fruit and a piece of cheese most days. Other days, I would be lucky enough to have some homemade oatmeal cookies and a glass of milk. My mother knew, instinctively, what was good for me. A healthy diet must be balanced with the proper ratios of proteins, favorable carbohydrates, favorable fats and enough water to maintain hydration.

THE DIGESTIVE PROCESS:

The first step in understanding what human beings need to eat to thrive and prevent disease, is understanding what happens to you biochemically when you eat. For every action a person takes, there is a reaction. So it is with the food you consume. Digestion begins with the first bite you eat. The salivary glands in your mouth secrete digestive juices (some of the same digestive juices the pancreas secretes) that begin breaking down food in your mouth. Food then passes down the throat, through the small intestines, which includes the stomach and on to the large intestines. In the stomach, usually over a two to four hour period, hydrochloric acid and pepsin reduce food to a semi-liquid state. This semi-liquid matter moves through the duodenum where digestive enzymes from the liver, the gallbladder and the pancreas further break down food. Eventually, after hundreds of chemical reactions in your body throughout the digestive process (a necessary process that utilizes the nutrients in the food you eat to preserve life and create energy) the waste products of digestion leave your body through the rectum and through urine.

As we age, the digestive process can become compromised. One reason for this is a decrease in hydrochloric acid. As many as 40% of adults do not secrete enough hydrochloric acid. A decrease in the secretion of hydrochloric acid can lead to serious problems since the breakdown and nutrient absorption from the food you eat will be severely sabotaged without sufficient hydrochloric acid. Some of the signs and symptoms associated with low hydrochloric acid secretion are:

- Bloating, belching, flatulence immediately after meals
- Indigestion, diarrhea or constipation
- Food allergies
- Weak, peeling and cracked fingernails
- Acne
- Iron deficiency
- Candida infections

BASIC NUTRIENTS:

In addition to water, there are three basic macronutrients all human beings need to sustain life. Those nutrients are protein, carbohydrates and fat. Human beings also need the proper amount of vitamins, minerals and other micronutrients for a healthy diet.

The overall term used to describe all biochemical actions in the body is called metabolism. Chemical actions in the body which breakdown and convert complex substances into simpler substances and usually produce energy is called catabolism. Chemical actions in the body which build-up and convert simple substances into more complex substances and utilize energy is called anabolism. Various endocrine hormones in the body control our metabolism.

Some type of hormonal response controls every activity in the body and that includes eating. According to Dr. Barry Sears, in his numerous Zone nutrition books, "The food you eat is probably the most powerful drug you will ever encounter. But to use this drug correctly you have to apply the hormonal rules about food that haven't changed in the past 40 million years, and are unlikely to change any time soon." More about the hormonal response of food later. First, we need to understand what the basic nutrients are and why they are necessary for life.

MACRONUTIRENTS:
PROTEIN:

Protein is necessary to build and repair systems in the body. Protein is vital for growth and development. Your muscles, your immune system, your skin, your hair, your tendons, your cartilage and every cell in your body, in some way, are dependent upon protein. Without protein you will die. When protein is consumed, it breaks down into amino acids and fat. Amino acids are the building blocks of protein made by the body. We need to consume protein to make protein.

Some sources of protein are called complete proteins. We find complete proteins (proteins which contain all the amino acids necessary for life) in soybeans, tofu, soymilk, plain yogurt, meat, poultry, fish, milk, cheese and eggs. Incomplete proteins (proteins that need to be combined with other proteins to make them complete) are found in nuts, beans, corn, brown rice and various types of seeds and legumes. Protein provides the necessary framework for biochemical actions and reactions to occur in the body. For the average adult, a diet whose total daily caloric intake consists of approximately 30 percent protein per day is considered adequate. Too much protein in a person's diet is not healthy and can cause the body to retain more fat than needed.

Every person's daily protein requirement is different. However, on average, the typical male needs about 30 grams of protein at each meal and the typical female needs about 20 grams of protein at each meal. To calculate your individual daily protein requirement, it is necessary to calculate your percent body fat, your lean muscle mass and your activity level. Please refer to Appendix A borrowed from Dr. Sears' book, The Soy Zone, where specific instructions and references are given for calculating your percent body fat, your lean muscle mass and your activity level. Once you know these values, it is easy to compute your individual daily protein requirements, as Dr. Sears tells us in his numerous Zone books. As a general rule however, we tell our patients to make protein the primary component of every meal or snack. Never eat more protein than the size and thickness of the palm of your hand and fill the rest of your plate with fruits and vegetables.

CARBOHYDRATES:

Almost all carbohydrates are converted into sugar. We need carbohydrates in our diet to provide energy. There are simple and complex carbohydrates. Simple carbohydrates, or simple sugars, are found in milk, milk products, fruit, beets, corn syrup and sugar cane. Complex carbohydrates, or whole-starch and fiber forms of carbohydrates, are found in grains, beans and vegetables.

When you eat carbohydrates, they are digested and become the body's blood glucose, which is the primary energy source for the brain, the red blood cells and all of the cells in the body. Simple carbohydrates enter the blood stream more quickly than complex carbohydrates, which cause a rise in blood sugar and a rise in insulin production in an attempt to normalize blood sugar levels. Carbohydrates, in the form of blood glucose, provide the body with energy. Excess carbohydrates that cannot be immediately used for energy are conserved in the liver for use later. Other carbohydrates are found in the muscles but are not readily assessable for future use in the rest of the body. When the body has too many carbohydrates and cannot use them, the carbohydrates are stored as fat. Unfortunately, the body can always find more fat cells to store excess carbohydrates. No wonder Americans are becoming obese; too many excess unfavorable carbohydrates.

Unrefined carbohydrates like vegetables, fruits and whole-grain products enter the blood stream more slowly than refined carbohydrates. Refined carbohydrates have very few vitamins or minerals and convert to blood glucose quite quickly. Some types of refined carbohydrates to avoid are pasta, sugar, desserts, many snack foods and soda pop.

A considerable number of unrefined carbohydrates provide the body with fiber, which is important for healthy digestion. Most fibers cannot be digested. As fiber passes through the digestive tract, it retains water, allowing stools to have more bulk and be softer in consistency. Fiber also binds with certain metabolic byproducts that if not bound to the fiber would form more cholesterol than the body needs. Therefore, fiber in our diet is very important in the prevention of heart disease and the prevention of colon cancer because it assists in keeping our arteries cleaned out and keeping our digestive system cleaned out. If you are eating enough healthy complex carbohydrates, in the form of fruits and vegetables, you will also be providing your body with fiber. A daily diet consisting of approximately 40 percent of your calories in the form of healthy carbohydrates, which should include at least 25 grams of fiber, is recommended.

FATS:

In nature fats never occur in a single form. All fats are some combination of saturated and unsaturated fats. Saturated fat is found in butter, cream, lard and can been seen on steak and other types of meat. Unsaturated fats are divided into two categories; monounsaturated fat and polyunsaturated fat. Monounsaturated fat is found in almonds, avocados, olive oil and canola oil. Polyunsaturated fat may be found in various vegetable oils such as corn oil and yes, margarine.

Polyunsaturated fat or partially hydrogenated oil is the worst kind of fat to eat. When cooked, polyunsaturated fat converts into trans fatty acids in the same way crude oil is converted into petroleum. Trans fatty acids are known to increase LDL cholesterol (we need some LDL but not too much) and lower HDL (the good form of cholesterol) Polyunsaturated fat oxidizes quickly and promotes the presence of more free radicals. Consuming polyunsaturated fat is like putting petroleum in your body. If that is not bad enough, it takes the body 51 days to get rid of these trans-oils. I do not know about you, but the vision of petroleum sloshing around in my body for almost two months, is not a pretty sight. This type of fat is found in many processed foods such as crackers and many snack foods which should be avoided.

The body needs fat to assist in normalizing the metabolism of carbohydrates. The slower you metabolize carbohydrates, the more your body releases stored fat for energy. We need fat to burn fat. Fat is what makes many foods more flavorable and it also helps release a hormone from the stomach, known as cholecystokinin (CCK) which tells the brain when you have had enough to eat.

Fatty acids are the building blocks of fat. Essential fatty acids cannot be produced in our bodies. Therefore, essential fatty acids must be obtained from the food we eat. Omega 6 oil or linoleic acid (LA) is an essential fatty acid that is found in cooking oil. Since cooking oil is abundant in our diet, we consume more than enough Omega 6 oils. Alpha-linolenic acid (ALA) or Omega 3 oil is found in cold-water plankton, algae or grass. Omega 3 oils are not plentiful in our diet The only animals that consume ALA are fish, therefore, taking Omega 3 fish oils daily (at least five to ten grams) and/or eating lots of fresh cold water fish, is important for a healthy diet.

ALA or Omega 3 oil converts into docosahexanenoic acid (DHA) and ecosapentaenoic acid (EPA), which are omega 3 fatty acids. DHA, which is found in the fatty tissue of the brain, is crucial for optimal brain functioning. Some research has shown that people with bipolar depression are deficient in DHA and when treated with DHA respond quite favorably. Fatty acids are the building blocks for eicosanoids in the body. Eicosanoids are the control systems that regulate all hormonal activities in the body. How we process the food we eat are dependent upon eicosanoids and the insulin/glucagon balance.

THE INSULIN CONNECTION:

We know that we need enough water, the right type and amount of proteins, carbohydrates and fats to maintain a healthy diet but what about insulin levels in our body and how it affects our health? Eating foods that keep insulin levels in a normal range, help the body stay healthy and fit. The cells in your body must have the proper amount of insulin, not too much and not too little, to stay alive. Too much insulin and too many calories can make you fat and decrease your chances for a longer and more healthful life.

Carbohydrates with a high glycemic index should be avoided. The glycemic index of carbohydrates, simply stated, means how much sugar is in the carbohydrate. The more sugar that is in a particular carbohydrate, the less healthful it is. Breads, potatoes, white rice, carrots, bananas, corn, raisins, shredded wheat, mangos, ice cream and various types of desserts containing sugar are all examples of foods with a high glycemic index.

Your brain uses more than two thirds of the carbohydrates in your body for energy. Unused carbohydrates are stored in the liver and the muscles in the form of glycogen. Only 40 to 90 grams of carbohydrates can be stored in the liver at any one time. If not replenished, the carbohydrates stored in the liver will deplete in about ten to twelve hours. About 300 to 400 grams of carbohydrates are stored in your muscles but these carbohydrates are not accessible for immediate energy requirements.

As stated earlier, eicosanoids are the hormonal regulators that control the function of all cells in the body. They are the starting point for all hormonal activity in the body. Controlling and balancing good and bad ecosanoid activity in the body can make the difference between health and illness. Good ecosanoid activity promotes vasodilatation, decreased clotting, improved immune response, decreased inflammation and decreased pain. Bad eicosanoid activity promotes vasoconstriction, increased clotting, decreased immune response, increased inflammation and increased pain. As you can see, we need more "good" eicosanoid than "bad" eicosanoid activity to stay healthy. If you wish to become an expert on these key eicosanoids please read the Zone books by Dr. Barry Sears. The key to balancing this hormonal activity is balancing our diets with the proper amounts of proteins, carbohydrates and fats. When we balance insulin and glucagon activity, by eating a hormonally correct diet, we are also properly balancing eicosanoid activity in the body.

Insulin and glucagon are hormones that are secreted by the pancreas. Insulin is a storage hormone and glucagon is a releasing hormone. Carbohydrates stimulate insulin activity and proteins stimulate glucagon activity. Glucagon releases glucose from the liver to ensure that the brain receives the right amount of glucose (energy) to function properly. Insulin tells the liver and muscles to store glucose. If there is not enough glucose circulating in the bloodstream and going to the brain, we become hypoglycemic (the term used to describe low blood sugar levels in the body). When we become hypoglycemic, the brain begins to shut down. Glugacon, to counteract hypoglycemia, releases glucose from the liver, to ensure that blood sugar levels increase.

What happens when we have too many carbohydrates and/or too much protein in our body? Insulin tells our body to store the excess carbohyrdrates and amino acids (the building blocks of protein) as fat. Over a period of time, increased insulin levels cause increased blood sugar levels because the target cells can no longer respond properly, to maintain the insulin/glucose balance. The result is increased body fat, which promotes heart disease and adult onset diabetes. This condition of too much insulin in the body and elevated blood sugar levels is known as hyperinsulinemia. Hyperinsulinemia is associated with the metabolic syndrome known as "Syndrome X". "Syndrome X" may be a combination of insulin resistance, unfavorable cholesterol and lipid levels in the blood, type II diabetes, hypertension (elevated blood pressure) and possibly ischaemic heart disease. When we consume too much protein, excess protein in our body turns to fat. Eating small meals (large meals can cause increased insulin levels) every four to five hours and eating the proper ratios of proteins, carbohydrates and fats at each meal or snack, can mean the difference between illness and good health.

Food is a drug and the sooner you accept this reality the better chance you have for improving your health. Everything you put in your mouth causes a biochemical action. You would never take the wrong amount of a prescription medication because there would be adverse affects. The same principle applies to food. If you are willing to eat the proper prescription of food, for your height, weight, body type and activity level, you have taken your first step towards improving your health. The choice is yours. We encourage you to read the Zone diet books by Dr. Sears. Especially helpful, are the Zone Meals in Minutes and The Soy Zone. We instruct our patients to eat in the "Zone" because we know that the body must be hormonally balanced to maintain one's proper weight, percent body fat and overall state of wellness. If the body is not hormonally balanced, it cannot receive the full benefits of the other anti-aging treatment modalities that we offer our patients. A proper diet is the foundation for a better quality of life and greater longevity.

MICRONUTRIENTS:

Micronutrients (vitamins and minerals) are also essential for life but in lesser quantities than macronutrients. The primary source of these micronutrients should come from the food you eat. If you are eating in the Zone, you will be getting many of the essential vitamins and minerals you need. However, many of today's foods are not as rich as they once were in vitamins and minerals. Therefore, dietary supplementation is an important addition to your diet.

IN A NUTSHELL OR SOYBEAN POD

We have tried to provide you with basic nutritional information and definitions for essential nutrients. Every patient we treat is unique. All patients, however, need to have a diet that is hormonally balanced and tailored to their specific nutritional requirements. We hope you will begin your own anti-aging program by starting to eat sensibly and hormonally correctly. You really are what you eat. The choice is yours.

Eating is one of the true pleasures in life. We think you can eat wisely and still have a pleasurable experience. Once you have the tools and know what your body needs, eating can be a fun and healthful experience. To assist you, we thought it might be helpful to share a few sample menus that are hormonally correct. The menus we prepare for our patients are, stated once again, based on their individual daily protein requirements. The following menus will give you some idea of what we recommend.

SAMPLE MENUS

Day One:
Breakfast:
Protein Smoothie
2 scoops protein powder (use one that is 100% protein)
1 cup fresh or frozen berries
Fructose powder if you need it sweetened
3/4 cup soymilk or 1% milk or water

Snack:
1/2 cup low fat cottage cheese
1/2 cup fresh berries
10 almonds
Water

Lunch:
Chicken salad
4 oz. lean chicken breast
2-3 cups lettuce
A few cucumber slices or mushrooms
2 tbsp. olive oil dressing
1 small whole pita bread
1 oz. low fat cottage cheese
Water

Snack:
1 Protein Bar
Water

Dinner:
4 oz grilled cold water salmon
1/2 cup steamed brown rice
Steamed asparagus (as much as you like)
1 tsp. butter or olive oil
1 cup plain yogurt and fresh fruit
Water

Bedtime Snack:
1/2 cup grapes
1 part skim mozzarella string cheese
Water

Day Two:
Breakfast:
1 boiled egg
1-cup low fat cottage cheese
6-10 nuts
1 orange or apple
Water

Snack:
1 protein bar
Water

Lunch:
Tuna Sandwich
4 oz. tuna with 1 tbsp. mayonnaise
1 slice rye bread
Lettuce, tomato, sprouts
1 large apple or other fruit
Water

Snack:
1 protein bar
Water

Dinner:
4 oz. chicken breast
2-3 cups vegetable stir-fry
2-tbsp. olive oil added to the vegetables
1/2 cup brown rice
Fresh fruit for desert
Water

Bedtime Snack:
1/3 cup unsweetened applesauce
1/2 cup low fat cottage cheese
6 almonds
Water

Day Three:
Breakfast:
Scrambled eggs (1 whole egg and 3 egg whites) with your favorite
seasonings
1 slice rye bread
1-tsp. butter or 2 oz. low fat cottage cheese
1 whole fresh fruit
Water

Snack:
1 protein bar
Water

Lunch:
Pita Sandwich
4 oz. turkey breast
Lettuce, sprouts, mustard, tomato
3 slices avocado
1 oz. low fat cottage cheese
1 whole fresh fruit
Water

Snack:
Protein bar
Water

Dinner:
Shrimp stir-fry
5 oz of shrimp
2-3 cups fresh or frozen vegetables
2 tbsp. olive oil
1/2 cup brown rice
Fresh fruit for desert
Water

Bedtime snack:
1 part string cheese
2 oz. deli meat (no added sugar)
1/2 cup grapes or other fruit
Water

REMEMBER THIS

- The cornerstone to improving your health and well being is good nutrition

- The number one cause of death in the world is from ischaemic heart disease, which is directly related to diet

- The biggest threat to your health today is what you put in your mouth

- You have the power to improve your health, your quality of life and your longevity by controlling what you eat and when you eat

- To maintain health and well being, human beings need to eat the proper ratios of proteins, carbohydrates and fats, at regular intervals

- Human beings are composed of about 70% water and need to stay well-hydrated at all times

- Drinking at least eight 8-ounce glasses of purified water every day is the minimum daily fluid requirement for an adult. Not drinking enough water may cause dehydration, which can lead to all sorts of health problems

- Digestion begins with the first bite you eat

- As we age, the digestive process can become compromised. One reason for this is a decrease in hydrochloric acid. As many as 40% of adults do not secrete enough hydrochloric acid

- Some of the signs and symptoms associated with low hydrochloric acid secretion are:
  - Bloating, belching, flatulence immediately after meals
  - Indigestion, diarrhea or constipation
  - Food allergies
  - Weak, peeling and cracked fingernails
  - Acne
  - Iron deficiency
  - Candida infections

- Consume a daily diet, which is comprised of about 1500 calories for the average adult male and about 1200 calories for the average adult female

- The daily caloric intake should consist of 40% favorable carbohydrates, 30% favorable proteins and 30% favorable fats at each meal and snack

- You need protein to stay alive. As a general rule eat a portion of protein about the size and thickness of the palm of your hand at every meal and snack

- Calculate your daily protein requirement based on your percent body fat, your lean muscle mass and your activity level (remember everyone's daily protein requirement is different)

- Avoid processed foods

- Avoid carbohydrates with a high glycemic index such as bread, pasta, potatoes, corn, and rice. Most fruits are just fine to eat except bananas, mangos and pineapple because they have too much sugar

- The glycemic index of carbohydrates means how much sugar is in the carbohydrate

- Avoid foods that contain partially hydrogenated oil

- Do not overcook your food

- Buy only "hormone-free" beef, poultry, pork, and eggs

- Avoid "farm-raised" salmon - make sure it comes from cold water

- Eat foods that are as fresh as possible

- Use Olive Oil in your dressings and canola oil for cooking

- Avoid "fat-free" products - they are usually loaded with sugars

- Limit caffeine - 2 cups per day

- Eat low on the food chain - avoid products with a long list of ingredients

- Take at least 5-10 grams of Omega Fish Oils daily (more for people with joint problems)

- The cells in your body must have the proper amount of insulin to stay alive

- Too much insulin and too many calories can make you fat and decrease your chances for a longer and more healthful life

- Carbohydrates are the body's main energy source

- Your brain uses more than two thirds of the carbohydrates in your body for energy

- Unused carbohydrates are stored in the liver and the muscles in the form of glycogen

- Only 40 to 90 grams of carbohydrates can be stored in the liver at any one time. If not replenished, the carbohydrates stores in the liver will deplete in about ten to twelve hours

- About 300 to 400 grams of carbohydrates are stored in your muscles but these carbohydrates are not accessible for immediate energy requirements

- Eicosanoids are the hormonal regulators that control the function of all cells in the body

- Controlling and balancing good and bad ecosanoid activity in the body can make the difference between health and illness

- The key to balancing many hormonal activities in the body is balancing your diet with the proper amounts of proteins, carbohydrates and fats

- When we balance insulin and glucagon activity, by eating a hormonally correct diet, we are also properly balancing eicosanoid activity in the body

- Carbohydrates stimulate insulin activity and proteins stimulate glucagon activity

- Glucagon releases glucose from the liver to ensure that the brain receives the right amount of glucose (energy) to function properly

- Insulin tells the liver and muscles to store glucose

- When we have too many carbohydrates and/or too much protein in our body, insulin tells our body to store the excess carbohydrates and amino acids (the building blocks of protein) as fat

- Over a period of time, increased insulin levels cause increased blood sugar levels because the target cells can no longer respond properly, to maintain the insulin/glucose balance. The result is increased body fat, which promotes heart disease and adult onset diabetes. This condition of too much insulin in the body and elevated blood sugar levels is known as hyperinsulinemia which can lead to "Syndrome X"

- Eating small meals (large meals can cause increased insulin levels) every four to five hours and eating the proper ratios of proteins, carbohydrates and fats at each meal or snack, can mean the difference between illness and good health

- Food is a drug and the sooner you accept this reality the better chance you have for improving your health

- A proper diet is the foundation for a better quality of life and greater longevity

- Micronutrients (vitamins and minerals) are also essential for life but in lesser quantities than macronutrients. The primary source of these micronutrients should come from the food you eat

CHAPTER EIGHT

VITAMINS, MINERALS AND OTHER SUPPLEMENTS

Micronutrients (vitamins and minerals) are also essential for life but in lesser quantities than macronutrients. The primary source of these micronutrients should come from the food you eat. If you are eating in the Zone, you will be getting many of the essential vitamins and minerals you need. However, many of today's foods are not as rich as they once were in vitamins and minerals. Therefore, dietary supplementation is an important addition to your diet. Significant doses of vitamins are one of the most important interventions you can make to maximize your healthspan. The government published recommended daily allowances (RDA) for vitamins and other supplements are just enough to keep you alive. The RDA's are not enough too prevent the degenerative changes associated with aging. The published medical data on the benefits of vitamins is overwhelming. We do not understand why the government and the media appear to be so opposed to supporting and promoting the benefits of vitamins. We do know, however, that vitamins, just like many other supplements are natural and therefore cannot be patented by the pharmaceutical companies. When a drug cannot be patented, the pharmaceutical companies cannot make the types of profits they are accustomed to making with drugs for which they hold the patent. A sad but true commentary that profit may come before health and well-being; you be the judge.

The doses we recommend for the following micronutrients are for our average adult patient.

VITAMINS

Vitamin C

Vitamin C, beta-carotene and vitamin E are known as the most important antioxidants. What is an antioxidant? We know that the body needs oxygen to survive. Free floating oxygen coverts into free radicals (unpaired electrons). We need some free radicals, but not too many, to fight disease. If too many free radicals stay in the body too long, they can cause damage. An antioxidant destroys free radicals by destroying itself. Since the lifespan of an antioxidant is quite short, they must be replaced continually. It is more important to realize that vitamins work together to quench free radicals. A free radical is consumed by its passage through a number of anti-oxidants, which include vitamin C, beta-carotene, selenium, etc. Because of this combined action of all the necessary vitamins, you cannot expect a single vitamin to do you much good; you need a balanced dose of all of the important anti-oxidants.

Vitamin C can help prevent cardiovascular disease and also improve outcomes for patients with coronary artery disease. Vitamin C helps regulate the release of insulin in the body. It also helps the healing process and promotes collagen growth. Depletion of vitamin C in the body can cause scurvy (rare today) whose symptoms may include bleeding gums, hemorrhages, dementia, muscle pain, joint pain and bone pain. Vitamin C may be found in many types of berries, oranges, various melons, green and red bell peppers, kiwi fruit, broccoli, cauliflower and tomatoes. Did you know that humans are one of the few animals that cannot make their own vitamin C? Goats, for example, make about twelve (12) grams of vitamin C daily. The daily dose of vitamin C recommended by the FDA is 60 mg. This dose, although better than nothing at all, will not do much for preventing cardiovascular disease. For effective antioxidant effects, we recommend 2000 mg per day of vitamin C, to be obtained from the food you eat and from supplementation. Since vitamin C has such a short half-life, we recommend that you divide your daily dose into two or three doses during the day.

Beta-carotene

Good dietary sources of beta-carotene are cantaloupe, spinach, various dark green leafy vegetables, romaine lettuce and apricots. Beta-carotene, a precursor to vitamin A, has been known for its antioxidant effects in the prevention of many cancers and heart disease. There is, however, some debate over the effectiveness of beta-carotene alone, in our diets. Recent research has shown that foods rich in beta-carotene are also rich in lycopene, lutein, zeaxanthin and alpha carotene, all strong disease fighting carotenoids. We recommend 20,000 IU of beta-carotene per day, to be obtained primarily from the food you eat and secondarily, from supplementation. It is important that your supplement contains natural beta-carotene or mixed carotenoids and the synthetic "trans" beta-carotene.

Vitamin E

There are actually eight fat-soluble plant compounds in the Vitamin E family. Vitamin E is a powerful antioxidant. It may be found in nut and vegetable oils, sunflower seeds, wheat germ and spinach. It is difficult to get enough Vitamin E from your diet, therefore supplementation is recommended. Vitamins E, taken in the proper dosage, has been shown to help prevent cancer, boost the immune system function, alleviate respiratory problems and help fight heart disease. Vitamin E reduces cellular aging, prevents abnormal blood clotting, protects the retina of the eye, protects the nervous system and reduces the risk for Alzheimer's disease. Vitamin E improves brain function through its antioxidant capabilities, which protect neurons in the brain from the effects of free radicals. Because Vitamin E is fat-soluble, it stays in the body longer than water soluble-vitamins such as the B vitamins and vitamin C. Since Vitamin E, stays in the body longer, it is important, not to take too much Vitamin E because it could interfere with blood coagulation. If you are taking any type of anticoagulant medication, it is important to consult your physician before taking Vitamin E. We recommend 400 to 800 IU of Vitamin E (Gamma E Tocopherol) per day.

Vitamin A

Vitamin A, a naturally occurring group of retinoids from plant sources, is one of the building blocks for a vibrant immune system. Vitamin A, an antioxidant, is a fat-soluble vitamin that helps prevent infection and also prevents macular degeneration. Vitamin A also helps slow the aging process and assists in protein metabolism. Taking too much vitamin A could be toxic, especially for the liver. Therefore, we recommend taking no more than 18,000 IU of vitamin A per day, to be obtained from your diet and supplementation. Pregnant women should never take more than 10,000 of vitamin A daily. Foods rich in vitamin A are carrots, cantaloupe, beet greens, pumpkin, sweet potatoes and spinach.

The B Vitamins

All of the B vitamins are important for proper metabolism. Vitamin B1, thiamin, helps convert carbohydrates into energy. Thiamin can be found in beef, pork, oatmeal, beans and oranges. Too little thiamin in the diet can cause the disease beriberi. Symptoms of thiamin deficiency include difficulty walking, swollen limbs, overall weakness, heart enlargement, depression and various mood changes. Severe thiamin deficiency can destroy brain cells and impair memory. We recommend 100 mg of thiamin daily.

Riboflavin, or Vitamin B2, is crucial for many activities in the body. Vitamin B2 is a powerful antioxidant and also helps convert amino acids (protein building blocks) into neurotransmitters, which are necessary for proper brain function. Vitamin B2 helps with growth and reproduction and assists with the metabolism of protein, carbohydrates and fats. Vitamin B2 promotes healthy hair, skin and nails. Vitamin B2 deficiency can impair vision and also result in severe dermatitis. Good sources of riboflavin are fish, poultry, asparagus, broccoli, yogurt and spinach. It would be difficult to get too much riboflavin since it is secreted in the urine, two hours after ingestion. It causes the urine to have a bright yellow color. Alcohol and birth control pills interfere with riboflavin absorption. We recommend 100 mg of Vitamin B2 daily to be obtained from your diet and from supplementation.

Vitamin B3, more commonly known as niacin, is found in tuna, chicken breasts, some fortified cereals and veal. Niacin, given in the proper dosage, assists in lowering cholesterol levels. Too much Niacin, however, may cause liver damage. Niacin has also proven useful in certain allergic conditions because it prevents the release of histamine. Niacin promotes relaxation, is necessary for orgasm, helps promote healthy skin, reduces blood pressure and increases circulation. Niacin also lowers cholesterol and triglycerides. Since niacin may cause flushing, nervousness, headache, itching, diarrhea and nausea, it should be taken under the supervision of a trained physician. We recommend 50 mg of niacin and 150 mg of niacinamide daily to be obtained from your diet and from supplementation. For cholesterol lowering effects, No-Flush Niacin may be recommended by your physician at a dose from 800 mg to 2400 mg daily. Niaspan, a long-acting prescription niacin is currently being used as the drug of choice for increasing HDL (the good cholesterol) and for increasing LDL particle size, which makes the "bad" cholesterol less dangerous.

Vitamin B5, Pantothenic Acid, is the anti-stress vitamin. Vitamin B5 helps with digestion, improves skin, is necessary in the production of the main neurotransmitter, acetylcholine and helps in removing age spots. Vitamin B5 is crucial for the formation of antibodies, essential for the production of adrenal hormones, assists in the proper utilization of vitamins by the body and helps convert protein, carbohydrates and fat into energy. Vitamin B5 may be found in saltwater fish, pork, nuts, mushrooms, various fresh vegetables, eggs, liver and whole wheat. We recommend 400-mg daily of Vitamin B5.

Pyridoxine or Vitamin B6 is found in avocados, chicken, beef, soybeans, brown rice, eggs, oats and peanuts. According to Dr. John Marion Ellis, "Vitamin B6 is as important to your body as oxygen and water." Vitamin B6 is necessary for proper metabolism, especially the metabolism of essential fatty acids, and assists in the creation of necessary neurotransmitters. Vitamin B6 is important in the formation of eicosanoids. A shortage of Vitamin B6 can lead to various types of nerve damage and insulin resistance. Patients taking L-dopa should consult their physician before taking Vitamin B6. Vitamin B6 should be taken in combination with the other B vitamins. Too much Vitamin B6 may cause various nerve disorders or photosensitivity. We recommend 100 mg of Vitamin B6 daily to be obtained from your diet and from supplementation.

The fatty covering that protects nerve fibers in your body is called the myelin sheath. Vitamin B12 is necessary in the production of the myelin sheath. Severe deficiencies of Vitamin B12 may cause a deterioration of the myelin sheath, which is evident in patients with multiple sclerosis. Adequate levels of Vitamin B12 can improve cognitive function. Low levels of Vitamin B12 may cause increased homocysteine (a substance that is formed from protein metabolism) levels, which, in turn, may cause more clotting in the arterial walls. Vitamin B12 is important in the production of red blood cells. Vitamin B12 can be found in ham, cooked oysters, crab, tuna, salmon, clams and herring. We recommend 400 mcg of Vitamin B12 daily to be obtained primarily from you diet and secondarily from supplementation.

Biotin, a B-complex vitamin, is needed to process the protein and fat we consume. Biotin can be manufactured by the body but is also found in eggs, various cereals and milk. People with elevated blood sugar levels seem to have lower biotin levels because "biotin lowers blood glucose levels. Biotin can assist in preventing hair loss and decrease the incidence of eczema and dermatitis. We recommend 600 mcg of Biotin daily to be obtained primarily from your diet.

Vitamin D

Vitamin D, a fat-soluble vitamin, is needed to transport phosphorus and calcium in the body so that bone growth occurs in children and bone remineralization occurs in adults. Vitamin D enhances the immune system (helps in the prevention of many cancers such as breast cancer and prostate cancer) assists in the regulation of a person's heartbeat, is needed for proper thyroid function, helps prevent muscle weakness and helps in normalizing the blood clotting process. Vitamin D is essential for a healthy skeletal system and healthy teeth. Vitamin D can be stored in body fat for up to nine months in an infant and for several months in a healthy adult. Experts say that ten minutes of summer sun provides the body with enough Vitamin D for the day. Other sources of vitamin D may be found in eggs, sardines, halibut, salmon, herring, tuna, sweet potatoes and fortified milk. Rickets, a disease causing bone deformation is caused by vitamin D deficiency. Vitamin D must always be taken in conjunction with calcium. We recommend 400 IU of vitamin D daily, to be obtained from your diet and supplementation.

Vitamin K

Vitamin K's primary responsibility is to help blood clot. Your intestinal bacteria makes approximately half of the Vitamin K you need. Since newborns do not have enough Vitamin K in their body at birth, they are usually given a shot of Vitamin K when they are born. Vitamin K is a fat-soluble vitamin. Vitamin K is needed for the metabolism of osteocalcin, which is the protein in bone tissue. Vitamin K also plays a role in transforming glucose into glycogen for storage in the liver. We recommend 60 mcg daily of Vitamin K. Good sources of Vitamin K are broccoli, green leafy vegetables, egg yolks, oatmeal and soybeans.

Folic Acid

Folic acid is an extremely important B vitamin that is involved in many activities in the body. Because folic acid is necessary for nerve formation and regulation and especially, nerve formation in the fetus, women, in their child bearing years, whether pregnant or not, should routinely take supplemental folic acid (400 mcg daily) to help prevent serious birth defects such as spina bifida and other neuronal disorders. Folic acid helps in the formation of red blood cells, the production of energy, the formation of white blood cells and is crucial for making DNA, which is the genetic code of your body. Adequate intake of folic acid has been shown to be helpful in treating some anxiety disorders and depression. Women with adequate folic acid levels in their bodies appear to have a lesser incidence of cervical dysplasia (abnormal cells in the cervix), which can be a precursor to cervical cancer. Folic acid may be found in many fruits and vegetables. Good sources of folic acid are navy beans, pinto beans, asparagus, broccoli, okra, spinach and brussel sprouts. We recommend 400 mcg to 800 mcg of folic acid daily to be obtained from your diet and from supplementation. Vitamin B6, vitamin B12 and folic acid are known to lower homocysteine levels, which is thought by many forward-thinking cardiologists to be more important in decreasing cardiovascular risk than lowering LDL cholesterol.

Lecithin (Phosphatidylcholine)

Cell membranes are primarily composed of lecithin, a fatty substance found in every cell in the body. Lecithin is composed of the B vitamin choline, linoleic acid and the vitamin inositol, which is needed for hair growth, helps reduce cholesterol levels and assists in preventing hardening of the arteries. Lecithin assists with fat metabolism, improves brain function and helps in the absorption of Vitamin A and Vitamin B1. Lecithin may be found in egg yolks, grains, fish and various legumes. We recommend 700-mg daily of lecithin and 200 mg daily of inositol, to be obtained from your diet and from supplementation.

Lycopene

Lycopene is the red pigment found in tomatoes, watermelon, red peppers and red grapefruit. It is a strong antioxidant carotenoid. Lycopene has many protective effects on the body including prostate cancer protection and brain protection and may be instrumental in preventing coronary artery disease. We recommend 10-mg daily of Lycopene. Have you ever thought about the reason why so many plants have anti-oxidants that protect humans? Plants need anti-oxidants to protect against free radical damage and secondly, during the evolutionary process, humans consumed large quantities of fresh fruits and vegetables as their only source of carbohydrates. As you will remember, carbohydrates produce energy. As a result "evolution" realized that since humans were eating all of these fruits and vegetables, they did not need to make many of their own anti-oxidants and the energy produced could be used for other things.

Para-Aminobenzoic Acid (PABA)

Para-Aminobenzoic Acid (PABA) is a primary ingredient in folic acid. It also helps in the metabolism of Vitamin B5. PABA is a powerful antioxidant that helps prevent sunburn and skin cancer. PABA helps with red blood cell formation, assists in protein metabolism and is integral in maintaining proper intestinal health. Some sources of PABA are various organ meats such as kidneys and liver, whole grains, spinach, molasses and mushrooms. We recommend 500 mg of PABA daily, to be obtained from your diet and from supplementation.

MINERALS

As with vitamins, various minerals are essential for a healthy life. Many minerals can be bound by fiber, which reduces their net effect. Therefore, taking the right type of minerals at the right time of the day is important. Low amounts of stomach acids, which can be a common condition as we age, may also cause some minerals to have a less than optimal effect. Low levels of certain minerals can be a contributing factor to anemia and other related diseases and cardiovascular disease. Adequate mineral levels assist various antioxidants in being more effective. Minerals are an important component in dietary supplementation.

Boron

Boron is a trace mineral that helps the body to more effectively utilize the minerals magnesium and calcium. Boron helps calcium get into the bone to prevent and/or treat osteoporosis. It also helps activate certain hormones in the body such as estrogen and testosterone. Boron assists in the metabolic process of Vitamin D. Boron can increase mental acuity. Healthy sources of boron may be found in apples, grapes, green leafy vegetables, cherries, beans and nuts. It is preferable to obtain at least 2 mg of boron per day from the food you eat.

Calcium

For our adult female patients, we recommend a daily dose of 3000 mg of calcium citrate. For our adult male patients, we recommend a daily dose of 1500 mg of calcium citrate. The body absorbs calcium better if daily doses are divided. Taking part of your daily calcium dose at bedtime can induce a better night's sleep. Some people experience gastric upset when taking calcium. If you have this problem, we recommend that you take your calcium with your meals. There are various anti-acid advertisements that state the particular anti-acid contains calcium. Be warned that if you take an anti-acid containing calcium, it will give you little benefit. The reason for this is that the anti-acid neutralizes stomach acids, which are necessary for the proper absorption of calcium. We all know that we need calcium to build strong bones. Calcium, when combined with phosphorus provides the framework for strong bones and teeth. Ninety-nine percent of all calcium is stored in your skeletal system and is essential for the creation of new bone and the removal of old bone. Adequate levels of calcium in the body help maintain a normal heart rhythm, assist with the blood clotting process and help with proper nerve and muscle function. Calcium also assists with serum cholesterol levels and is important in protein manufacturing when the body is making RNA and DNA; the substances that comprise your genetic makeup. Calcium assists in lowering serum iron levels. Good sources of calcium are broccoli; salmon that still has the bones, sardines, green leafy vegetables and yogurt.

Chromium
Most Americans do not get enough chromium in their diet. Chromium, a trace mineral is necessary for the body to utilize insulin correctly, which subsequently allows blood sugar (blood glucose) levels to stay within an optimum range. People with hyperinsulinemia (glucose intolerance), which means that glucose and insulin levels are too high in the body, can benefit from the proper amount of chromium in their diets. Because of its glucose-balancing effect, chromium can help with weight loss. People with low chromium levels, in addition to experiencing glucose intolerance, may suffer from fatigue, high cholesterol levels and anxiety. Chromium may be found in ham, brown rice, grape juice and broccoli. We recommend 400mcg of chromium daily.

Copper
Believe it or not, copper is necessary for our survival. Too much copper in the body can contribute to the formation of senile plaques found in Alzheimer's disease. The level of copper in the body is directly proportional to the amount of vitamin C and zinc in the body. Too much vitamin C and zinc will cause a low copper level. Conversely, too much copper in the body will cause low levels of vitamin C and zinc. Osteoporosis can be partially traced to low copper levels because copper is necessary for collagen formation, which is an essential protein that makes our bones, skin and connective tissue. Copper is also involved in the metabolism of iron. Copper is an important component of one of our built-in antioxidants, superoxide dismutase (SOD). Copper may be found in avocados, almonds, broccoli, mushrooms, cooked oysters, cocoa powder, green leafy vegetables, salmon and soybeans. We recommend 2 mg of copper daily.

Iodine
Iodine is needed to produce the necessary thyroid hormone, thyroxine. Thyroxine regulates body temperature, metabolism, muscle tone and breathing. Too little thyroxine can lead to an enlarged thyroid gland, which is called a goiter. Too little iodine in the diet can cause hypothyroidism, fatigue, weight gain and has also been associated with breast cancer. Most of us get enough iodine in our diet by using iodized table salt. Foods rich in iodine are garlic, sesame seeds, summer squash, soybeans, lobster, shrimp and spinach. We recommend 150 mcg of iodine daily.

Magnesium

Did you know that magnesium has been used successfully in decreasing the risk for heart attack, preventing high blood pressure, asthma, kidney stones, lessening the symptoms of PMS (premenstrual syndrome) and preventing various irregular heart rhythms? Epsom salts, long known for its healing properties is primarily composed of magnesium. Magnesium is necessary for making all the muscles in your body flex and for assisting in energy production. Magnesium also ensures that the body utilizes calcium correctly. Many cardiac drugs, diuretics, coffee and alcohol can cause magnesium deficiency. Stress can also cause magnesium deficiency. Patients with heart disease or kidney problems need to consult their primary care physician before taking magnesium. We recommend 400 mg of magnesium daily. Food sources of magnesium are spinach, oatmeal, broccoli, yogurt, avocados, brown rice, most dairy products, blueberries and green leafy vegetables.

Manganese

Strong bones, collagen formation and proper brain function are all dependent upon adequate levels of manganese in the body. Low levels of manganese can cause muscle contractions, vision and/or hearing loss, convulsions, rapid heart rate and atherosclerosis. We recommend 10 mg of manganese daily. Dietary sources of manganese may be found in blueberries, various nuts, shellfish, egg yolks, pineapple, avocados and nuts.

Molybdenum

Molybdenum is needed to make certain biochemical reactions occur in the body. This trace mineral helps the body detoxify sulfites, which are found in many preservatives. It also helps in the production of certain genetic material, the production of protein and the creation of uric acid, which is a vital metabolic waste product. We recommend 200-mcg daily of molybdenum. Eating a well balanced diet can usually supply the body with enough molybdenum. Food sources for molybdenum may be found in dark green leafy vegetables, whole grains, milk products and beans.

Potassium

Potassium interacts with sodium to ensure that fluid balances in the body are correct. Potassium is necessary for maintaining optimal levels of blood pressure, proper muscle contractions, regular heart rhythm and proper nerve transmissions throughout the body. We need to eat more fruits and vegetables daily to get enough potassium in our diet. Good sources of potassium are brown rice, cantaloupe, spinach, dried apricots, poultry, avocados, raisins, potatoes and bananas. We recommend 200-mg daily of potassium aspartate.

Selenium

Selenium is a crucial antioxidant and essential in the creation of one of our built-in antioxidants, glutathione peroxidase. Selenium works with vitamin E in ridding the body of unwanted free radicals. Selenium keeps many viruses in check and this may be its most vital role in addition to inhibiting the oxidation of lipids in the body and detoxifying heavy metals. Selenium has been shown to help prevent colon, breast and prostate cancer. Brazil nuts are so rich in selenium that only two or three nuts, eaten daily, may provide an adequate dose of selenium. We recommend 200-400 mcg of selenium daily. Be warned that taking too much selenium can have toxic effects. Lobster, crab, whole grains, broccoli, brown rice, molasses, onions, tuna and many vegetables contain selenium.

Vanadium

Vanadium, not easily absorbed by the body, can deplete chromium levels but small amounts are needed for bone and teeth formation and for cellular metabolism. Low levels of vanadium have been associated with kidney disease and cardiovascular disease. Sources of vanadium include fish, olives, radishes and whole grains. We recommend 200 mcg of vanadium daily.

Zinc

Zinc has many functions. Zinc helps in the formation of superoxide dismutase (SOD), which is one of the body's built-in antioxidants. Too much zinc in the body can contribute to the formation of senile plaques found in Alzheimer's disease. Proper amounts of zinc are necessary for prostate health, maintaining immune system function (too much zinc, however, will decrease immunity) and producing

many of the cells you need to stay healthy. Zinc is needed to metabolize protein, help prevent acne by controlling oil gland activity,
promote healing and help with collagen formation. Zinc is necessary for bone formation, prevents the creation of certain free radicals, helps the body maintain adequate levels of vitamin E and
enhances a person's sense of taste and sense of smell. Zinc is important to reproduction because it assists with organ development and
sperm motility. Zinc may be found in egg yolks, fish, red meat, soybeans, sunflower seeds, whole grains, nuts and yogurt. We recommend 30-50 mg of zinc daily. Taking more than 100 mg of zinc daily
can decrease a person's immunity, as mentioned previously and it
will also decrease copper levels in the body. Zinc lozenges have
been shown to cure or prevent the common cold. The average dose
of zinc is 14 mg per lozenge but every brand may be different and it
is best to follow the directions for dose on the box of the particular
brand of zinc lozenges you purchase.

OTHER NUTRIENTS

As you can see, your body is a complex organism and requires
many nutrients to function properly. In addition to the macronutrients; protein, carbohydrates and fat and the micronutrients; vitamins and minerals, there are other nutrients your body needs. The
following are some of the "other" nutrients we recommend to our
patients.

Alpha Lipoic Acid
Alpha lipoic acid is an important overall body antioxidant. It
increases cell levels of the built-in antioxidant glutathione. Alpha
lipoic acid increases energy levels, reduces heavy metal levels in the
body, including iron levels. It enhances the activity of other antioxidants such a vitamin C, vitamin E, coenzyme Q10, and assists with
maintaining normal growth and metabolism. This nutrient has been
useful in treating patients with iron toxicity, ALS, cataracts, chronic
fatigue syndrome, diabetic retinopathy, diabetic nerve disease, macular degeneration and multiple sclerosis. To date, there are no
adverse effects from taking alpha lipoic acid. We recommend 250
mg of alpha lipoic acid two times per day and for our diabetic
patients we recommend 250 mg three to four times per day.

Aspirin

Baby aspirin, 81 mg daily, can provide many health benefits. Chronic inflammation of any type may cause a wide range of health problems. Elevated C-reactive protein levels can be an indication of inflammation, especially in the coronary arteries. Taking 81 mg of aspirin daily can lower C-reactive protein levels and thereby decrease the risk associated with coronary artery disease. Low doses of aspirin help keep the blood thinned, which decreases the risk for heart attacks and strokes. When taking aspirin it should be taken with food to prevent possible stomach upset. Patients taking any type of anti-coagulant medications should consult their physician before taking aspirin. Aspirin and non-steroidal anti-inflammatories (NSAIDS) also play a role in preventing Alzheimer's dementia and colon cancer.

Betaine HCL

As we age, the production of hydrochloric acid and pepsin in the stomach may decrease causing a variety of symptoms, which include bloating, belching, flatulence immediately after meals, indigestion, diarrhea or constipation, food allergies, weak, peeling and cracked fingernails, acne, iron deficiency and Candida infections. Taking Betaine HCL, when clinically indicated can restore stomach acids to a healthful level. We recommend 648 mg of Betaine HCL and 130 mg of pepsin daily.

Bifidobacterium bifidum

It has been known for years that the bowel contains many types of bacteria. Some are good and others may contribute to certain disease processes including adult onset diabetes, meningitis, myasthenia gravis, arthritis, Grave's disease and ulcerative colitis. We need the proper type of bacteria in our colon to digest food and assist with various metabolic processes. Fungal infections in the intestinal tract are not uncommon. To prevent fungal/yeast infections in the digestive tract, a proper diet is important and also taking bifido bacteria supplements. Bifo bacteria feed on sugar, which is a primary cause of fungal infections in the digestive tract. A daily dose of 2 billion parts of bifido bacteria is recommended for good intestinal health

Bilberry

Bilberry, also known as blueberry, assists in maintaining the proper insulin levels in the body. Bilberry may help in preventing macular degeneration and acts as a natural diuretic, which assists in maintaining a healthy urinary tract. Bilberry is a plant and we recommend a daily dose of 100 mg of bilberry extract, found in many good multivitamins. Consuming blueberries in your diet is even more beneficial.

Carnosine

Carnosine is an amino acid intermediate that has amazing antioxidant, anti-glycating (glucose that accumulates in our tissues causes cross-links in proteins, enzymes and cell membranes, which leads to loss of function of our cells) aldehyde quenching (aldehydes are by-products of protein metabolism) and metal chelating actions. Carnosine can give old cells new life and prevent other cells from becoming damaged as a result of aging protein metabolism, which is one of the reasons cells age or die. Protein is needed for life but oxidation and interactions with sugars and aldehydes cause destructive changes in protein metabolism. Carnosine is a broad-spectrum agent that can protect the body from the unwanted effects of modified protein metabolism. Carnosine is one of the most important supplements, in addition to CoQ10 that we recommend for our patients. Carnosine can help prevent: skin aging, LDL oxidation, DNA damage, neurological degeneration, muscle wasting, the accumulation of damaged proteins in the body, cell aging, circulatory problems in the brain, the build-up of glycation end products and the cross-linking of protein in the lens of the eyes. Carnosine can improve wound healing and inhibit amyloid plaque formation, which is found in abundance in the brains of Alzheimer's patients. Carnosine also buffers against the effects of too much zinc or too much copper in the body. To be effective, Carnosine must be taken in adequate doses. We recommend 500 mg of Carnosine three times per day.

Cetyl Myristoleate

This fatty substance acts like an essential fatty acid and helps decrease the pain caused by osteoarthritis, rheumatoid arthritis and psoriasis because it helps lubricate joints and bones. It works by "reprogramming" harmful "T" cells that attack the body. Dosage is dependent upon a patient's symptoms.

Chitosan

Chitosan is a source of fiber made from the shells of shellfish. Chitosan binds with fat and cholesterol and is effective, for some patients, on a weight-loss program. When Chitosan is combined with vitamin C, it is even more effective in absorbing fat. When indicated, we recommend 250-mg of Chitosan at each meal. The dose may gradually be increased to three 250-mg capsules at each meal. Chitosan should never be used by pregnant women and should be stopped if nausea, vomiting or abdominal pain occur.

Citrus Bioflavinoids

Bioflavinoids are considered vitamins and are useful in reducing pain, preventing asthma, promoting circulation, lowering cholesterol levels and when taken in conjunction with vitamin C, may decrease the symptoms associated with oral herpes. We recommend 400mg daily of citrus bioflavinoids. Good sources of bioflavinoids include grapes, cherries, apricots, oranges and lemons.

Coenzyme Q10 (CoQ10)

CoQ10 is found naturally in every cell in the body. It is a fat-soluble vitamin that is an antioxidant and vital for energy metabolism. Since CoQ10 levels may deplete as we get older or we do not get enough of this vitamin from our diets, we strongly encourage our patients to take 60 mg of Solanova' CoQ10 daily. Adequate levels of CoQ10 can improve cardiovascular health, increase energy levels, boost the immune system, lower high blood pressure and may reverse gum disease. CoQ10 has also been shown to decrease tumors in breast cancer patients.

Conjugated Linoleic Acid

Conjugated linoleic acid (CLA) is a fatty acid that enhances the immune system through its antioxidant and anti-cancer effects. It is twice as potent as the antioxidant beta-carotene. It protects against many diseases such as cancer and atherosclerosis. Fiber can interfere with the absorption of CLA. Therefore, CLA should not be taken with high-fiber meals. When clinically indicated we recommend three to six 500-mg capsules of CLA daily, in divided doses and for cancer patients, six to twelve 500 mg capsules, in divided doses, may be recommended daily.

Fiber Food

Getting enough fiber in our diet is important. Fruits and vegetables offer the most healthful form of fiber. Since most humans eat meat, which is difficult for humans to digest, they may need additional fiber in their diet. Fiber Food is a good source of dietary fiber. We recommend 6 capsules of Fiber Food with each meal. When taking fiber, at least eight to ten ounces of water should be consumed.

Garlic

As far back as biblical times, garlic has been recognized as one of the most useful foods. Garlic can help lower blood pressure, assists in preventing blood clots, lowers cholesterol levels, improves the immune system function, acts as an antibiotic, an anti-fungal and an anti-viral agent and helps with the digestive process. We recommend at least 500 mg of garlic daily.

Ginger

Small amounts of ginger daily, 200 mg can help in maintaining a healthy colon. Ginger is also a powerful antioxidant and may be used to help wounds and sores heal. Ginger has been used successfully in decreasing or eliminating nausea and vomiting, hot flashes, indigestion and abdominal cramping.

Ginkgo Biloba

This nutrient comes from the leaves of the Ginkgo Biloba tree. Ginkgo Biloba improves blood circulation and increases the oxygen supply to all parts of the body, especially the brain and the heart. Known as the "smart" herb, ginkgo biloba may improve memory, reduce blood pressure, improve hearing loss and may slow some of the symptoms of Alzheimer's disease. Because of its anti-clotting effects, patients taking anti-coagulant medications should consult their physician before taking ginkgo biloba. We recommend between 120 mg and 240 mg daily for our patients.

Ginseng

Ginseng, an herb, has been widely used in Chinese medicine for centuries. The benefits of ginseng are numerous. Generally speaking, ginseng promotes better health, improves energy and increases physical performance. Ginseng is useful for relieving some of the symptoms associated with stress because it assists in normalizing cortisol levels. Ginseng may be a beneficial adjunct in treating elevated blood pressure, low blood pressure, stress-related illnesses, diabetes, depression, insomnia and atherosclerosis. We recommend three 300-mg capsules of Ginseng daily, two capsules taken in the morning and one in the afternoon. We also recommend taking this dose for two weeks and then taking a respite for two weeks, before starting the dose again.

Glucosamine

Glucosamine is involved in the mucous secretions of the urinary tract, the digestive tract and the respiratory system. Glucosamine has proven effective in treating the symptoms of various joint ailments, asthma, vaginitis and certain skin problems. Glucosamine is a naturally occurring amino sugar. Glucosamine helps tissue cells stay together. Glucosamine is necessary for the building and maintaining of all connective tissue and for the lubricating fluid needed by the body, especially joints. We recommend Glucosamine Sulfate 750 mg one to three times per day, depending on a patient's symptoms as they relate to joint pain.

Glutamine

An amino acid that is found in the muscles of the body, glutamine is mandatory for proper brain function. Glutamine helps the digestive tract stay healthy and it is also necessary for the metabolism of RNA and DNA. Glutamine is needed for nitrogen metabolism. Glutamine has been used in treating patients with arthritis, intestinal disorders and patients with sugar cravings such as alcoholics. Raw parsley and spinach are good sources of glutamine. We recommend 1000-mg daily of this amino acid.

Glutathione

Produced in the liver, glutathione is a strong antioxidant. Glutathione detoxifies harmful substances in the liver and also helps red blood cells stay healthy and protects white blood cells.

Glutathione additionally helps to properly metabolize fat. Glutathione levels decrease as a person ages. Low levels of glutathione in the body may cause various mental disorders, a lack of coordination and difficulty in maintaining one's balance. We recommend 50 mg of glutathione daily.

Grape Seed Extract
Grape seed oil, which is low in saturated fat, is a natural fatty acid that does not contain cholesterol, sodium or trans fatty acids. Grape seed extract comes from the seeds and skins of grapes. It is a more powerful antioxidant than vitamin C and vitamin E. Grape seed extract also relaxes smooth muscle and may be effective in combating hypertension. We recommend 50-mg daily of this nutrient.

Green Tea Extract
Green tea has antioxidant properties and may help in the prevention of stomach and colon cancer. Green tea has anti-clotting properties that assist in the prevention of arteriosclerosis. There is also some evidence that green tea may be useful in promoting weight loss since it assists in maintaining proper glucose and insulin levels. We recommend 400-mg daily of this nutrient.

Indole 3 Carbinol (I3C)
Indole 3 Carbinol (I3C) is a dietary supplement made from cruciferous vegetables such as broccoli and cauliflower. I3C may decrease cancer cell growth, especially breast and prostate cancers that are linked to higher estrogen levels in the body. I3C provides antioxidant protection and provides protection from harmful environmental toxins. We recommend 200 mg two times per day for patients weighing 120 pounds or less, 200 mg three times per day for patients weighing between 120 and 180 pounds and 200 mg four times per day for patients weighing more than 180 pounds.

Lactobacillus acidophilus
Lactobacillus acidophilus is a friendly bacterium that helps maintain a normal environment in your digestive tract. This type of bacteria aids in the metabolism of vitamin K and the B vitamins. Lactobacillus acidophilus also helps fight against yeast infections. Having friendly bacteria in your intestinal tract can do much for improving your health. Even if you eat properly, there will still be

many byproducts of the food you eat that need to be destroyed by healthy bacteria. We recommend 2 billion parts of lactobacillus acidophilus daily.

Milk Thistle
This extract, found in various leaves, fruits and seeds, has excellent antioxidant properties. It protects the liver against free radical damage and is also known to protect the kidneys. It may also help in the treatment of psoriasis. We recommend 200 mg daily.

Methyl Sulfonylmethane (MSM)
MSM is a bio-available sulfur that has many anti-inflammatory properties. MSM is also known to improve the immune system function and provide relief from many allergies. For our patients with joint pain, we recommend 2000-mg daily of the supplement. For MSM to be effective it must be taken with at least 2000 mg of vitamin C daily.

N-Acetyl-L-Cysteine (NAC)
NAC, an amino acid that can break down excessive amounts of mucous and also has antiviral properties, acts as an antioxidant that suppresses free radicals in the liver and the lungs. We recommend 250 mg of NAC daily.

Red Grape Skin Extract (Anthocyanins)
A vitamin, red grape skin extract can work with vitamin C to suppress allergic reactions. Grape seed extract is a wonderful antioxidant. Grape seed extract can also enhance collagen production and decrease skin aging. We recommend 400-mg daily of this nutrient.

Saw Palmetto, Pygeum and Urtica
Saw palmetto is a plant extract that assists in alleviating the symptoms associated with an enlarged prostate gland. Saw palmetto blocks prostate cell growth by binding dihydrotestosterone and it relaxes smooth muscle, which helps with the symptoms of urinary frequency and urinary flow. Pygeum, another plant extract helps the prostate gland shrink and inhibits prostate cell growth, which can lead to prostate cancer. Urinary flow and complete emptying of the bladder can be a result of prostate enlargement. Urtica, an herbal extract from the nettle root improves urinary flow and bladder emp-

tying. We recommend to all of our male patients a combination of saw palmetto, pygeum and urtica. The dose is 160 mg of saw palmetto two times per day, pygeum 50 mg two times per day and urtica (stinging nettle extract) 120 mg two times per day.

Silibinin

Silibinin is an extract derived from milk thistle and known for its liver protection, anti-cancer and anti-cardiovascular disease effects. Milk thistle enhances cell growth when needed and decreases it when needed. When clinically indicated, we recommend 375-mg daily of this supplement. Patients with prostate cancer may benefit from the actions of this supplement by taking six capsules daily, in three divided doses.

Soy Extract

Derived from the soybean, this dietary supplement has been proven to be beneficial for improving bone density, lowering LDL cholesterol, increasing HDL cholesterol, decreasing menopausal symptoms, decreasing prostate growth, helping the thyroid gland function more effectively and assisting in the prevention of colon and breast cancers. When clinically indicated, we recommend 270 mg daily. Ingesting soybeans, which are delicious when steamed, is an even better way to get the wonderful benefits of soy.

Trimethylglycine (TMG)

TMG improves methylation and thereby may improve health and slow aging. Methylation is defined as the constant enzyme changes that occur to our cellular DNA, which is needed to maintain and repair our DNA. Aging compromises healthy methylation. Poor methylation can result in cancer, liver disease and loss of brain cell function. An indication of poor methylation is elevated serum homocysteine levels. TMG helps lower homocysteine levels. We recommend three 500-mg capsules daily, when clinically indicated.

Tumeric

This nutrient has antioxidant properties and also acts as a natural antibiotic. It helps in preventing blood clots, protects the liver against many toxic substances and has anticancer effects. We recommend 300 mg daily.

REMEMBER THIS

- Micronutrients (vitamins and minerals) are essential for life but in lesser quantities than macronutrients (protein, carbohydrates and fat)

- The primary source of your micronutrients should come from the food you eat

- We need some free radicals, but not too many, to fight disease

- If too many free radicals stay in the body too long, they can cause damage

- An antioxidant destroys free radicals by destroying itself. Since the lifespan of an antioxidant is quite short, they must be replaced continually

- Vitamin C can help prevent cardiovascular disease and also improve outcomes for patients with coronary artery disease

- Vitamin C helps regulate the release of insulin in the body

- Vitamin C helps the healing process and promotes collagen growth

- Vitamin C may be found in many types of berries, oranges, various melons, green and red bell peppers, kiwi fruit, broccoli, cauliflower and tomatoes

- For effective antioxidant effects, we recommend 2000 mg per day of Vitamin C, to be obtained from the food you eat and from supplementation

- Beta-carotene, a precursor to vitamin A, has been known for its antioxidant effects in the prevention of many cancers and heart disease

- Sources of beta-carotene are cantaloupe, spinach, various dark green leafy vegetables, romaine lettuce and apricots

- We recommend 20,000 IU of beta-carotene per day, to be obtained primarily from the food you eat and secondarily, from supplementation

- There are eight fat-soluble plant compounds in the Vitamin E family

- Vitamin E is a powerful antioxidant

- Vitamin E is found in nut and vegetable oils, sunflower seeds, wheat germ and spinach

- It is difficult to get enough Vitamin E from your diet, therefore supplementation is recommended

- Vitamin E has been shown to help prevent cancer, boost the immune system function, alleviate respiratory problems and help fight heart disease

- Vitamin E reduces cellular aging, prevents abnormal blood clotting, protects the retina of the eye, protects the nervous system and reduces the risk for Alzheimer's disease

- Vitamin E improves brain function through its antioxidant capabilities

- Vitamin E is fat-soluble and stays in the body longer than water soluble-vitamins such as the B vitamins and vitamin C

- Since Vitamin E, stays in the body longer, it is important, not to take too much Vitamin E because it could interfere with blood coagulation

- If you are taking any type of anticoagulant medication, it is important to consult your physician before taking Vitamin E

- We recommend 400 to 800 IU of Vitamin E (Gamma E Tocopherol) per day

- Vitamin A, an antioxidant, is a fat-soluble vitamin that helps prevent infection and also prevents macular degeneration

- Vitamin A slows the aging process and assists in protein metabolism

- Taking too much vitamin A could be toxic, especially for the liver

- We recommend taking no more than 18,000 IU of vitamin A per day, to be obtained from your diet and supplementation

- Foods rich in vitamin A are carrots, cantaloupe, beet greens, pumpkin, sweet potatoes and spinach

- Vitamin B1, thiamin, helps convert carbohydrates into energy

- Thiamin can be found in beef, pork, oatmeal, beans and oranges

- Severe thiamin deficiency can destroy brain cells and impair memory

- We recommend 100 mg of thiamin daily

- Riboflavin, or Vitamin B2, is a powerful antioxidant and also helps convert amino acids (protein building blocks) into neurotransmitters, which are necessary for proper brain function

- Vitamin B2 helps with growth and reproduction and assists with the metabolism of protein, carbohydrates and fats

- Vitamin B2 promotes healthy hair, skin and nails

- Good sources of riboflavin are fish, poultry, asparagus, broccoli, yogurt and spinach

- Alcohol and birth control pills interfere with riboflavin absorption

- We recommend 100 mg of Vitamin B2 daily to be obtained from your diet and from supplementation

- Vitamin B3, niacin, is found in tuna, chicken breasts, some fortified cereals and veal

- Niacin assists in lowering cholesterol levels

- Too much Niacin may cause liver damage

- Niacin has proven useful in certain allergic conditions because it prevents the release of histamine

- Niacin promotes relaxation, is necessary for orgasm, helps promote healthy skin, reduces blood pressure and increases circulation

- Niacin lowers cholesterol and triglycerides

- Niacin may cause flushing, nervousness, headache, itching, diarrhea and nausea

- Niacin should be taken under the supervision of a trained physician

- We recommend 50 mg of niacin and 150 mg of niacinamide daily to be obtained from your diet and from supplementation

- For cholesterol lowering effects, No-Flush Niacin may be recommended by your physician at a dose from 800 mg to 2400 mg daily

- Niaspan, a long-acting prescription niacin is currently being used as the drug of choice for increasing HDL (the good cholesterol)

- Vitamin B5, Pantothenic Acid, is the anti-stress vitamin

- Vitamin B5 helps with digestion, improves skin, is necessary in the production of the main neurotransmitter, acetylcholine and helps in removing age spots

- Vitamin B5 is crucial for the formation of antibodies, essential for the production of adrenal hormones, assists in the proper utilization of vitamins by the body and helps convert protein, carbohydrates and fat into energy

- Vitamin B5 may be found in saltwater fish, pork, nuts, mushrooms, various fresh vegetables, eggs, liver and whole wheat

- We recommend 400-mg daily of Vitamin B5

- Pyridoxine or Vitamin B6 is found in avocados, chicken, beef, soybeans, brown rice, eggs, oats and peanuts

- Vitamin B6 is as important to your body as oxygen and water"

- Vitamin B6 is necessary for proper metabolism, especially the metabolism of essential fatty acids, and assists in the creation of necessary neurotransmitters

- Vitamin B6 is important in the formation of eicosanoids

- Vitamin B6 should be taken in combination with the other B vitamins

- Too much Vitamin B6 may cause various nerve disorders or photosensitivity

- We recommend 100 mg of Vitamin B6 daily to be obtained from your diet and from supplementation

- Vitamin B12 is necessary in the production of the myelin sheath

- Adequate levels of Vitamin B12 can improve cognitive function

- Low levels of Vitamin B12 may cause increased homocysteine levels

- Vitamin B12 is important in the production of red blood cells

- Vitamin B12 can be found in ham, cooked oysters, crab, tuna, salmon, clams and herring

- We recommend 400 mcg of Vitamin B12 daily to be obtained primarily from you diet

- Biotin, a B-complex vitamin, is needed to process the protein and fat we consume

- Biotin can be manufactured by the body but is also found in eggs, various cereals and milk

- Biotin lowers blood glucose levels

- Biotin assists in preventing hair loss and decreases the incidence of eczema and dermatitis

- We recommend 600 mcg of Biotin daily to be obtained primarily from your diet

- Vitamin D is a fat-soluble vitamin

- Vitamin D is needed to transport phosphorus and calcium in the body so that bone growth occurs in children and bone remineralization occurs in adults

- Vitamin D enhances the immune system (helps in the prevention of many cancers such as breast cancer and prostate cancer) assists in the regulation of a person's heartbeat, is needed for proper thyroid function, helps prevent muscle weakness and helps in normalizing the blood clotting process

- Vitamin D is essential for a healthy skeletal system and healthy teeth

- Vitamin D can be obtained from the sun. Other sources of vitamin D are eggs, sardines, halibut, salmon, herring, tuna, sweet potatoes and fortified milk

- Vitamin D must always be taken in conjunction with calcium

- We recommend 400 IU of vitamin D daily, to be obtained from your diet and supplementation

- Vitamin K's primary responsibility is to help blood clot

- Vitamin K also plays a role in transforming glucose into glycogen for storage in the liver

- We recommend 60 mcg daily of Vitamin K

- Good sources of Vitamin K are broccoli, green leafy vegetables, egg yolks, oatmeal and soybeans

- Folic acid is necessary for nerve formation and regulation and especially, nerve formation in the fetus

- Women, in their child bearing years, whether pregnant or not, should routinely take supplemental folic acid (400 mcg daily) to help prevent serious birth defects such as spina bifida

- Folic acid helps in the formation of red blood cells, the production of energy, the formation of white blood cells and is crucial for making DNA

- Women with adequate folic acid levels in their bodies appear to have a lesser incidence of cervical dysplasia (abnormal cells in the cervix) which can be a precursor to cervical cancer

- Folic acid may be found in many fruits and vegetables

- Good sources of folic acid are navy beans, pinto beans, asparagus, broccoli, okra, spinach and brussel sprouts

- We recommend 400 mcg to 800 mcg of folic acid daily to be obtained from your diet and from supplementation

- Lecithin is composed of the B vitamin choline, linoleic acid and the vitamin inositol, which is needed for hair growth

- Lecithin helps reduce cholesterol levels and assists in preventing hardening of the arteries

- Lecithin assists with fat metabolism, improves brain function and helps in the absorption of Vitamin A and Vitamin B1

- Lecithin may be found in egg yolks, grains, fish and various legumes

- We recommend 700-mg daily of lecithin and 200-mg daily of inositol, to be obtained from your diet and from supplementation

- Lycopene is the red source found in tomatoes, watermelon, red peppers and red grapefruit

- Lycopene is a strong antioxidant carotenoid

- Lycopene has many protective effects on the body including prostate and brain protection and may be instrumental in preventing coronary artery disease

- We recommend 10 mg daily of Lycopene

- Para-Aminobenzoic Acid (PABA) is a primary ingredient in folic acid

- PABA helps in the metabolism of Vitamin B5

- PABA is a powerful antioxidant that helps prevent sunburn and skin cancer

- PABA helps with red blood cell formation, assists in protein metabolism and is integral in maintaining proper intestinal health

- Sources of PABA are various organ meats such as kidneys and liver, whole grains, spinach, molasses and mushrooms

- We recommend 500 mg of PABA daily, to be obtained from your diet and from supplementation

- As with vitamins, various minerals are essential for a healthy life

- Adequate mineral levels assist various antioxidants in being more effective

- Minerals are an important component in dietary supplementation

- Boron is a trace mineral that helps the body to more effectively utilize the minerals magnesium and calcium

- Boron helps activate certain hormones in the body such as estrogen and testosterone

- Boron assists in the metabolic process of Vitamin D

- Boron can increase mental acuity

- Sources of boron may be found in apples, grapes, green leafy vegetables, cherries, beans and nuts

- It is preferable to obtain at least 2 mg of boron per day from the food you eat

- For adult female patients, we recommend a daily dose of 3000 mg of calcium citrate

- For our adult male patients, we recommend a daily dose of 1500 mg of calcium

- We need calcium to build strong bones

- Adequate levels of calcium in the body help maintain a normal heart rhythm, assist with the blood clotting process and help with proper nerve and muscle function

- Calcium assists with serum cholesterol levels and is important in protein manufacturing when the body is making RNA and DNA; the substances that comprise your genetic makeup

- Calcium assists in lowering serum iron levels

- Good sources of calcium are broccoli, salmon that still has the bones, sardines, green leafy vegetables and yogurt

- Chromium, a trace mineral is necessary for the body to utilize insulin correctly

- Chromium can help with weight loss

- Chromium may be found in ham, brown rice, grape juice and broccoli

- We recommend 400mcg of chromium daily

- Copper is necessary for our survival

- The level of copper in the body is directly proportional to the amount of vitamin C and zinc in the body

- Osteoporosis, can be partially traced to low copper levels because copper is necessary for collagen formation which is an essential protein that makes our bones, skin and connective tissue

- Copper is involved in the metabolism of iron

- Copper may be found in avocados, almonds, broccoli, mushrooms, cooked oysters, cocoa powder, green leafy vegetables, salmon and soybeans

- We recommend 2 mg of copper daily

- Iodine is needed to produce the necessary thyroid hormone, thyroxine

- Most of us get enough iodine in our diet by using iodized table salt

- Foods rich in iodine are garlic, sesame seeds, summer squash, soybeans, lobster, shrimp and spinach

- We recommend 150 mcg of iodine daily

- Magnesium is necessary for making all the muscles in your body flex and for assisting in energy production

- Magnesium ensures that the body utilizes calcium correctly

- Stress can cause magnesium deficiency

- We recommend 400 mg of magnesium daily

- Food sources of magnesium are spinach, oatmeal, broccoli, yogurt, avocados, brown rice, most dairy products, blueberries and green leafy vegetables

- Strong bones, collagen formation and proper brain function are all dependent upon adequate levels of manganese in the body

- Low levels of manganese can cause muscle contractions, vision and/or hearing loss, convulsions, rapid heart rate and atherosclerosis

- We recommend 10 mg of manganese daily

- Dietary sources of manganese may be found in blueberries, various nuts, shellfish, egg yolks, pineapple, avocados and nuts

- Molybdenum is needed to make certain biochemical reactions occur in the body

- Molybdenum helps in the production of certain genetic material, the production of protein and the creation of uric acid

- We recommend 200-mcg daily of molybdenum

- Eating a well balanced diet can usually supply the body with enough molybdenum

- Food sources for molybdenum may be found in dark green leafy vegetables, whole grains, milk products and beans

- Potassium is necessary for maintaining optimal levels of blood pressure, proper muscle contractions, regular heart rhythm and proper nerve transmissions throughout the body

- Good sources of potassium are brown rice, cantaloupe, spinach, dried apricots, poultry, avocados, raisins, potatoes and bananas

- We recommend 200-mg daily of potassium aspartate

- Selenium is a crucial antioxidant

- Selenium keeps many viruses in check and this may be its most vital role in addition to inhibiting the oxidation of lipids in the body and detoxifying heavy metals

- Brazil nuts are so rich in selenium that only two or three nuts, eaten daily, may provide an adequate dose of selenium

- Too much selenium can have toxic effects

- Lobster, crab, whole grains, broccoli, brown rice, molasses, onions, tuna and many vegetables contain selenium

- Vanadium is needed for bone and teeth formation and for cellular metabolism

- Sources of vanadium include fish, olives, radishes and whole grains

- We recommend 200 mcg of vanadium daily

- Proper amounts of zinc are necessary for prostate health, maintaining immune system function (too much zinc will decrease immunity) and producing many of the cells you need to stay healthy

- Zinc is needed to metabolize protein, help prevent acne by controlling oil gland activity, promote healing and help with collagen formation

- Zinc is necessary for bone formation, prevents the creation of certain free radicals, helps the body maintain adequate levels of vitamin E and enhances a person's sense of taste and sense of smell

- Zinc is important to reproduction because it assists with organ development and sperm motility

- Zinc may be found in egg yolks, fish, red meat, soybeans, sunflower seeds, whole grains, nuts and yogurt

- We recommend 30 mg of zinc daily

- Taking more than 100 mg of zinc daily can decrease a person's immunity

- Too much zinc decreases copper levels in the body

- In addition to the macronutrients; protein, carbohydrates and fat and the micronutrients; vitamins and minerals, there are other nutrients your body needs

- Alpha lipoic acid is an important overall body antioxidant

- Alpha lipoic acid increases energy levels, reduces heavy metal levels in the body, including iron levels

- Alpha lipoic acid enhances the activity of other antioxidants such a vitamin C, vitamin E, coenzyme Q10, and assists with maintaining normal growth and metabolism

- We recommend 250 mg of alpha lipoic acid two times per day and for our diabetic patients we recommend 250 mg three to four times per day

- Baby aspirin, 81 mg daily, can provide many health benefits

- Taking 81 mg of aspirin daily can lower C-reactive protein levels and thereby decrease the risk associated with coronary artery disease

- Low doses of aspirin help keep the blood thinned

- Taking Betaine HCL, when clinically indicated, can restore stomach acids to healthy levels

- We recommend 648 mg of Betaine HCL and 130 mg of pepsin daily

- A daily dose of 2 billion parts of bifido bacteria is recommended for good intestinal health

- Bilberry, also known as blueberry, assists in maintaining the proper insulin levels in the body

- We recommend a daily dose of 100 mg of bilberry extract and consuming blueberries in your diet

- Carnosine is an amino acid intermediate that has amazing antioxidant, anti-glycating (glucose that accumulates in our tissues causes cross-links in proteins, enzymes and cell membranes, which leads to loss of function of our cells) aldehyde quenching (aldehydes are by-products of protein metabolism) and metal chelating actions

- Carnosine can give old cells new life and prevent other cells from becoming damaged as a result of aging protein metabolism, which is one of the reasons cells age or die

- Carnosine is one of the most important supplements, in addition to CoQ10 that we recommend for our patients

- To be effective, Carnosine must be taken in adequate doses. We recommend 500 mg of Carnosine three times per day

- Cetyl Myristoleate helps decrease the pain caused by osteoarthritis, rheumatoid arthritis and psoriasis because it helps lubricate joints and bones

- The dose for Cetyl Myristoleate is dependent upon a patient's symptoms

- Chitosan is a source of fiber made from the shells of shellfish

- When indicated, we recommend one 250-mg of Chitosan at each meal

- Bioflavinoids are useful in reducing pain, preventing asthma, promoting circulation, lowering cholesterol levels and when taken in conjunction with vitamin C, may decrease the symptoms associated with oral herpes

- We recommend 400 mg daily of citrus bioflavinoids

- Good sources of bioflavinoids include grapes, cherries, apricots, oranges and lemons

- CoQ10 is found naturally in every cell in the body

- CoQ10 is a fat-soluble vitamin that is an antioxidant and vital for energy metabolism

- We recommend 60 mg of Solanova' CoQ10 daily

- Adequate levels of CoQ10 can improve cardiovascular health, increase energy levels, boost the immune system, lower high blood pressure and may reverse gum disease

- CoQ10 has also been shown to decrease tumors in breast cancer patients

- Conjugated linoleic acid (CLA) is a fatty acid that enhances the immune system through its antioxidant and anti-cancer effects

- When clinically indicated we recommend three to six 500 mg capsules of CLA daily, in divided doses and for cancer patients, six to twelve 500 mg capsules, in divided doses, may be recommended daily

- Getting enough fiber in our diet is important

- Fruits and vegetables offer the most healthful form of fiber

- Fiber Food is a good source of dietary fiber

- We recommend 6 capsules of Fiber Food with each meal

- Garlic can help lower blood pressure, assists in preventing blood clots, lowers cholesterol levels, improves the immune system function, acts as an antibiotic, an anti-fungal and an anti-viral agent and helps with the digestive process

- We recommend at least 500 mg of garlic daily

- Small amounts of ginger daily, 200 mg can help in maintaining a healthy colon

- Ginger is a powerful antioxidant and may be used to help wounds and sores heal

- Ginkgo Biloba improves blood circulation and increases the oxygen supply to all parts of the body, especially the brain and the heart

- Ginkgo biloba may improve memory, reduce blood pressure, improve hearing loss and may slow some of the symptoms of Alzheimer's disease

- We recommend between 120 mg and 240 mg daily for our patients

- Ginseng promotes better health, improves energy and physical performance

- Ginseng may be a beneficial adjunct in treating elevated blood pressure, low blood pressure, stress-related illnesses, diabetes, depression, insomnia and atherosclerosis

- We recommend three 300 mg capsules of Ginseng daily

- Glucosamine helps tissue cells stay together

- Glucosamine is necessary for the building and maintaining of all connective tissue and for the lubricating fluid needed by the body, especially joints

- We recommend Glucosamine Sulfate 750 mg one to three times per day, depending on a patient's symptoms as they relate to joint pain

- Glutamine is mandatory for proper brain function

- Glutamine helps the digestive tract stay healthy and it is also necessary for the metabolism of RNA and DNA

- Glutamine is needed for nitrogen metabolism

- Raw parsley and spinach are good sources of glutamine

- We recommend 1000-mg daily of glutamine

- Glutathione is a strong antioxidant

- Glutathione detoxifies harmful substances in the liver and also helps red blood cells stay healthy and protects white blood cells

- Glutathione helps to properly metabolize fat

- We recommend 50 mg of glutathione daily

- Grape seed extract is a more powerful antioxidant than vitamin C and vitamin E

- Grape seed extract also relaxes smooth muscle and may be effective in combating hypertension

- We recommend 50-mg daily of grape seed extract

- Green tea has antioxidant properties and may help in the prevention of stomach and colon cancer

- Green tea has anti-clotting properties that assist in the prevention of arteriosclerosis

- Green tea may be useful in promoting weight loss

- We recommend 400-mg daily of Green Tea

- Indole 3 Carbinol (I3C) is a dietary supplement made from cruciferous vegetables such as broccoli and cauliflower

- I3C decreases cancer cell growth, especially breast and prostate cancers which are linked to higher estrogen levels in the body

- I3C provides antioxidant protection and provides protection from harmful environmental toxins

- For I3C, we recommend 200 mg two times per day for patients weighing 120 pounds or less, 200 mg three times per day for patients weighing between 120 and 180 pounds and 200 mg four times per day for patients weighing more than 180 pounds

- Lactobacillus acidophilus is a friendly bacterium that helps maintain a normal environment in the digestive tract

- We recommend 2 billion parts of lactobacillus acidophilus daily

- Milk thistle is found in various leaves, fruits and seeds

- Milk thistle has excellent antioxidant properties

- We recommend 200 mg daily

- MSM is a bio-available sulfur and has many anti-inflammatory properties

- For our patients with joint pain, we recommend 2000-mg daily of the supplement

- For MSM to be effective it must be taken with vitamin C daily

- NAC, is an amino acid that can break down excessive amounts of mucous

- We recommend 250 mg of NAC daily

- Red grape skin extract (anthocyanins) is a vitamin that works with vitamin C to suppress allergic reactions

- Red grape skin extract is a wonderful antioxidant

- Red grape skin extract can enhance collagen production and decrease skin aging

- We recommend 400-mg daily of red grape skin extract

- Saw palmetto is a plant extract that assists in alleviating the symptoms associated with an enlarged prostate gland

- Saw palmetto blocks prostate cell growth by binding dihydrotestosterone

- Saw palmetto relaxes smooth muscle, which helps with the symptoms of urinary frequency and urinary flow

- Pygeum, another plant extract helps the prostate gland shrink and inhibits prostate cell growth

- Urtica, an herbal extract from the nettle root improves urinary flow and bladder emptying

- We recommend to all of our male patients a combination of saw palmetto, pygeum and urtica. The dose is 160 mg of saw palmetto two times per day, pygeum 50 mg two times per day and urtica (stinging nettle extract) 120 mg two times per day

- Silibinin is an extract derived from milk thistle and known for its liver protection, anti-cancer and anti-cardiovascular disease effects

- When clinically indicated, we recommend 375 mg daily of Silibinin

- Soy extract has been proven to be beneficial for improving bone density, lowering LDL cholesterol, increasing HDL cholesterol, decreasing menopausal symptoms, decreasing prostate growth, helping the thyroid gland function more effectively and assisting in the prevention of colon and breast cancers

- When clinically indicated, we recommend 270 mg daily of soy extract

- TMG improves methylation and thereby may improve health and slow aging

- TMG helps lower homocysteine levels

- We recommend three 500-mg capsules daily of TMG, when clinically indicated

- Tumeric has antioxidant properties and also acts as a natural antibiotic

- We recommend 300 mg daily of Tumeric

Listed below are the basic supplements we recommend for our patients. Other supplements (some that were discussed in this chapter) may be added to a patient's regime depending on their symptoms, certain blood levels or other standard assessment criteria

- Use supplements wisely, when needed, and approved by your anti-aging physician

  - Vitamin C 2000 mg daily
  - Beta Carotene 20,000 IU daily
  - Vitamin E 400 to 800 IU daily
  - Vitamin A 18,000 IU daily
  - Vitamin B1 (Thiamin) 100 mg daily
  - Vitamin B2 (Riboflavin) 100 mg daily
  - Vitamin B3 (Niacin) 50 - 150 mg daily
  - Vitamin B5 400 mg daily
  - Vitamin B6 100 mg daily
  - Vitamin B12 400 mcg daily
  - Biotin 600 mcg daily
  - Vitamin D 400 IU daily
  - Vitamin K 60 mcg daily
  - Folic Acid 400 - 800 mcg daily
  - Lecithin 700 mg daily
  - Inositol 200 mg daily
  - Lycopene 10 mg daily
  - PABA 500 mg daily
  - Boron 2 mg daily
  - Calcium Citrate 1500 mg daily (men) and 3000 mg daily (women)
  - Chromium 400 mcg daily

- Copper 2 mg daily
- Iodine 150 mcg daily
- Magnesium 400 mg daily
- Manganese 10 mg daily
- Molybdenum 200 mcg daily
- Potassium Aspartate 200 mg daily
- Selenium 200 mcg daily
- Vanadium 200 mcg daily
- Zinc 30 mg daily
- Alpha Lipoic Acid 250 mg 2x/ day (If diabetic 250 mg 3-4 times/day)
- Baby aspirin 81 mg daily
- Bifobacterium bifidum 2 billion parts daily
- Bilberry 100 mg daily
- Carnosine 500 mg 3x/day
- Citrus Bioflavinoids 400 mg daily
- CoQ10 60 mg daily (Solanova brand)
- Garlic 500 mg daily
- Ginger 200 mg daily
- Ginkgo Biloba 120 - 240 mg daily
- Ginseng 300 mg three times per day
- Glucosamine 750 mg daily (more if joint pain)
- Glutamine 1000 mg daily
- Glutathione 50 mg daily
- Grape Seed Extract 50 mg daily
- Green Tea Extract 400 mg daily
- Indole 3 Carbinol (I3C) 200 mg 2x/day (weight 120 pounds or less) 200 mg 3x/day (weight 120-180 pounds) 200 mg 4x/day (weight > 180spounds
- Lactobacillus acidophilus 2 billion parts daily
- Milk Thistle 200 mg daily
- NAC 250 mg daily
- Red Grape Skin Extract 400 mg daily
- MEN ONLY (prostate health):
  Saw palmetto 160 mg 2x/day
  Pygeum 50 mg 2x/day
  Urtica 120 mg 2x/day
- Tumeric 300 mg daily

CHAPTER NINE

EXERCISE

Now you know why eating a hormonally correct diet and taking the right amount and kind of vitamins, minerals and other supplements is the cornerstone to improving your health and well being. The next building block for achieving and maintaining good health is exercise. Knowing what type of exercise your body needs and how often you should exercise is important. Too much exercise or the wrong type of exercise can be just as harmful as no exercise at all. The human body needs to "move" in order to prosper. Physical activity can improve your health. Exercise can make your heart stronger, increase circulation, lower LDL cholesterol levels, decrease body fat, lower blood pressure, decrease the risk of breast, colon, prostate and endometrial cancers, help prevent adult onset diabetes (type II diabetes) and osteoporosis, plus exercise increases back strength and mobility. The human body needs to stay active to remain healthy. So, start your exercise program today. A healthier more youthful future awaits you.

As a person ages, mobility, strength and flexibility decrease because we lose muscle fiber. When muscle fiber is lost, muscle mass and strength decline. This loss of strength causes a decrease in mobility and flexibility. To counter these effects, you need to maintain a proper diet, an effective exercise program and, when clinically indicated, begin natural hormone replacement therapy. By modifying your lifestyle through diet, exercise and natural hormone replacement therapy, you may slow or even reverse the loss of muscle fiber, which will allow your body and your mind to remain healthy and energized for years to come.

Our bodies are living organisms that respond to a variety of stimuli. This was true from the beginning of time and it is true today. Feeling hungry is a stimulus that tells us when to eat. If we eat food that is not good for us, our bodies will respond accordingly. If we do not exercise or exercise inappropriately, our bodies will also respond accordingly.

Today, in our modern environment, exercise has become optional because our activities of daily living do not force us to stay physically fit. The physical demands placed on the human body through the acts of work and survival have decreased and our bodies have suffered. Osteoporosis is on the rise in both men and women. The number of people suffering from obesity is climbing and the increasing incidence of back ailments is alarming. It is evident that to keep healthy, our bodies need exercise just as much today as they did in times past.

When we exercise, we are compelling our bodies to become stronger and more efficient. We are forcing our bones to become denser, our muscles stronger and our internal organs to work more effectively.

Exercise produces microscopic tears in muscle fibers. As a result, the body constantly works to repair the muscular tissue, which results in making muscle fibers denser and stronger. Therefore, exercising regularly ensures that the body is in a constant state of cellular regeneration. This constant state of cellular regeneration promotes the production and release of hormones such as human growth hormone (the master hormone of the body) and testosterone. These major hormones, in conjunction with many other major and minor hormones in the body, contribute to an improved body image, improved strength, increased libido and a more youthful appearance, in general.

You now know why the body needs exercise just as much as it needs the right type of food for a better quality of life. Let's discuss what types of exercise the body needs to improve and maintain health and well being. Your body needs three types of exercise to stay optimally fit. The three types of exercise you need are aerobic training, anaerobic training and flexibility training.

AEROBIC EXERCISE:

Aerobic exercise is also known as cardiovascular training. Aerobic training requires oxygen as its primary catalyst for energy production. This energy source can be sustained for a long duration because of the abundant levels of oxygen taken into the body, but lacks in explosive power. Aerobic training increases your heart rate and promotes greater amounts of oxygen to flow through your body thereby improving circulation. Increased oxygen absorption also creates an atmosphere conducive to a higher metabolic rate, allowing the body to maintain more optimal levels of body fat and a better exchange of oxygen and carbon dioxide.

If you have not exercised for some time, begin by walking fifteen minutes per day. Gradually increase your walking time to thirty minutes per day. If your schedule permits, try walking for one hour per day. Once you are in the routine of walking daily, increase your pace, so that your heart rate is elevated to at least 55% of your maximum heart rate. Try to maintain some type of rhythm to your walking which will give your body greater benefits from your exercise efforts. Other aerobic exercises that are beneficial in improving cardiovascular fitness include distance running, stair climbing, skating and basketball.

ANAEROBIC EXERCISE (RESISTANCE TRAINING):

Anaerobic exercises are typically associated with strength, agility and quick bursts of power. One of the best forms of anaerobic exercise is "resistance training". Unlike aerobic training, where the primary energy source is oxygen, the anaerobic training energy source is an energy system known as the ATP/CP (Adenosine Triphosphate and Creatine Phosphate) system. In this system, Creatine Phosphate combines with ADP (the precursor of ATP) and allows for the formation of ATP and creatine. The process provides enough energy to contract muscles maximally for a short duration of time because there is a limited supply of CP molecules. When CP is depleted, ATP can no longer be synthesized in this way, so muscular strength and power decrease.

Resistance training produces increased muscle mass and explosive strength. With increased muscle mass, a person's metabolic rate is heightened due to the additional energy needed to maintain a higher level of muscle mass. By increasing your muscle strength you may lower your blood pressure, decrease unfavorable cholesterol levels, help your insulin and glucose levels stay within healthful ranges, increase your bone density and improve your cardiovascular system.
You do not have to be a body builder and "pump iron" to reap the

benefits of resistance training. Weight lifting or resistance bands provide a stimulus that forces the body to respond to physical stress. Once the body has adapted to a certain resistance exercise routine, it is important to change the routine periodically, so the body will continue to adapt and maintain strength.

For someone who is in fairly good shape physically, adaptation to the physical stress caused by resistance training usually takes approximately two weeks. For someone, who is not well conditioned, adaptation can take up to six weeks.

The body has six major muscle groups: the chest, the back, the legs, the shoulders, the arms and the abdominal (also known as core muscles). With resistance training, each of the major muscle groups can be isolated or used in conjunction with other muscles. The goal of resistance training is to control movement by using the proper biomechanical form through the contraction (concentric movement) and extension (eccentric movement) of the muscle being worked. These actions will create maximum muscle fiber recruitment, which promotes strength and muscular gains.

Using proper biomechanics and appropriate body positioning, when performing resistance training, will protect your skeletal structure and create balance in the specific muscle being exercised. When you exercise, having good posture is important. Beginning at the top of your body, you need to have your cervical spine straight. This may be accomplished by keeping your head straight, looking forward and placing your tongue on the roof of your mouth, while performing resistance training. Your chest should be held high and your shoulders need to be pulled back and down by squeezing your shoulder blades together. Next, your lower back should be slightly arched. If you find it difficult to place your body in the aforementioned positions, you will need to create strength and flexibility in these areas through the use of stretching and resistance training. As we move further down the body, the hips must be squared, which means when you are facing forward, there is no rotation of the hips in any direction. Your knees need to be slightly bent and your feet should be squared approximately shoulder to hip width apart. If you are lying on a bench, the points of contact on the bench will be the back of your head, your shoulder blades and your buttocks. Your feet need to be planted on the floor with your heels directly below your knees. These positioning guidelines may be applied to almost any form of resistance training whether they are performed lying, seated or standing.

Today, many trainers are using a Swiss ball for resistance training. The Swiss ball is portable and versatile. The Swiss ball is made in a number of different sizes and you will usually see them in the abdominal training area of your local gym. The Swiss balls used for resistance training will not burst but some exercise balls found in gyms do not meet this anti-burst specification. Before using a Swiss ball, make sure it is an ABS ball that is guaranteed not to burst. Training on a Swiss ball can provide the stimulus needed to make you stronger, improve the functions of your nervous system and improve the stability of your spine and your joints.

Some of the advantages of Swiss ball training are improved balance, improved neuromuscular response and improved "core strength" (core muscles include the abdominal, the lower back and the hip muscles). Strength training on the Swiss ball helps strengthen abdominal, hip and lower back muscles, which in turn reduces back pain. Pain reduction in the lower back is not the only benefit of Swiss ball training; it also helps facilitate a better exercise exhaustion of the muscles and wards off unwanted tension on shoulder joints, which can be common when weight lifting.

You want your resistance training to be effective. Therefore, make sure your training is helping you become stronger and more agile. To assist you in achieving your exercise goals, we recommend that you consult with a qualified trainer for a fitness evaluation before you begin any type of resistance training, either using weights and/or the Swiss ball. You can hurt yourself if you do not know what you are doing.

FLEXIBILITY:

Flexibility training is an exercise process by which muscles, tendons and ligaments are stretched. Stretching allows connective tissue to be lengthened, which increases range of motion. Stretching also increases circulation by increasing the surface area of muscles. Stretching improves flexibility, assists in decreasing muscular pain and increases cellular regeneration.

Now that you have a basic understanding of the three major types of exercise, the following pages in this chapter will be dedicated to sharing some examples of the types of exercises we recommend to our patients.

Flexibility Training:

Warming-up before and after any exercise routine is important. Jogging or running in place can be done before you begin your flexibility workout. HOLD EACH STRETCH FOR AT LEAST 30 SECONDS OR LONGER. The following are some basic examples of effective stretching exercises using a Swiss ball when appropriate:

UPPER BODY STRETCHES

1. PRONE TRUNK TRACTION:

2. TRUNK TRACTION:

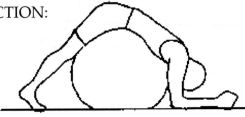

3. THE CAT:

4. LATERAL STRETCH:

5. SIDE LATERAL STRETCH:

6. CHEST STRETCH:

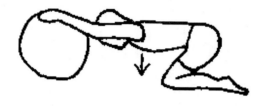

7. SIDE STRETCH:

8. REACHING SIDE STRETCH:

9. TRUNK ROTATION STRETCH:

10. TRICEPS STRETCH:

LOWER BODY STRETCHES

1. CALVE STRETCH:

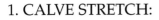

2. SIT AND REACH STRETCH:

3. KNEES TO CHEST STRETCH:

4. SITTING ADDUCTOR STRETCH:

5. QUAD STRETCH:

6. HIP AND GROIN STRETCH:

Resistance Training:

If the purpose of your resistance training is to just stay physically fit, do a series of the following exercises until you feel the "burn" as our trainers say. If you want longer, leaner muscles do at least twenty (20) repetitions of each exercise followed by three stretching exercises of the worked muscle. If you want bigger, stronger muscles do about twelve (12) repetitions of each exercise at an increased weight. The actual number of repetitions for your exercise regime should be determined by what your fitness goals are. We recommend consulting with a qualified trainer to determine your exact workout regime. The following are some of the resistance training exercises that our trainers recommend to many of our patients: Our trainers use the Swiss balls, free weights, rubber exercise bands and other training tools when consulting with patients.

CORE MUSCLE GROUP
1. SWISS BALL CRUNCHES:

Starting Position:
• Ball placed mid-back
• Arms placed behind head or across the chest
• Head placed a fist-length from chest
• Knees bent at 90 degree angle

Action Sequence:
• Flexing of the abdominal muscles
• Slight upward movement of the chest

Return Sequence:
• Slowly relax the abdominal muscles
• Slow downward movement of the chest to the staring position

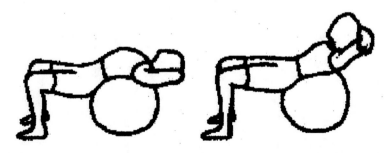

2. SIDE LATERAL FLEXION:

Starting Position:

- Hip placed on ball
- Upper leg placed forward
- Rear leg placed back
- Lower arm resting on ball
- Bend upper arm, hand on head
- Body straight with shoulders, aligned with hips

Action Sequence:

- Pull with the oblique muscles, bend at sides. Shoulders rise (Do not push with arm on ball or pull with arm on head)

Return Sequence:

- Slowly relax oblique muscles, lowering upper body back to the starting position

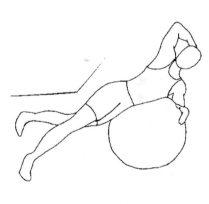

3. KICK OUTS:
Starting Position: ·
- Seated on bench, buttocks at bench's edge
- Hands holding onto bench at hip level
- Knees bent and held up into upper body

Action Sequence:
- Extend knees away from body
- Slightly move upper body away from legs
- Body should be bent to about 160 degrees

Return Sequence:
- Pull knees back into upper body
- Raise upper body back into knees

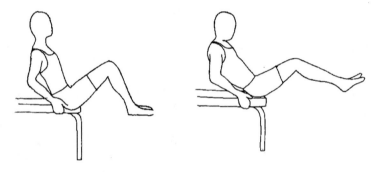

4. BRIDGES:
Starting Position:
- Upper shoulders placed on ball
- Head resting on ball with no tension
- Hips help up in alignment with the body
- Knees bent at 90 degrees

Action Sequence:
- Lower hips downward, towards Swiss ball

Return Sequence:
• Press hips upward, back to the starting position
• HOLD AT THE STARTING POSITION FOR A FEW SECONDS

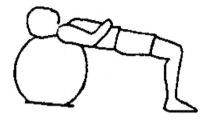 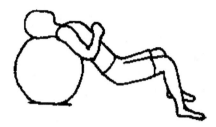

5. SUPER PEOPLE:
Starting Position:
• Lie on ball, chest down
• Ball placed in stomach region
• Legs extended
• Arms extended
• Head in neutral position (not up and not down)

Action Sequence:
• Raise opposing limbs (i.e., right arm, and left leg)
• Arm extended straight ahead of shoulder
• Leg held at hip level
• Hold limbs up for the count of five

Return Sequence:
• Lower limbs to floor
• Raise opposing limbs and repeat sequence

 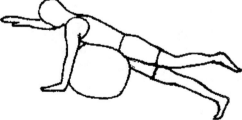

CHEST

1. SWISS BALL DUMBELL PRESS:

Starting Position:
- Lie on ball, chest up and at shoulder level
- Head resting flat on ball
- Hips held up
- Feet on floor, shoulder width apart
- Elbows bent at 90 degrees

Action Sequence:
- Pressing with chest, raise weight up
- Arms should slightly extend up, in an arching motion
- Do not press straight up, or extend arms fully

Return Sequence:
- Slowly lower arms back to 90 degree angle

2. SWISS BALL PUSH-UPS:

Starting Position:
- Body placed on ball, face down (body may be placed anywhere between the stomach (easiest position) and the feet (hardest position)
- Hands placed on floor, twice your shoulder width apart

Action Sequence:
- Bend elbows at 90 degrees
- The body acts like a teeter-totter and rises

Return Sequence:
• Press down with chest, extending the arms and lowering the legs

BICEPS

1. STANDING DUMBELL CURLS:

Starting Position:
• Use the correct posture guidelines mentioned earlier in this chapter
• Arms not fully extended, weights at your side

Action Sequence:
• Flexing biceps, alternate, raising and lowering arms to a 45 degree bend
• Elbows must be held close to the body at your side
Return Sequence:
• Slowly extend the arms beck to the starting position

2. STANDING HAMMER CURLS:

Starting Position:
- Use the correct posture guidelines mentioned earlier in this chapter
- Arms are not fully extended, weights at your side

Action Sequence:
- Flexing biceps, raise arms to 45 degree bend
- Keep palms facing one another. Do not rotate palms of hands
- Keep elbows held close into the sides of your body

Return Sequence:
- Slowly extend arms down, back to the starting position

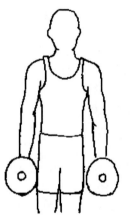 

TRICEPS

1. SWISS BALL TRIPCEP'S DIP:

Starting Position:
- Hands placed on the forward 1/3 of the Swiss ball
- Body extended out in front of the ball
- Hips down
- Legs bent

Action Sequence:
- Lower body by bending elbows to 90 degree angle

Return Sequence:
- Pressing down with triceps, extend the arms back to the starting position. Do not press with legs

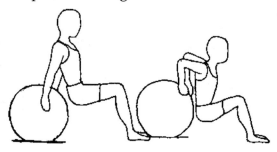

2. BEHIND THE HEAD TRICEPS EXTENSIONS:
(May be done with weights or exercise band)

Starting Position:
- Use the correct posture guidelines mentioned earlier in this chapter
- In a standing position, raise weight-bearing arm up, in line with your head
- Flex the elbow, to a 90 degree bend
- Weight should now be behind your head
- Opposite arm may be held at your side or placed on the other tricep

Action Sequence:
- Flex the triceps and extend the arm upward
- Hold the elbow in a fixed position (no forward or backward movements)

Return Sequence:
- Slowly lower the weight back behind the head to a 90 degree angle

BACK

1. LATERAL PULL-DOWNS:

Starting Position:
- Body seated
- Hands evenly spaced on the handle bars
- Arms bent at 90 degrees
- Shoulders held down

Action Sequence:
- Pull the bars down until they touch the upper chest
Return Sequence:
- Slowly allow the bar to rise back to the starting position
- Keep shoulders down and do not fully extend the arms

2. SWISS BALL SEATED ROW:

Starting Position:
- Place elastic exercise band around a fixed object
- Sit on Swiss ball with chest out and shoulders back
- Arms should be slightly bent and shoulder width apart
- Feet width will be up to the individual

Action Sequence:
- Pull shoulder blades together
- Arms pulled back into body
- Elbows can be flared out or held close to the body

Return Sequence:
- Slowly extend the arms and shoulder blades
- Do not fully extend the arms or roll shoulders forward

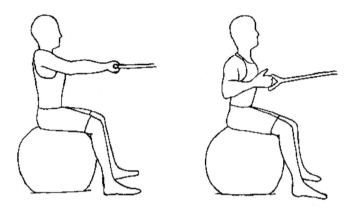

3. SWISS BALL BACK EXTENTIONS:

Starting Position:
- Kneel facing the Swiss ball
- Drape body over the Swiss ball in a prone position so that stomach is resting on the ball
- Bend head down
- Place hands behind head

Action Sequence:
- Raise head up, pulling abdominal muscles in
- Keep the back straight

Return Sequence:
- Slowly return to the starting position

SHOULDERS
1. SEATED DUMBELL PRESS:

Starting Position:
- Sitting on ball, chest out, shoulders back
- Feet spread to a comfortable position
- Arms held up at shoulder level
- Elbows bent at 90 degrees

Action Sequence:
- Press up with shoulders, raising arms
- Arms should be raised in an arcing motion
- Weights should be held in alignment with shoulders

Return Sequence:
- Slowly lower arms back to the starting position

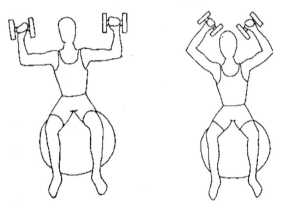

2. SIDE LATERAL RAISES:

Starting Position:
- Use the correct posture guidelines mentioned earlier in this chapter
- Hold weights at sides

Action Sequence:
- Pulling with shoulders, raise your arms up and out, at shoulder level

Return Sequence:
- Slowly lower weights back down to the starting position by slowly relaxing the shoulders

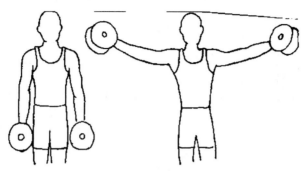

LEGS
1. SWISS BALL SQUATS:

Starting Position:
- Place Swiss ball mid back or at the arch in the back
- Place feet shoulder width apart
- Feet should be slightly forward
- There should be very little weight placed on the Swiss ball

Action Sequence:
- Flex hips back, immediately followed by your knees
- Press your chest upward
- Push buttocks back and underneath ball
- Flex knees to 90-degree angle
- Make sure your knees do no extend further than the toes on your feet

Return Sequence:
- Press with heels, extending the legs upward

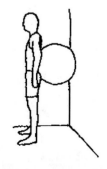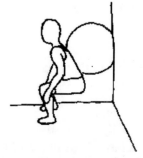

2. SWISS BALL LEG CURLS:

Starting Position:
- Lie on the floor, chest up
- Place feet on top of Swiss ball
- Raise your hips up and off of the floor
- Keep your head on the floor
- Extend your arms out to the side for stability

Action Sequence:
- Press down with your heels
- Pull knees into your body
- Keep your hips off of the floor

Return Sequence:
- Extend the knees back to the starting position
- Keep your hips off of the ground

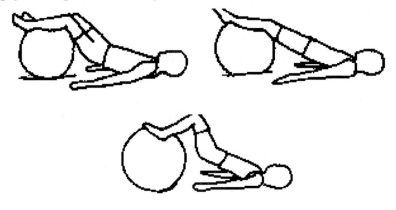

3. LUNGES:

Starting Position:
- Standing straight, hold weights in both hands

Action Sequence:
- Keeping the back straight, squat so that your right leg moves forward and your left leg move back
- Knees of both legs will be bent
- Return to standing position
- Repeat sequence, moving leg left forward and right leg back

Return Sequence:
- Return to the starting position

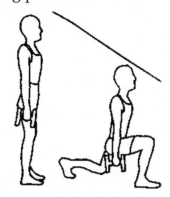

4. SWISS BALL ADDUCTION/ABDUCTION:

Starting Position:
- Lie on floor, on your side
- Place upper foot on top of the Swiss ball
- Extend lower foot, in front of the ball, keeping the foot on the floor
- Bend the lower arm and rest palm of hand on head to support your head
- Bend upper arm across stomach and place on floor in front of stomach

Action Sequence:
- Press down on ball with upper leg
- Raise the lower leg off of the floor (knee up)

Return Sequence:
- Slowly lower the leg back to the floor

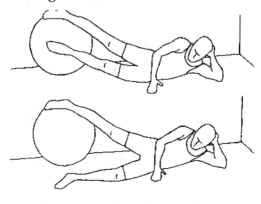

5. STANDING CALVE RAISES:

Starting Position:
- Use the correct posture guidelines mentioned earlier in this chapter
- Hold weights in hands at your side
- Feet should be placed on a raised platform

Action Sequence:
- Press down on the ankles, raising the body upward (there should be no movement in the knees)

Return Sequence:
- Slowly lower the body to the starting position by relaxing the calve muscles

SUMMARY:
The information contained in this chapter is meant to be an overview and to let you know why exercise is so important in maintaining good health. We always recommend that our patients meet with one of our trainers before beginning any type of intense exercise program. Exercise is vital to good health and well being. You should learn as many exercises as you can, so you may vary your workout. If you do the same exercise routine all of the time, you will reach an exercise plateau and your efforts will not be maximized. Remember that you want to stimulate your body. Exercise will keep you fit and give you more energy. Through exercise you can have greater mobility and better muscle and tendon strength. As with a proper diet, (the first building block in maintaining good health), exercise is the second building block in maintaining good health and is crucial in improving your quality of life. Start exercising today; you deserve the best quality of life you can have.

REMEMBER THIS

- Knowing what type of exercise your body needs and how often you should exercise is important

- Too much exercise or the wrong type of exercise can be just as harmful as no exercise at all

- The human body needs to "move" in order to prosper

- Physical activity can improve your health

- Exercise can make your heart stronger, increase circulation, lower LDL cholesterol levels, decrease body fat, lower blood pressure, decrease the risk of breast, colon, prostate and endometrial cancers, help prevent adult onset diabetes (type II diabetes) and osteoporosis, plus exercise increases back strength and mobility

- The human body needs to stay active to remain healthy

- As a person ages, mobility, strength and flexibility decrease because we lose muscle fiber

- When muscle fiber is lost, muscle mass and strength decline

- The loss of strength causes a decrease in mobility and flexibility

- By modifying your lifestyle through diet, exercise and natural hormone replacement therapy, you may slow or even reverse the loss of muscle fiber, which will allow your body and your mind to remain healthy and energized for years to come

- Osteoporosis is on the rise in both men and women. Exercise can help in the prevention of osteoporosis

- The number of people suffering from obesity is climbing and the increasing incidence of back ailments is alarming. Exercise can decrease the incidence of both obesity and back problems

- Exercise produces microscopic tears in muscle fibers. As a result, the body constantly works to repair the muscular tissue, which results in making muscle fibers denser and stronger

- Exercising regularly ensures that the body is in a constant state of cellular regeneration

- Aerobic exercise is also known as cardiovascular training

- Aerobic training requires oxygen as its primary catalyst for energy production

- Aerobic training increases your heart rate and promotes greater amounts of oxygen to flow through your body thereby improving circulation

- Increased oxygen absorption also creates an atmosphere conducive to a higher metabolic rate, allowing the body to maintain more optimal levels of body fat and a better exchange of oxygen and carbon dioxide

- If you have not exercised for some time, begin by walking fifteen minutes per day

- Other aerobic exercises that are beneficial in improving cardiovascular fitness include distance running, stair climbing, skating and basketball

- Anaerobic exercises are typically associated with strength, agility and quick bursts of power

- One of the best forms of anaerobic exercise is "resistance training"

- The main energy source for anaerobic training is an energy system know as ATP/CP (Adenosine Triphosphate and Creatine Phosphate)

- Resistance training produces increased muscle mass and explosive strength

- By increasing your muscle strength you may lower your blood pressure, decrease unfavorable cholesterol levels, help your insulin and glucose levels stay within healthful ranges, increase your bone density and improve your cardiovascular system

- For someone who is in fairly good shape physically, adaptation to the physical stress caused by resistance training usually takes approximately two weeks. For someone, who is not well conditioned, adaptation can take up to six weeks

- The body has six major muscle groups: the chest, the back, the legs, the shoulders, the arms and the abdominal (also known as core muscles)

- The goal of resistance training is to control movement by using the proper biomechanical form through the contraction (concentric movement) and extension (eccentric movement) of the muscle being worked. These actions will create maximum muscle fiber recruitment, which promotes strength and muscular gains

- Using proper biomechanics and appropriate body positioning, when performing resistance training, will protect your skeletal structure and create balance in the specific muscle being exercised

- Today, many trainers are using a Swiss ball for resistance training. The Swiss ball is portable and versatile

- Some of the advantages of Swiss ball training are improved balance, improved neuromuscular response and improved "core strength" (core muscles include the abdominal, the lower back and the hip muscles)

- Flexibility training is an exercise process by which muscles, tendons and ligaments are stretched

- Stretching allows connective tissue to be lengthened, which increases range of motion

- Stretching increases circulation by increasing the surface area of muscles

- Stretching improves flexibility, assists in decreasing muscular pain and increases cellular regeneration

- Warming-up before and after any exercise routine is important

- Jogging or running in place can be done before you begin your flexibility workout

- If the purpose of your resistance training is to just stay physically fit, do the recommended exercises only until you feel the "burn" as our trainers say

- If the purpose of your resistance training is longer, leaner muscles, do at least twenty (20) repetitions of each recommended exercise

- If the purpose of your resistance training is bigger, stronger muscles, do about twelve (12) repetitions of each exercise

- Preferably, the number of repetitions for your exercise regime should be determined by what your fitness goal is. We recommend consulting with a qualified trainer to determine your exact workout regime

- Exercise is vital to good health and well being

- You should learn as many exercises as you can, so you may vary your workout

- Start exercising today; you deserve the best quality of life you can have

CHAPTER TEN

Supplements for Athletic Performance and Bodybuilding

We are frequently asked by many of our patients what they can do, in addition to bio-identical hormone replacement and eating a hormonally correct diet, to improve their exercise performance. In this chapter we will briefly discuss three exercise enhancing supplements that have been documented in the scientific literature to improve exercise performance and may also build muscle mass and decrease body fat. The three supplements that will be discussed are creatine, conjugated linoleic acid (CLA) and beta-hydroxy beta-methyl butyrate (HMB). Before discussing these supplements, there are some basic facts you should know before beginning any type of rigorous exercise routine.

We know that proper exercise improves immune system function, increases strength, improves cognition, increases muscle mass, decreases total body fat and improves metabolism overall. However, there are some unwanted effects of exercise that must be addressed. Exercise causes the production of more free radicals and adequate amounts of antioxidants must be taken to offset this result. Depending on your height, weight, diet, age, activity level and the intensity, type and length of your exercise workout, you will need to adjust your daily doses of antioxidants. We recommend at least two (2) grams of vitamin C daily but if you are exercising vigorously, you can safely take up to ten (10) grams of vitamin C intermittently throughout the day. We recommend 400 to 800 IU of vitamin E daily but if you are exercising vigorously, you can take up to 1200 IU of vitamin E daily. Remember that vitamin E is a fat-soluble vitamin and it is stored in the body much longer than water-soluble vitamins like vitamin C. We also recommend CoEnzyme 10 (CoQ10) the inherent and very important antioxidant, 60 mg daily if made by Solanova or 100 to 200 mg daily if you are taking another brand.

Exercise causes added stress to the body, so taking the proper amounts of B-vitamins is important. Taking a good B-complex vitamin with your vitamin C at each meal can decrease the stress placed on your body from vigorous exercise. We recommend 100 mg daily of vitamin B1, 100 mg daily of vitamin B2, 150 mg daily of vitamin B3, 400 mg vitamin B5 daily, 100 mg vitamin B6 daily, 400 mcg of vitamin B12 daily, 600 mcg of biotin daily and 400 - 800 mcg daily of folic acid.

You will also need to supplement your diet with adequate amounts of proteins, carbohydrates and fats to complement your exercise effort. Calculating your daily protein requirements (Appendix A) will assist you in making sure you are not getting too much or too little protein, carbohydrates and fat in your diet. The more active you are, the more protein you will need but you do not want to consume too much protein, either.

Exercise also decreases mineral stores in the body and adequate amounts of minerals must be taken to counteract this effect of exercise. Make sure you are getting enough calcium (unless contraindicated, we recommend men take 1500 mg daily and women take 3000 mg daily) magnesium (400 mg daily) potassium (200 mg daily) selenium (200 to 400 mcg daily) and other trace minerals. Remember that selenium is a trace mineral and it is also an important antioxidant.

Some forms of exercise cause wear and tear on joint cartilage. Therefore, supplements that help fight against cartilage degeneration, such as glucosamine and chondroitin should also be considered. The dose of these two supplements is dependent upon the amount of joint pain you are experiencing.

The benefits of exercise far outweigh any negative effects and if you are taking therapeutic doses of antioxidants, minerals and other supplements, you can avoid the negative effects of exercise just mentioned. If you wish to increase your exercise performance, the following supplements may assist you in accomplishing your goals. We caution you, however, to consult your physician before taking any of the following supplements and we also caution you never to take more than a therapeutic dose of these supplements. Taking too much of any supplement or medication can have untoward effects on the body.

Creatine:

Creatine is a naturally occurring compound (an amino acid) that is stored in skeletal muscle and is mandatory for the transmission of phosphate-bound energy in both the brain and muscle tissues. Creatine is a by-product of kidney, liver and pancreas metabolism. Low creatine levels can cause problems with motor control and mentation. Creatine has been used for some time by body-builders to increase muscle size. Although most studies have proven creatine supplementation to be safe and effective, we caution any patient with impaired renal function to avoid this supplement and once again, we caution you to use this supplement only after you have checked with your physician and to never use more than the recommended dose.

In study after study, creatine has been shown to increase muscle size and improve exercise performance and is most effective for improving strength in high-intensity aerobic and anaerobic (resistance) activities. Creatine causes the body to retain more fluid in the muscles and as a result the muscle size increases. Since creatine causes fluid retention, weight gain can be a concern or a benefit, depending upon your exercise goals. Creatine can also cause muscle cramping because of the fluid retention in the muscles. Drinking six additional 8-ounce glasses of water daily can eliminate the muscle cramping that may be caused by creatine. Creatine is used widely in sports-related nutrition programs. The normal loading dose for creatine is 20 grams daily for two weeks but we prefer to recommend 10 grams of creatine for two weeks, followed by 5 grams daily for six weeks. After you have been on creatine for eight weeks total, it is important to discontinue this supplement for sixteen weeks and then, if so desired, you can begin the on and off cycle once again.

Conjugated Linoleic Acid (CLA):

CLA is a fatty acid that has both anabolic (building up) and lypolitic (fat breakdown) effects. CLA supplementation can increase total body mass while reducing fat mass. CLA is a naturally occurring fatty acid, which is predominately found in dairy products and beef. Since we are consuming less beef and dairy products today, we may have less CLA in our diets. Also, cattle are being fed more forage today than in times past, when most cattle fed upon pasture grass. Cattle that have been fed pasture grass convert linoleic acid into CLA. More than any other fatty acid, CLA has powerful antioxidant and anti-cancer effects. CLA may provide significant breast cancer and prostate cancer protection and it also protects against atherosclerosis and may reduce the incidence of asthma.

Using CLA during resistance training has been shown to increase bone density over a period of time and it also improves immune system performance during exercise training. Using CLA during resistance training can improve body composition and increase strength. Unlike creatine, CLA does not cause water retention and does not increase fat. CLA has overall health benefits as well as improving exercise performance. The recommended dose for CLA is 3000 mg daily.

Beta Hydroxy Beta Methyl Butyrate (HMB):

HMB is a metabolite of leucine, an amino acid and is a popular supplement among body-builders. HMB is found in various animal and plant foods and is also found naturally in the body. Supposedly, HMB works by decreasing the breakdown of muscle tissue. During resistance training HMB increases lean muscle mass and strength. HMB increases a cell's oxygen capabilities and lowers the levels of the enzyme lactic dehydrogenase (LDH). LDH is associated with pancreatic function and glucose metabolism and levels may increase during resistance training due to muscle damage. Creatine kinase (CK) is an enzyme found primarily in skeletal muscle, brain and heart tissue. During resistance training CK levels increase. Elevated CK levels are associated with muscle damage and HMB is known to decrease levels of CK, thereby protecting cells from injury during resistance training. HMB may also enhance the activity of certain muscle-specific proteins. The recommended dose of HMB, when participating in resistance training or some other form of vigorous exercise is three (3) grams daily.

There are several other supplements that may improve your exercise performance. Dehydroepiandrosterone (DHEA) the "mother" steroidal hormone in the body, discussed in Chapter Twelve, has also been known to decrease body fat, lower LDL cholesterol and increase muscles mass. DHEA should not be taken unless your physician is monitoring your DHEA Sulfate levels. The daily dose for DHEA is dependent upon serum DHEA Sulfate levels.

Phosphatidylserine, found in the cortex of the brain repairs damaged nerve fibers and removes waste products from the brain. As you know, exercise causes increased cortisol levels in the brain because exercise causes added stress on the body. Phosphatidylserine 100-mg daily can significantly reduce the elevated cortisol levels in the brain associated with physical stress.

We believe that your energy level, your mental clarity and your overall sense of well-being will improve greatly if you eat a hormonally correct diet, exercise sensibly and balance your hormone levels. However, if one of your goals is to build more muscle mass than is typically associated with following your anti-aging program, the previously mentioned supplements may help you achieve your goals.

REMEMBER THIS

• Three supplements that enhance exercise performance are creatine, conjugated linoleic acid (CLA) and beta-hydroxy beta-methyl butyrate (HMB

• Proper exercise improves immune system function, increases strength, improves cognition, increases muscle mass, decreases total body fat and improves metabolism overall

• Exercise causes the production of more free radicals and adequate amounts of antioxidants must be taken to offset this result

• Depending on your height, weight, diet, age, activity level and the intensity, type and length of your exercise workout, you will need to adjust your daily doses of antioxidants

• We recommend at least two (2) grams of vitamin C daily but if you are exercising vigorously, you can safely take up to ten (10) grams of vitamin C intermittently throughout the day

• We recommend 400 to 800 IU of vitamin E daily but if you are exercising vigorously, you can take up to 1200 IU of vitamin E daily. Remember that vitamin E is a fat-soluble vitamin and it is stored in the body much longer than water-soluble vitamins like vitamin C

• We recommend CoEnzyme 10 (CoQ10) the inherent and very important antioxidant, 60 mg daily if made by Solanova or 100 to 200 mg daily if you are taking another brand

• Exercise causes added stress to the body, so taking the proper amounts of B-vitamins is important. Taking a good B-complex vitamin with your vitamin C at each meal can decrease the stress placed on your body from vigorous exercise. We recommend 100 mg daily of vitamin B1, 100 mg daily of vitamin B2, 150 mg daily of vitamin B3, 400 mg vitamin B5 daily, 100 mg vitamin B6 daily, 400 mcg of vitamin B12 daily, 600 mcg of biotin daily and 400 - 800 mcg daily of folic acid

- You need to supplement your diet with adequate amounts of proteins, carbohydrates and fats to complement your exercise effort

- Calculating your daily protein requirements (Appendix A) will assist you in making sure you are not getting too much or too little protein, carbohydrates and fat in your diet. The more active you are, the more protein you will need but you do not want to consume too much protein

- Exercise decreases mineral stores in the body and adequate amounts of minerals must be taken to counteract this effect of exercise

- Make sure you are getting enough calcium, unless contraindicated. We recommend men take 1500 mg daily and women take 3000 mg daily

- We recommend magnesium (400 mg daily) potassium (200 mg daily) selenium (200 to 400 mcg daily) and other trace minerals

- Selenium is a trace mineral and it is also an important antioxidant

- Some forms of exercise cause wear and tear on joint cartilage

- Supplements that help fight against cartilage degeneration, such as glucosamine and chondroitin should also be considered. The dose of these two supplements is dependent upon the amount of joint pain you are experiencing

- The benefits of exercise far outweigh any negative effects and if you are taking therapeutic doses of antioxidants, minerals and other supplements, you can avoid the negative effects of exercise

- If you wish to increase your exercise performance, the following supplements may assist you in accomplishing your goals. We caution you, however, to consult your physician before taking any of the following supplements and we also caution you never to take more than a therapeutic dose of these supplements. Taking too much of any supplement or medication can have untoward effects on the body

Creatine:

- Creatine is a naturally occurring compound (an amino acid) that is stored in skeletal muscle and is mandatory for the transmission of phosphate-bound energy in both the brain and muscle tissues

- Creatine is a by-product of kidney, liver and pancreas metabolism

- Low creatine levels can cause problems with motor control and mentation

- Creatine has been used for some time by body-builders to increase muscle size

- Any patient with impaired renal function should not use creatine

- Creatine has been shown to increase muscle size and improve exercise performance and is most effective for improving strength in high-intensity aerobic and anaerobic (resistance) activities

- Creatine causes the body to retain more fluid in the muscles and as a result the muscle size increases

- Since creatine causes fluid retention, weight gain can be a concern or a benefit, depending upon your exercise goals

- Creatine can cause muscle cramping because of the fluid retention in the muscles

- Drinking six additional 8-ounce glasses of water daily can eliminate the muscle cramping that may be caused by creatine

- The normal loading dose for creatine is 20 grams daily for two weeks but we prefer to recommend 10 grams of creatine for two weeks, followed by 5 grams daily for six weeks. After you have been on creatine for eight weeks total, it is important to discontinue this supplement for sixteen weeks and then, if so desired, you can begin the on and off cycle once again

Conjugated Linoleic Acid (CLA):

- CLA is a fatty acid that has both anabolic (building up) and lypolitic (fat breakdown) effects

- CLA supplementation can increase total body mass while reducing fat mass

- CLA is a naturally occurring fatty acid, which is predominately found in dairy products and beef

- CLA has powerful antioxidant and anti-cancer effects

- CLA may provide significant breast cancer and prostate cancer protection and it also protects against atherosclerosis and may reduce the incidence of asthma

- Using CLA during resistance training has been shown to increase bone density over a period of time and it also improves immune system performance during exercise training

- Using CLA during resistance training can improve body composition and increase strength

- CLA does not cause water retention and does not increase fat

- CLA has overall health benefits as well as improving exercise performance

- The recommended dose for CLA is 3000 mg daily

Beta Hydroxy Beta Methyl Butyrate (HMB):

- HMB is a metabolite of leucine, an amino acid and is a popular supplement among body-builders

- HMB is found in various animal and plant foods and is also found naturally in the body

- HMB works by decreasing the breakdown of muscle tissue

- During resistance training HMB increases lean muscle mass and strength

- HMB increases a cell's oxygen capabilities and lowers the levels of the enzyme lactic dehydrogenase (LDH)

- LDH is associated with pancreatic function and glucose metabolism and levels may increase during resistance training due to muscle damage

- Creatine kinase (CK) is an enzyme found primarily in skeletal muscle, brain and heart tissue. During resistance training CK levels increase

- Elevated CK levels are associated with muscle damage and HMB is known to decrease levels of CK, thereby protecting cells from injury during resistance training

- HMB may enhance the activity of certain muscle-specific proteins

- The recommended dose of HMB, when participating in resistance training or some other form of vigorous exercise is three (3) grams daily

- Dehydroepiandrosterone (DHEA) the "mother" steroidal hormone in the body, has been known to decrease body fat, lower LDL cholesterol and increase muscles mass

- DHEA should not be taken unless your physician is monitoring your DHEA Sulfate levels

- The daily dose for DHEA is dependent upon serum DHEA Sulfate levels

- Phosphatidylserine, found in the cortex of the brain repairs damaged nerve fibers and removes waste products from the brain

- Exercise causes increased cortisol levels in the brain because exercise causes added stress on the body

- Phosphatidylserine 100-mg daily can significantly reduce the elevated cortisol levels in the brain associated with physical stress

CHAPTER ELEVEN

HUMAN GROWTH HORMONE

O f all the interventions that anti-aging medicine has brought to medicine and the patients who wish to slow and reverse the aging process, human growth hormone (HGH) is perhaps the most profound and the most controversial. In this chapter we will teach you the science, the physiology of human growth hormone, and we will ask and answer the following questions:

- Is growth hormone decline a major cause of "aging"?
- What are the benefits of HGH replacement therapy?
- What are the risks and side effects of HGH replacement therapy?
- What is the information on HGH replacement therapy in the medical literature?
- What are the practical aspects of HGH replacement therapy?

HGH Physiology Lesson:
Okay, here comes the physiology. You may wish to skip this section if you are impatient, but we encourage you to continue reading. You already know that hormones are compounds created by various endocrine glands that travel to other sites in the body to cause their effects. It is useful to view the neuroendocrine and immune systems as one combined system, which includes the brain, endocrine glands and the immune system. Let's follow the hormones in the growth hormone family. The hypothalamus in the brain produces Growth Hormone Releasing Hormone (GHRH) that travels to the anterior pituitary gland and signals the anterior pituitary gland to release human growth hormone (HGH) into the blood. Another hormone produced by the hypothalamus, Somatostatin, or growth hormone inhibiting hormone (GHIH) tells the anterior pituitary gland not to release growth hormone.

There are other hormones known as growth hormone releasing peptides that also signal the pituitary to release growth hormone. When HGH is released into the bloodstream it has effects on virtually all organs of the body. One of the major effects of HGH is to direct the liver to produce insulin-like growth factor 1 (IGF-1).

HGH also causes the body to produce binding proteins that carry IGF-1and act as hormones in their own right. When we assess a patient's blood for growth hormone, we look at the IGF-1 level. The reason for this is that growth hormone is produced in spurts and also disappears from the blood very rapidly. To measure growth hormone accurately you would need an intravenous catheter withdrawing blood all day. Since this is not practical, the next best lab test for evaluating human growth hormone levels is IGF-1. IGF-1 is not a perfect test for HGH levels but we know that if the IGF-1 level is low, the patient is not producing enough HGH.

HGH is a peptide hormone and consists of a chain of 191 amino acids. HGH is a relatively large molecule with a complicated three-dimensional structure. This is one of the reasons why HGH cannot be taken by mouth at this time. If you took HGH by mouth, you would digest it in the stomach and it would not have the exact structure needed to accurately fit into its receptor sites throughout the body. To be effective, HGH needs to work the same way as a lock and key set and that is why the only current effective route for HGH is by injection.

Most of the HGH produced by the pituitary gland is secreted at night, during deep sleep, which is known as stage III and stage IV sleep. This deep phase of sleep occurs after the rapid eye movement (REM) sleep during which we dream. GHRH is released constantly during deep sleep and Somatostatin (GHIH) is inhibited during deep sleep. So the inhibitor is inhibited and the net result is more HGH in the body.

One of the problems that often occurs, as we age is a poorer quality of sleep and less deep sleep. A side effect of less sleep or less deep sleep as we become older, is less HGH secretion, which is necessary for our well-being and perhaps even for deep sleep. Therefore, with less sleep and less deep sleep, a viscous cycle starts. The typical prescribed sleep medications or the over-the-counter sleeping pills do not increase stage III and IV sleep and are not useful in increasing our HGH output at night.

HGH and IGF-1 affect all organs and tissues of the body. Here is a partial list of how HGH affects various parts of the body:

- Brain: HGH improves cognitive function and mood
- Heart: HGH improves blood flow and cardiac output
- Carotid arteries: HGH promotes less atherosclerosis and narrowing
- Lungs: HGH increases lung function
- Body composition: HGH promotes less fat, especially abdominal fat, more muscle, stronger bones
- Exercise: HGH increases exercise capacity
- Immune: HGH increases immune system function

HGH Replacement Therapy:

Where did the idea of HGH replacement therapy for normal aging come from? First, remember the concept that we age because our key hormones decline, our hormones don't decline because we age. In Chapter One, we discussed the ideas from evolutionary biology and natural selection that declining hormones and declining mental and physical function cannot benefit an animal and cause him or her to have more offspring and cannot help an animal through survival of the fittest. Evolution put all of an animal's energy into reaching reproductive age and reproducing; what happened afterwards did not matter. That was then, but today, in the era of adequate nutrition, sanitation, vaccines and anti-aging medicine we are able to survive way beyond reproductive age. The goal of anti-aging medicine is improved health and well-being by maximizing mental and physical functioning in the years past reproductive age from age forty (40) through ages seventy (70) eighty (80) ninety (90) and beyond.

The decline in HGH is known as somatopause. Every hormone has a pause and human growth hormone is no different. The somatopause or decline in HGH levels begins at age twenty-five to thirty-five and is usually completed by age forty. Age forty was the maximum life expectancy before modern civilization. Evolution did not include youthful levels of HGH past age forty since hardly anyone lived past the age of forty.

Human Growth hormone obtained its name from the fact that HGH is necessary to make children grow. Children with pituitary dwarfism can and have been treated with HGH for years to reach normal adult heights. Children with other causes of growth retardation have also been successfully treated with HGH. Perhaps "growth hormone" is not really a good name for this hormone since it is also necessary for a vigorous and healthy adult life. A better name for HGH might be tissue repair and control hormone or youth preserving hormone.

It is now standard practice in endocrinology to treat adults with "adult growth hormone deficiency syndrome." What is adult growth hormone deficiency syndrome and how do you get it? Adults who have had their pituitary gland damaged through surgery or radiation and adults with childhood HGH deficiency are some examples of people with adult growth hormone deficiency. These conditions are often called "pathological" growth hormone deficiency. When we look at the mental and physical functioning of these patients it looks a lot like "aging." Listed below are some of the symptoms that are common for adults with "adult growth hormone deficiency syndrome."

Mental:	Decreased quality of life, intelligence, memory, mood, well-being
Sleep:	Decreased and/or poor quality
Body Composition:	Decreased muscle, increased fat especially abdominal fat, increased osteoporosis
Lung function:	Decreased
Exercise ability:	Decreased, strength decreased
Immune function:	Decreased, increased infections
Heart function:	Decreased, less cardiac output
Cholesterol & lipids:	Becomes worse
Sexual function:	Decreased
Glucose &insulin function:	Increased insulin resistance
Flexibility:	Decreased joint cartilage mobility and increased arthritis
Skin:	Decreased skin thickness
Healing:	Decreased rate of wound healing

These symptoms are a model of aging. We know we can reverse these problems with HGH therapy in patients who have "adult growth hormone deficiency". Now what about "normal aging?"

"Normal aging" is also a state of growth hormone deficiency. Growth hormone released by the pituitary gland decreases steadily after thirty or forty years of age and the HGH levels of a normal fifty or sixty year old may be as low as an adult with pathological deficiency form pituitary disease. In fact, almost everyone over forty has a human growth hormone deficit compared to twenty to thirty year olds. This is where the paradigm shift of anti-aging medicine diverges from traditional endocrinology. In anti-aging medicine, the decline of HGH with normal aging is treated in the same way as pathological HGH deficiency. In the next section we will look at some of the articles in the medical literature to support this idea.

What The Medical Literature Says About HGH Replacement Therapy:

Let's look at some of the HGH research in recent years. It all started when Daniel Rudman, M.D., published an article in the prestigious New England Journal of Medicine in 1990. Dr. Rudman replaced HGH in normal men between 60 and 80 years of age. He noted improvement in skin thickness and body composition and concluded, "The overall deterioration of the body that comes with growing old is not inevitable...We now realize that some aspects of it can be prevented or reversed." You would imagine that this statement would take the medical world by storm. This was the first statement in a medical journal that documented that some aspects of aging could actually be reversed. Well, what happened in the medical world? Nothing, absolutely nothing. There is usually a generation between a breakthrough discovery and changes in the practice of medicine. Examples of this include the discovery of penicillin, the discovery of limes to prevent scurvy, the discovery of sterile operating technique for surgeons.

In the past ten years there have been many studies on patients with HGH deficiency and the results of HGH replacement therapy. Some studies published in major medical journals in the past few years are listed below:

Johannsson study in 1997 showed that 9 months of HGH treatment decreased abdominal and subcutaneous fat, improved insulin sensitivity, improved cholesterol and lipids and improved blood pressure

Looking at how HGH replacement therapy improves the different systems of the body:

Brain:

Riddle: IGF-1, which is increased by HGH, increases connections of brain neurons

Aleman: HGH deficiency is correlated with poor emotional and psychosocial function

IGF-1 is correlated with cognitive function:

Nyberg: HGH improves cognitive capabilities, memory, alertness, work capacity

Bone:

Longobardi: Bone density is significantly improved with HGH therapy

Sugimoto: Decreased osteoporosis, increased strength, and decreased waist/hip ratio

Baum: Increased bone density, decreased fat

Van de Lely: Increased rate of returning to pre-fracture living after hip fracture

Heart:

Gibney: Improved cardiovascular function, reverses athero sclerosis, opens up narrowed carotid arteries, improves cardiomyopathy

Fazio: Improves cardiac performance

Immune system:

Clark: Improves immune system

Burgess: Improves immune system

Body composition:

Christiansen: Decreases fat and increases muscle

TerMatten: Abdominal fat decreased 50%

Exercise capacity:
Johansson: Increased exercise capacity

Quality of Life:
Gibney: Increased sense of well being and quality of life

HGH replacement therapy has the potential to improve many illnesses and medical conditions. Included in the illnesses where
HGH replacement has produced a significant improvement as documented in the medical literature are fibromyalgia, Chron's disease,
burns and other injuries. HGH also promotes improved healing.
HGH replacement therapy has been found to be safe in children in
over twenty-five (25) years of research and in adults in over eighteen (18) years of research at this point. Given these facts of the prolonged and successful use of HGH, we think that healthy skepticism
also has its place. The skeptic may ask, "Where is the 50 year study
showing that HGH replacement is safe?" Of course, there is no such
study at this point. If we always stayed the same, without any
degeneration of mental and physical abilities as we aged why
would we want to mess with a perfect system? But it is not a perfect
system and we are all aware of the declines that occur with aging.

We know that every individual is on a different path and there are
many preventive measures that we can (and must) do such as eating a hormonally correct diet, engaging in effective forms of exercise
and taking the proper amount and type of supplements. But the
tremendous benefits of youthful hormone levels, including HGH,
offer a chance to alter the process of aging and to keep us strong and
vigorous until we die. Is it experimental? Yes. However, not keeping
HGH levels youthful has known consequences that are dangerous.
Without youthful HGH levels, most of us will become frail, with
declining mental and physical abilities, our immune systems will
become inadequate and we will most likely live many years with
chronic illnesses before we die. Personally, the data that exists is
convincing enough for us, our families, the CHI staff and our hundreds of patients to take this route of HGH replacement therapy and
alter the normal process of aging. Perhaps, HGH replacement therapy is not the conservative thing to do but not intervening in this
process we call aging usually has drastic consequences.

Practical Aspects of HGH Replacement Therapy:
What is it like taking human growth hormone replacement therapy? As my neighbor, attorney Mike Goldstein says, "When you are twenty years old you don't wake up each morning and say "Wow I'm twenty, I feel great, I have energy, stamina, I recover quickly from injuries, my memory is great, my sexual performance is super, I'm optimistic and I'm enthusiastic". At twenty, you just feel good and you live your life. This is how I feel with HGH replacement therapy. I feel good and I live my life." My neighbor's statement gives you a little insight of how HGH can make you feel. The changes a person can experience with HGH replacement therapy may vary from subtle to dramatic. HGH replacement therapy provides a solid foundation for health and anti-aging. Aging is a catabolic process; tissues are being broken down, muscle, bone and even brain. The actions of human growth hormone are anabolic, which means it helps build new cells and tissues and helps the body to constantly repair itself.

The physical changes that occur with HGH therapy are obvious; more muscle and less fat, especially abdominal fat. Up to 50% of excess abdominal fat can be lost in six months. This process works especially well with exercise and as always, hormone replacement therapy is built on a foundation of diet, exercise, and supplements. There can be cosmetic changes as a result of HGH replacement therapy. More than 50% of patients will experience a decrease in facial wrinkles, a decrease in the graying of hair and even a decrease in hair loss in men. We refer to these wonderful effects from HGH replacement therapy as plastic surgery from the inside out.

Energy changes with HGH replacement therapy are sometimes described as a feeling of limitless energy; both physical and mental. With HGH replacement therapy, there is sometimes a feeling that there is no limit to what you can do; a feeling of optimism like you had when you were younger.

The mental and psychological changes, with HGH replacement therapy, can include reversal of depression, a positive outlook on life and increased memory and intellectual functioning. Patients have reported increased esthetic awareness as well. We have had comments from some of our patients that music sounds better, colors are brighter and their sense of smell and their hearing have improved. Our patients also tell us that they seem to have a heightened sense of awareness to their surroundings and the events in their every day lives. A consistent comment from our patients on HGH replacement therapy is the increased ability to focus even later in the day. At CHI, because we are doing exactly what our patients are doing, we have also experienced the same sensations and feelings that our patients share with us.

Side Effects of HGH Replacement Therapy:
The side effects of human growth hormone replacement therapy, if any, are usually minor and are reversible by decreasing the dose or in a few cases discontinuing the treatment. The side effects actually are only occasionally seen when the low/frequent-dose method of HGH treatment is used. In some studies, the total dose of HGH is given as two or three injections per week. This is for the convenience of the people in the study and the investigators since in this situation patients cannot administer the HGH themselves because every aspect of the study must be documented. However, in anti-aging medical practice, the HGH is self-administered by the patient, six or seven days a week and this method has rare side effects.

Possible side effects of HGH administration may include edema (swelling) paresthesias (numbness and tingling in hands) arthralgias (joint aching) and glucose intolerance where the blood sugar is higher for a given amount of sugar or equivalent consumed. To explain further, swelling may appear in the ankles or the hands. Numbness and tingling can be seen in the hands and is sometimes similar to carpal tunnel syndrome. There may be numbness in the hands or the arms after sleeping in one position during the night. Joint aching can be experienced in the wrists, knees or other joints.

Even though most studies on HGH replacement therapy have shown decreased insulin resistance with HGH, there can be an increase in insulin resistance in some patients. What this means is that the blood sugar will be higher for a given amount of carbohydrates consumed. This situation can usually be prevented by following a Zone diet or decreasing the dose of HGH. In men when testosterone is used along with HGH, the complication of increased insulin resistance is avoided. At any rate, we monitor our patients closely for these possible side effects and adjust the HGH dose accordingly.

What about other side effects from HGH replacement therapy. We know there are no adverse effects on heart function; every study shows improved cardiovascular function.

Acromegaly is a disease caused by the pituitary gland secreting too much HGH. It can result in distorted facial features, enlargement of hands and feet and is associated with other medical problems. There is no chance of developing acromegaly from HGH replacement therapy since the dose and effects are closely monitored.

What about cancer? Because HGH is an anabolic hormone and makes things grow could a small cancer hiding somewhere grow because of HGH replacement therapy? This question has been investigated thoroughly in the medical literature. The conclusion from Vance in the New England Journal of Medicine, October 1999, "There is no evidence that HGH replacement therapy affects the risk of cancer." A fascinating study was recently published in the Journal of Clinical Endocrinology and Metabolism. This study looked at children who had brain cancer and had the brain cancer treated. Some of the children received HGH therapy after the treatment and some did not. The group that received the HGH had less recurrence of the brain cancer than the group who did not receive HGH.

HGH Administration:

How is human growth hormone taken? The only effective way to significantly increase growth hormone levels in the body is to use recombinant HGH by injection. You will undoubtedly see a barrage of advertisements on the Internet and in magazines and newspapers for "growth hormone" pills and sprays. As of this moment, in our opinion, all of these products are frauds and scams. There is no evidence in any peer reviewed medical publication that any of these over-the-counter products are effective.

Since HGH is a prescription drug, it cannot legally be sold over the counter and products that claim to contain HGH do not have a significant amount to do much good. Some HGH products claim that the HGH comes from plants. We find this interesting since there are no plants that contain HGH. Some products claim to be "homeopathic." Again, these products cannot contain a useful amount of HGH.

Our patients learn to give themselves injections with tiny needles and a very small insulin syringe. Our patients administer their HGH six days per week, once a day. The HGH injection is subcutaneous which means that it goes just under the skin, in the fat. Since HGH has some local fat dissolving effect, we recommend that it be given in the "love handle" region of the body. After being on HGH replacement therapy for a while, you may not be able to find the love handle because it will be gone. That's the breaks. You can also give HGH subcutaneously (slightly under the skin) in the abdomen, thighs or anywhere.

The prescription HGH is made by the recombinant DNA technique. The gene for production of HGH is inserted into another organism such as bacteria. The bacteria produce the exact HGH that humans produce. This HGH is purified and administered by injection.

As stated earlier, the injections are given with very tiny needles, gauge 28 to 30, and you can hardly feel this tiny needle going through the skin. Our patients learn to give themselves these shots on their Evaluation Day and they become "experts" in five minutes. In the near future there will be prescription oral products, which will be effective, but as of 2001 there are none. Of course, we want to keep our minds open and perhaps there will be an over the counter product which is effective, but to be convinced, we must see some independent data that does not come from the manufacturer of the product.

You may have heard that there is something dangerous about HGH injections. In the past there was. Before the recombinant DNA technique was available, the only way HGH could be obtained was from the pituitary glands of human cadavers. Years ago, this form of HGH was used for children who were not growing due to HGH deficiency. Some of this supply of HGH obtained from human cadavers was contaminated with the virus from Creutzfeld-Jacov disease, the human equivalent for "Mad-cow disease." Tragically, some of these children, who took this form of contaminated HGH, developed this brain disease years later. Many people and some physicians are not aware of the difference between modern recombinant HGH and this older form of HGH from dead people's pituitaries. There is absolutely no danger of Creutzfeld-Jacov disease from modern recombinant HGH.

HGH Cost:
What about cost? Although recombinant HGH is made by the same techniques as insulin, which is very inexpensive, HGH replacement therapy is currently quite expensive. If a person can possibly afford HGH replacement therapy he or she has to decide on priorities. What is more important, a new car, a cruise, or preventing the deterioration that comes with aging?

What about current prices for HGH? First, we would like to explain our philosophy about pricing. In our practice we charge our patients our cost of HGH and also charge a "medical supervision fee" for administering their anti-aging program. Because we pass on discounted prices for supplements and medications to our patients, we have to charge something to cover overhead expense; otherwise we would be working for free and could not keep our doors open. Every physician may have different pricing practices, so it is important to learn what the cost of your anti-aging program is going to be from the physician you choose to supervise your anti-aging program. As an example, some physicians prefer to mark up the price of the growth hormone instead of charging a professional oversight fee.

To continue to educate you about HGH pricing, it is important to know how HGH is measured. HGH is measured in "international units" or IU's and milligrams. One milligram (mg) of HGH equals 3 IU's of HGH. Vials of HGH can contain between 4 and 18 IU's of HGH, depending on the pharmaceutical manufacturer. Various pharmaceutical manufacturers charge different prices for their HGH. HGH must be obtained by prescription through a reputable pharmacy. If you are obtaining your HGH from any other source, we caution you to be careful. You do not know where that HGH has been, if it is the real thing or if, in fact, it has been damaged or is outdated.

Now, let's figure out prices. Most patients will require between 4 to 12 IU's of HGH per week, with some patients needing up to 15 IU's of HGH per week. Currently, HGH costs about $12.50 to $15.50 per IU. If a patient required 4 IU's of HGH/week it would cost 4 x $12.50 = $50 a week or about $2500 a year. To continue, 8 IU's per week, which is an average dose, would cost about $5000 per year, 12 IU's per week would cost about $7500 per year and so on. As the bad joke goes, "It's cheaper than payments on a Lexus lease."

Once again, we do not recommend just taking HGH alone to maximize heath and fitness. For better health, wellness and more vitality, you need to start with lifestyle changes, which include diet, exercise, supplements and balancing all of the key hormones, including HGH. The results of this combination can be profound. You can reinvent yourself. You can have the physiology that you had in your 20's and the wisdom and experience of your chronological age. The rest is up to you.

REMEMBER THIS

- Of all the interventions that anti-aging medicine has brought to medicine human growth hormone (HGH) is perhaps the most profound and the most controversial

- Hormones are compounds created by various endocrine glands that travel to other sites in the body to cause their effects

- The hypothalamus in the brain produces Growth Hormone Releasing Hormone (GHRH) that travels to the anterior pituitary gland and signals the anterior pituitary gland to release human growth hormone (HGH) into the blood

- Another hormone produced by the hypothalamus, Somatostatin, or growth hormone inhibiting hormone (GHIH) tells the anterior pituitary gland not to release growth hormone

- There are other hormones known as growth hormone releasing peptides that also signal the pituitary to release growth hormone

- When HGH is released into the bloodstream it has effects on virtually all organs of the body

- One of the major effects of HGH is to direct the liver to produce insulin-like growth factor 1 (IGF-1)

- HGH also causes the body to produce binding proteins that carry IGF-1 and act as hormones in their own right

- When we assess a patient's blood for growth hormone, we look at the IGF-1 level. The reason for this is that growth hormone is produced in spurts and also disappears from the blood very rapidly

- To measure growth hormone accurately you would need an intravenous catheter withdrawing blood all day. Since this is not practical, the next best lab test for evaluating human growth hormone levels is IGF-1

- IGF-1 is not a perfect test for HGH levels but we know that if the IGF-1 level is low, the patient is not producing enough HGH

- HGH is a peptide hormone and consists of a chain of 191 amino acids

- HGH is a relatively large molecule with a complicated three-dimensional structure. This is one of the reasons why HGH cannot be taken by mouth at this time

- If you took HGH by mouth, you would digest it in the stomach and it would not have the exact structure needed to accurately fit into its receptor sites throughout the body. To be effective, HGH needs to work the same way as a lock and key set and that is why the only current effective route for HGH is by injection

- Most of the HGH produced by the pituitary gland is secreted at night, during deep sleep, which is known as stage III and stage IV sleep. This deep phase of sleep occurs after the rapid eye movement (REM) sleep during which we dream

- GHRH is released constantly during deep sleep and Somatostatin (GHIH) is inhibited during deep sleep. So the inhibitor is inhibited and the net result is more HGH in the body

- One of the problems that often occurs, as we age is a poorer quality of sleep and less deep sleep

- A side effect of less sleep or less deep sleep as we become older, is less HGH secretion

- Typical prescribed sleep medications or the over-the-counter sleeping pills do not increase stage III and IV sleep and are not useful in increasing our HGH output at night

- HGH and IGF-1 affect all organs and tissues of the body. Here is a partial list of how HGH affects various parts of the body:

- Brain: HGH improves cognitive function and mood

- Heart: HGH improves blood flow and cardiac output

- Carotid arteries: HGH promotes less atherosclerosis and narrowing

- Lungs: HGH increases lung function

- Body composition: HGH promotes less fat, especially abdominal fat, more muscle, stronger bones

- Exercise: HGH increases exercise capacity

- Immune: HGH increases immune system function

- We age because our key hormones decline, our hormones don't decline because we age

- Evolution put all of an animal's energy into reaching reproductive age and reproducing; what happened afterwards did not matter. That was then, but today, in the era of adequate nutrition, sanitation, vaccines and anti-aging medicine we are able to survive way beyond reproductive age

- The goal of anti-aging medicine is improved health and well-being by maximizing mental and physical functioning in the years past reproductive age from age forty (40) through ages seventy (70) eighty (80) ninety (90) and beyond

- The decline in HGH is known as somatopause

- Every hormone has a pause and human growth hormone is no different. The somatopause or decline in HGH levels begins at age twenty-five to thirty-five and is usually completed by age forty

- Age forty was the maximum life expectancy before modern civilization. Evolution did not include youthful levels of HGH past age forty since hardly anyone lived past the age of forty

- Human Growth hormone obtained its name from the fact that HGH is necessary to make children grow

- Children with pituitary dwarfism can and have been treated with HGH for years to reach normal adult heights. Children with other causes of growth retardation have also been successfully treated with HGH

- It is now standard practice in endocrinology to treat adults with "adult growth hormone deficiency syndrome"

- Adults with childhood HGH deficiency are some examples of people with adult growth hormone deficiency. These conditions are often called "pathological" growth hormone deficiency. When we look at the mental and physical functioning of these patients it looks a lot like "aging." Listed below are some of the symptoms that are common for adults with "adult growth hormone deficiency syndrome."

Mental:	Decreased quality of life, intelligence, memory, mood, well-being
Sleep:	Decreased and/or poor quality
Body Composition:	Decreased muscle, increased fat especially abdominal fat, and increased osteoporosis
Lung function:	Decreased
Exercise ability:	Decreased, strength decreased
Immune function:	Decreased, increased infections
Heart function:	Decreased, less cardiac output
Cholesterol & lipids:	Becomes worse
Sexual function:	Decreased
Glucose & insulin function:	Increased insulin resistance
Flexibility:	Decreased joint cartilage mobility and increased arthritis
Skin:	Decreased skin thickness
Healing:	Decreased rate of wound healing

- The symptoms above are a model of aging. We know we can reverse these problems with HGH therapy in patients who have "adult growth hormone deficiency

- "Normal aging" is also a state of growth hormone deficiency

- Growth hormone released by the pituitary gland decreases steadily after thirty or forty years of age and the HGH levels of a normal fifty or sixty year old may be as low as an adult with pathological deficiency form pituitary disease

- Everyone over forty has a human growth hormone deficit compared to twenty to thirty year olds

- In anti-aging medicine, the decline of HGH with normal aging is treated in the same way as pathological HGH deficiency

What The Medical Literature Say About HGH Replacement Therapy:

- Daniel Rudman, M.D., published an article in the prestigious New England Journal of Medicine in 1990. Dr. Rudman replaced HGH in normal men between 60 and 80 years of age. He noted improvement in skin thickness and body composition and concluded, "The overall deterioration of the body that comes with growing old is not inevitable...We now realize that some aspects of it can be prevented or reversed." In the past ten years there have been many studies on patients with HGH deficiency and the results of HGH replacement therapy

- HGH replacement therapy has the potential to improve many illnesses and medical conditions. Included in the illnesses where HGH replacement has produced a significant improvement as documented in the medical literature are fibromyalgia, Chron's disease, burns and other injuries. HGH also promotes improved healing

- HGH replacement therapy has been found to be safe in children in over twenty-five (25) years of research and in adults in over eighteen (18) years of research at this point

- We know that every individual is on a different path and there are many preventive measures that we can (and must) do such as the eating a hormonally correct diet, engaging in effective forms of exercise and taking the proper amount and type of supplements

- The tremendous benefits of youthful hormone levels, including HGH, offer a chance to alter the process of aging and to keep us strong and vigorous until we die

- Not keeping HGH levels youthful has known consequences that are dangerous. Without youthful HGH levels, most of us will become frail, with declining mental and physical abilities, our immune systems will become inadequate and we will most likely live many years with chronic illnesses before we die

- Perhaps, HGH replacement therapy is not the conservative thing to do but not intervening in this process we call aging usually has drastic consequences

- When you are twenty years old you don't wake up each morning and say "Wow I'm twenty, I feel great, I have energy, stamina, I recover quickly from injuries, my memory is great, my sexual performance is super, I'm optimistic and I'm enthusiastic". At twenty, you just feel good and you live your life. This is how you may feel with HGH replacement therapy

- The changes a person can experience with HGH replacement therapy may vary from subtle to dramatic

- HGH replacement therapy provides a solid foundation for health and anti-aging

- Aging is a catabolic process; tissues are being broken down, muscle, bone and even brain

- The actions of human growth hormone are anabolic, which means it helps build new cells and tissues and helps the body to constantly repair itself

- The physical changes that occur with HGH therapy are obvious; more muscle and less fat, especially abdominal fat. Up to 50% of excess abdominal fat can be lost in six months

- Hormone replacement therapy is built on a foundation of diet, exercise, and supplements

- There can be cosmetic changes as a result of HGH replacement therapy. More than 50% of patients will experience a decrease in facial wrinkles, a decrease in the graying of hair and even a decrease in hair loss in men. We refer to these wonderful effects from HGH replacement therapy as plastic surgery from the inside out

- Energy changes with HGH replacement therapy are sometimes described as a feeling of limitless energy; both physical and mental

- With HGH replacement therapy, there is sometimes a feeling that there is no limit to what you can do; a feeling of optimism like you had when you were younger

- The mental and psychological changes, with HGH replacement therapy, can include reversal of depression, a positive outlook on life and increased memory and intellectual functioning. Patients have reported increased esthetic awareness as well

- A consistent comment from our patients on HGH replacement therapy is the increased ability to focus even later in the day

- The side effects of human growth hormone replacement therapy, if any, are usually minor and are reversible by decreasing the dose or in a few cases discontinuing the treatment

- The side effects actually are only occasionally seen when the low/frequent-dose method of HGH treatment is used

- In anti-aging medical practice, the HGH is self-administered by the patient, six or seven days a week and this method has rare side effects

- Possible side effects of HGH administration may include edema (swelling) paresthesias (numbness and tingling in hands) arthralgias (joint aching) and glucose intolerance where the blood sugar is higher for a given amount of sugar or equivalent consumed

- Even though most studies on HGH replacement therapy have shown decreased insulin resistance with HGH, there can be an increase in insulin resistance in some patients. What this means is that the blood sugar will be higher for a given amount of carbohydrates consumed. This situation can usually be prevented by following a Zone diet or decreasing the dose of HGH. In men when testosterone is used along with HGH, the complication of increased insulin resistance is avoided

- We monitor our patients closely for these possible side effects and adjust the HGH dose accordingly

- What about other side effects from HGH replacement therapy. We know there are no adverse effects on heart function; every study shows improved cardiovascular function

- Acromegaly is a disease caused by the pituitary gland secreting too much HGH. It can result in distorted facial features, enlargement of hands and feet and is associated with other medical problems

- There is no chance of developing acromegaly from HGH replacement therapy since the dose and effects are closely monitored

- What about cancer? Because HGH is an anabolic hormone and makes things grow could a small cancer hiding somewhere grow because of HGH replacement therapy? This question has been investigated thoroughly in the medical literature. The conclusion from Vance in the New England Journal of Medicine, October 1999, "There is no evidence that HGH replacement therapy affects the risk of cancer." A fascinating study was recently published in the Journal of Clinical Endocrinology and Metabolism. This study looked at children who had brain cancer and had the brain cancer treated. Some of the children received HGH therapy after the treatment and some did not. The group that received the HGH had less recurrence of the brain cancer than the group who did not receive HGH

- The only effective way to significantly increase growth hormone levels in the body is to use recombinant HGH by injection

- You will undoubtedly see a barrage of advertisements on the Internet and in magazine and newspapers for "growth hormone" pills and sprays. As of this moment, in our opinion, all of these products are frauds and scams. There is no evidence in any peer reviewed medical publication that any of these over-the-counter products are effective

- Since HGH is a prescription drug, it cannot legally be sold over the counter and products that claim to contain HGH do not have a significant amount to do much good

- Some HGH products claim that the HGH comes from plants. We find this interesting since there are no plants that contain HGH. Some products claim to be "homeopathic." Again, these products cannot contain a useful amount of HGH

- Our patients learn to give themselves injections with tiny needles and a very small insulin syringe. Our patients administer their HGH six days per week, once a day

- The HGH injection is subcutaneous which means that it goes just under the skin, in the fat. Since HGH has some local fat dissolving effect, we recommend that it be given in the "love handle" region of the body

- After being on HGH replacement therapy for a while, you may not be able to find the love handle because it will be gone

- You can also give HGH subcutaneously (slightly under the skin) in the abdomen, thighs or anywhere

- The prescription HGH is made by the recombinant DNA technique. The gene for production of HGH is inserted into another organism such as bacteria. The bacteria produce the exact HGH that humans produce. This HGH is purified and administered by injection

- HGH injections are given with very tiny needles, gauge 28 to 30, and you can hardly feel this tiny needle going through the skin.

Our patients learn to give themselves these shots on their Evaluation Day and they become "experts" in five minutes

- In the near future there will be prescription oral products which will effective but as of 2001 there are none

- You may have heard that there is something dangerous about HGH injections. In the past there was. Before the recombinant DNA technique was available, the only way HGH could be obtained was from the pituitary glands of human cadavers. Years ago, this form of HGH was used for children who were not growing due to HGH deficiency. Some of this supply of HGH obtained from human cadavers was contaminated with the virus from Creutzfeld-Jacov disease, the human equivalent for of "Mad-cow disease." Tragically, some of these children, who took this form of contaminated HGH, developed this brain disease years later. Many people and some physicians are not aware of the difference between modern recombinant HGH and this older form of HGH from dead people's pituitaries

- There is absolutely no danger of Creutzfeld-Jacov disease from modern recombinant HGH

- Although recombinant HGH is made by the same techniques as insulin, which is very inexpensive, HGH replacement therapy is currently quite expensive

- If a person can possibly afford HGH replacement therapy he or she has to decide on priorities. What is more important, a new car, a cruise, or preventing the deterioration that comes with aging?

- What about current prices for HGH? First, we would like to explain our philosophy about pricing. In our practice we charge our patients our cost of HGH and also charge a "medical supervision fee" for administering their anti-aging program. Because we pass on discounted prices for supplements and medications to our patients, we have to charge something to cover overhead expense; otherwise we would be working for free and could not keep our doors open. Every physician may have different pricing practices, so it is important to learn what the cost of your anti-aging program is going to be from the physician you choose to supervise your anti-aging program. As an example, some physicians prefer to mark up the price of the growth hormone instead of charging a professional oversight fee

- To continue to educate you about HGH pricing, it is important to know how HGH is measured. HGH is measured in "international units" or IU's and milligrams. One milligram (mg) of HGH equals 3 IU's of HGH. Vials of HGH can contain between 4 and 18 IU's of HGH, depending on the pharmaceutical manufacturer. Various pharmaceutical manufacturers charge different prices for their HGH

- HGH must be obtained by prescription through a reputable pharmacy. If you are obtaining your HGH from any other source, we caution you to be careful. You do not know where that HGH has been, if it is the real thing or if, in fact, it has been damaged or is outdated

- Most patients will require between 4 to 12 IU's of HGH per week, with some patients needing up to 15 IU's of HGH per week. Currently, HGH costs about $12.50 to $15.50 per IU. If a patient required 4 IU's of HGH/week it would cost 4 x $12.50 = $50 a week or about $2500 a year. To continue, 8 IU's per week, which is an average dose, would cost about $5000 per year, 12 IU's per week would cost about $7500 per year and so on

- We do not recommend just taking HGH alone to maximize heath and fitness

- For better health, wellness and more vitality, you need to start with lifestyle changes, which include diet, exercise, supplements and balancing all of the key hormones, including HGH. The results of this combination can be profound. You can re-invent yourself. You can have the physiology that you had in your 20's and the wisdom and experience of your chronological age. The rest is up to you.

CHAPTER TWELVE

OTHER HORMONES

One of the major themes throughout this book is, "We age because our hormones decline, our hormones do not decline because we age." What are hormones? Hormones are chemical substances in our bodies that are released to have an effect on tissues somewhere else in the body. Hormones control our response to illness by controlling our immune system, our response to stress, our sexual development, our growth and our metabolism. When hormone levels are balanced in our bodies, we are more likely to enjoy good health provided our lifestyle choices are also healthful. Most people in their twenties, have optimal hormonal levels.

As we age, our hormone levels begin to decline. For example, estrogen levels in women decline drastically, over a one to three year period at the time of menopause. In men, testosterone levels decline slowly over a thirty-year period. Usually the secretion of human growth hormone in both sexes decreases steadily between the ages of forty and ninety. DHEA decreases to very low levels in both men and women and insulin sensitivity becomes much less as we age or we are affected by obesity. We usually do not feel the effects of these declining hormone levels until our late thirties, early forties or occasionally, late forties or early fifties. In the past, we associated aging with the decline of our mental and physical capabilities. We now know that natural (bioidential) hormone replacement therapy, when clinically indicated, can improve a person's physical and mental status to that of a person ten to twenty years younger; provided that person also eats a hormonally correct diet and exercises appropriately at least three to five times per week.

Osteoporosis:

Before we discuss the major hormones in the body, a word about osteoporosis because your hormone levels affect the incidence of osteoporosis. Did you know that osteoporosis is preventable? Many of us in the medical field are deeply saddened when we see the effects that osteoporosis can have on the body.

Osteoporosis is more common in women than men. Osteoporosis causes bones to become more brittle and less dense, which increases the chance for fractures. Osteoporosis is the leading cause of hip fractures in the U.S. Annually, forty percent of the American population between the ages of eighty and ninety die from complications arising from a hip fracture. In the United States, 4 to 6 million menopausal women have osteoporosis and approximately 13 to 17 million women have osteopenia, which is the beginning stage of osteoporosis. Annually, osteoporosis accounts for about 14 billion dollars in direct medical expenses, 400,000 hospital admissions, more than 180,000 nursing home admissions and 2.5 million physician visits.

What is osteoporosis? Osteoporosis is an imbalance in new bone formation and bone resorption. There may be a genetic predisposition to the disease but many other factors contribute to the occurrence of the disease. Low estrogen levels in women, low testosterone levels in both men and women, low growth hormone levels in both sexes, calcium and vitamin D deficiencies, lack of exercise, alcohol consumption, tobacco, caffeine, beverages containing phosphate and certain medications such as some anti-seizure and some cortisone drugs can all be contributing factors to the incidence of osteoporosis. Since osteoporosis interferes with bone remineralization and bone formation, people with osteoporosis may experience bone deformities. Please continue to read and learn about many of the hormones in your body and why it is so important to keep hormone levels in a youthful range. You do not have to be the next person to have osteoporosis.

Your Hormones:
There are many hormones produced by the body. We will discuss the major hormones in the body and what they do.

Human Growth Hormone (HGH):
Please refer to Chapter Eleven, which discusses Human Growth Hormone (HGH), the "master hormone" in the body.

Testosterone:

Currently, according to Unimed Pharmaceuticals more than 5 million men in the United States suffer from the effects of hyopgonadism or low testosterone levels. We have discussed many of the effects of hypogonadism in Chapter Two, which addresses male and female menopause but we felt it necessary to mention testosterone once again, since it is such an important total body hormone.

When we think of testosterone, we think of men, big hunks of muscle and aggressive behavior but testosterone is a crucial hormone in both men and women. Testosterone, primarily a male sex hormone, is also found in females. Testosterone, produced in the testes and adrenal glands in males, is needed for male sexual development and plays a primary role in libido, cardiovascular health, lung function, improved bone mass, brain health (memory enhancer) erectile function of the penis, mood enhancement and a person's overall energy level.

As a person ages, his/her testosterone levels decline. In men, the "free" testosterone level (the testosterone that is available for use in the body and not bound) begins to decline gradually in a person's thirties. This decline in available testosterone in males is known as andropause or male menopause. Because andropause occurs gradually over a thirty-year period, the medical community in comparison to female menopause has given less attention to this condition. In addition to aging, stress can also lower testosterone levels. Low levels of testosterone are associated with increased body fat (especially abdominal fat) decreased energy levels, depression, sexual dysfunction, wasting of bones and muscles, increased blood pressure and increased incidence of heart disease. A man in his eighties has about one-fifth the amount of testosterone in his body as he had in his youth.

As stated earlier, women need a certain amount of testosterone, too. Testosterone, in women, is produced primarily in the ovaries and is known to improve clitoral and nipple sensitivity, increase libido, improve the quality of orgasm and can increase muscle strength and bone density. Testosterone may also improve various symptoms of menopause including "hot flashes," weight gain, fatigue, lethargy and may decrease the risk of breast cancer.

When testosterone levels decline, a man's prostate gland will enlarge. An enlarged prostate gland has been associated with a greater risk for cancer of the prostate. Natural testosterone replacement therapy has been shown to improve prostate health.

In addition to natural testosterone replacement therapy, there are other medications and supplements that improve prostate health. Saw palmetto, an extract from the berries of the saw palmetto palm tree, which is indigenous to the southern regions of the American Atlantic coast has been known to improve the symptoms associated with an enlarged prostate such as frequent nighttime urination and decreased flow of urine. Proscar (finasteride) a prescription medication has been used successfully in decreasing serum levels of dihyrotestosterone (DHT) which, when too high have typically been associated with enlargement of the prostate gland. Other herbal supplements that improve prostate health include Pygeum and Urtica. Indole 3 Carbinol, a dietary supplement made from cruciferous vegetables like broccoli and cauliflower, also has a protective effect on the prostate because of its anti-cancer properties. Zinc is a mineral that is needed, in proper amounts, for optimum prostate health.

Natural testosterone replacement therapy can improve energy levels, increase bone density, decrease blood pressure, increase sexual drive and performance, decrease heart disease, lower LDL cholesterol levels, raise HDL cholesterol levels, enhance blood glucose levels, improve muscle strength, improve brain function and decrease body fat. In both our male and female patients, we prescribe natural testosterone transdermal creams or gels, which are easily absorbed and are quite efficient at returning serum testosterone levels to youthful levels. The dose for every patient is different depending upon a person's serum testosterone levels. Testosterone doses for women are much lower than testosterone doses for men.

Estrogen:

We discussed estrogen in Chapter Two but it is important to once again discuss this major hormone. Estrogen, in females, is made primarily in the ovaries. For approximately thirty-five years of a woman's life, estrogen, progesterone and testosterone usually maintain a healthy equilibrium throughout the reproductive years. During the first half of a woman's menstrual cycle, estradiol levels increase before ovulation. Once ovulation occurs, progesterone levels increase, making the uterus ready for impregnation. If a woman does not become pregnant, progesterone levels decrease and eventually when the woman has her menses or period, the waste products of the menstrual cycle are expelled.

"Estrogens" are the primary female sex hormones. The three major estrogens found in the female are estradiol, estriol and estrone. Estradiol is the most active estrogen in the body but may not be well absorbed. Estrone, known to relieve some of the symptoms of menopause has been associated with some forms of cancer and is selectively used in natural (bioidentical) hormone replacement therapy. Estriol has been shown to have anti-cancer effects and inhibits breast cancers.

Adequate levels of natural estrogens can prevent heart disease, decrease cholesterol levels, control carbohydrate metabolism, assist with blood clotting, improve memory, prevent osteoporosis and prevent or decrease the incidence of Alzheimer's disease. Additionally, adequate estrogen levels in the bloodstream will help decrease the symptoms associated with menopause (hot flashes, vaginal dryness, mood swings, increased urination at night, incontinence) and prevent strokes.

Low estrogen levels can cause a women to have symptoms of anxiety, migraine headaches, decreased memory, decreased skin thickness, hot flashes and depression while estrogen levels that are too high can cause symptoms of irritability, fluid retention, food cravings, hot flashes, urinary frequency, fatigue, breast tenderness and anxiety. As you probably noted, hot flashes can occur when estrogen levels are either too high or too low.

Almost all, postmenopausal women need natural hormone replacement therapy, which includes estrogen, progesterone, testosterone and thyroid. It is the rare exception that will not need natural hormone replacement therapy. Many soy products contain natural plant estrogens and may be beneficial for all women because of possible anti-cancer effects. When clinically indicated we prescribe natural (bioidentical) estrogen transdermal creams for our female patients that are comprised of estradiol and estriol.

Some of the side effects of natural estrogen replacement therapy may be fluid retention, increased body fat (usually 5-10 pounds) and increased risk of breast and uterine cancer if not given in conjunction with natural progesterone. When clinically indicated, we prescribe natural progesterone to our female patients. The dosage for the estrogen cream is dependent upon a woman's serum estradiol level. Natural estrogens comes from soy products which are derived from phytoestrogens, which, when synthesized, have an identical molecular structure as the estrogens produced in our bodies. We do not recommend oral estrogens because they interfere with insulin/glucose metabolism in the body and with human growth hormone metabolism and we never prescribe synthetic estrogens such as Premarin, which is made from the urine of pregnant mares.

Progesterone:
Progesterone, primarily a female hormone but also found in males in small amounts, is made in the corpus luteum in the ovaries, the adrenal glands and in pregnancy, it is produced in the placenta. Progesterone helps estrogen levels stay in a therapeutic range and therefore, can protect against endometrial (the lining of the uterus) cancer, which can be caused by too much estrogen in the body. Progesterone also protects against osteoporosis, protects against breast cancer, decreases fluid retention, normalizes blood clotting, helps maintain normal blood sugar levels, assists in lowering LDL cholesterol levels, improves libido, decreases vaginal dryness and has a sedative effect on the central nervous system.

Like estrogen, progesterone levels decline as we age. Synthetic progestins (i.e., Provera) produce unwanted side effects such as fluid retention, weight gain, depression and breast tenderness. We prescribe oral micronized natural (bioidentical) progesterone (made from the wild yam) lozenges or pills for our female patients. The dosage of progesterone is different for every patient, depending upon the serum progesterone level.

Thyroid Hormones:

The thyroid gland is located in the neck, below your voice box, which is known as the larynx. The thyroid gland affects every function in the body because it controls metabolism. Since the thyroid hormones control metabolism, they tell the body how fast or slow it should use the fuel we eat, especially carbohydrates and fat.

The thyroid hormones thyroxine (T4) and triiodothyronine (T3) and calcitonin regulate metabolism and the amount of calcium in the body, respectively. Approximately 80% of the thyroid hormone produced in the body is T4. Thyroxine (T4) however, is not readily available and is stored by the body, only to be released when T3 levels are low. Triiodothyronine (T3) is approximately four times more powerful than T4 and is the active thyroid hormone in the body. Having thyroid levels in a youthful range is critical for good health. When thyroid levels are too high in the bloodstream, the hypothalamus, in the brain, secretes more thyroid-releasing hormone (TRH), which causes the pituitary gland in the brain to release less thyroid-stimulating hormone (TSH). When thyroid levels in the bloodstream are too low, more TRH is released by the hypothalamus and more TSH is released by the pituitary gland. All of these actions occur because the body is trying to get thyroid hormone levels within a normal range.

Smoking, a toxic environment, stress, chronic antibiotic therapy, congenital defects, genetic disorders, infection, nutritional disorders, radiation, hormonal imbalances and tumors can all affect thyroid function. When thyroid levels are too high, it is called hyperthyroidism, which can cause anxiety, fatigue, heart palpitations, weight loss, heat intolerance, diarrhea and sweating. When thyroid levels are too low, it is called hypothyroidism, which may cause hair loss, fatigue, dry skin, constipation, weight gain and sensitivity to cold.

In children, low thyroid levels can retard normal growth and development. Hypothyroidism has been found in some children that are hyperactive and in many adults with compromised cardiac function. Low thyroid levels in some women can cause irregular menstrual cycles or even cessation of menstrual bleeding. Elevated cholesterol levels, elevated triglyceride levels, fluid retention, sexual disorders, memory problems, depression, recurrent upper respiratory infections, joint stiffness and soreness, severe nighttime muscle cramps, low back pain, osteoporosis and anemia may also be caused by hypothyroidism. Patients with severe cases of hypothyroidism may experience epileptic seizures.

Broda O. Barnes, M.D., Ph.D., who spent over 50 years researching thyroid function, stated that the health of the cells in our body depend on a study supply of nutrients, oxygen and thyroid hormones. Adequate levels of the thyroid hormones also enhance night vision because thyroid hormones assist in the production of retinine, which is needed for nighttime visual acuity.

Many synthetic thyroid replacement medications only replace T4 and not T3 (i.e., Synthyroid). Since adequate amounts of both T3 and T4 are needed for proper thyroid function, we prescribe Amour Desiccated Thyroid (a combination of T3 and T4) or Thyrolar to our patients who need thyroid supplementation. Armour Desiccated Thyroid is a natural substance derived from the thyroid glands of pigs and Thyrolar is an effective and safe synthetic mixture of T3 and T4. The dose prescribed for thyroid replacement is dependent upon the serum TSH, free T4 and free T3 levels. As you can surmise, a properly functioning thyroid gland is key for maintaining optimal health and well being.

Pregnenolone:

Pregnenolone is produced in the mitochondria (the energy producing power plants of our cells) in the brain and in the adrenal glands. As we age, our pregnenolone levels decline by as much as 60% by the time we are 75 years old. Pregnenolone is known as the "grandmother" hormone in the body because it is a precursor to progesterone and to DHEA (dehydroepiandrosterone), which is a precursor to the sex hormones testosterone and estrogen. Pregnenolone is derived from cholesterol, as are all other steroidal hormones. Our steroidal hormones are the body's best source of defense against stress. Pregnenolone also plays an important role in neutralizing cellular toxins.

Large concentrations of pregnenolone are found in the brain and are known to improve all of our mental functions. Some patients with bipolar disorders (manic depression) have very low levels of Pregnenolone. Since pregnenolone is known to have a protective effect on the neurons in the brain, adequate levels of pregnenolone have been shown to improve memory and deep rapid eye movement (REM) sleep.

Pregnenolone has also been used successfully to treat many of the symptoms of arthritis including muscle and joint pain, decreased energy levels, decreased strength and decreased mobility without any of the unwanted side effects associated with the current standard cortisone treatments prescribed so frequently today. Pregnenolone has a protective action against the unwanted effects of elevated cortisol levels. Pregnenolone has been shown to improve mood, decrease fatigue, enhance memory and improve a person's ability to cope with stress. Pregnenolone may also be an important component in repairing the fatty layer that protects nerves, known as the myelin sheath. As you may know, patients with multiple sclerosis, where the myelin sheath is destroyed, experience many debilitating symptoms.

When clinically indicated, we prescribe Pregnenolone to our patients. Dosage usually ranges from 100 mg to 200 mg per day and should be taken in the morning.

DHEA (dehydroepiandrosterone):

We know from the amount of scientific literature on DHEA, that all people over the age of forty (40) years of age are deficient in DHEA. Our DHEA levels can decline as much as 90% by the time we are seventy (70) years of age. DHEA, the "mother" hormone of the body, is made in the brain and in the adrenal cortex. DHEA is one of the most plentiful hormones in the body. Just as you need cholesterol to make pregnenolone, you need pregnenolone to make DHEA and progesterone. From progesterone, we make cortisol. From DHEA, we make androstenedione, which turns into estrone and testosterone. Estrone is then converted into estriol and estradiol but estradiol can also be made from testosterone. As you can see, all of the steroidal hormones are inter-dependent upon one another;

therefore maintaining healthful levels of all the major hormones in the body is essential.

Adequate levels of DHEA can improve sexual function (in women, adequate levels of DHEA can increase testosterone levels) increase muscle mass, decrease body fat (by speeding up the metabolism and decreasing muscle insulin resistance) improve memory, improve mental acuity, decrease depression and improve the immune system response (by controlling cortisol levels and adrenaline levels).

When your DHEA levels are in an optimal range, you have less risk of developing: arteriosclerosis because DHEA lowers cholesterol levels. Since DHEA lowers insulin levels there is less risk for developing adult onset diabetes. DHEA also decreases the risk of malignant tumors or cancers because it enhances the immune system response. DHEA can help prevent the decrease in mental functioning, which can be a precursor to Parkinson's disease or Alzheimer's disease, since it protects the neurons in the brain. Due to DHEA's protective benefit in so many areas of the body, it assists in improving symptoms associated with learning disabilities, impaired memory, HIV infection, obesity and autoimmune diseases such as chronic fatigue syndrome, arthritis, lupus, herpes and Epstein-Barr.

DHEA may also play a role in treating and/or preventing osteoporosis. As stated earlier, DHEA is manufactured in the adrenal glands but DHEA, along with testosterone, estrogen and progesterone is produced in the ovaries in females. Since we know that testosterone and progesterone stimulate bone formation and estrogen inhibits bone resorption, DHEA, like estrogen, may also inhibit bone resporption. Further, because DHEA, like testosterone, is an androgen hormone, DHEA may additionally play a role in bone formation. Therefore, DHEA may have a dual role in preventing osteoporosis because it is capable of stimulating bone formation and inhibiting bone resorption.

In some animal studies, DHEA slowed the aging process. Mice treated with DHEA had glossier coats, less gray hair and looked and acted younger than mice not treated with DHEA.

DHEA should never be given to male patients with existing prostate disease because DHEA is converted into testosterone and estrogen and these hormones may cause unwanted cell growth in the already diseased prostate. If, however, a male patient has a normal PSA level and a normal digital rectal exam, the use of DHEA can be of great benefit in preventing prostate cancer.

As stated previously, DHEA supplementation in female patients can sometimes raise testosterone levels and DHEA may also raise estrogen levels enough, so that estrogen replacement therapy may not be needed. Women with breast cancer should consult their physician before taking DHEA. There are studies, which indicate that higher DHEA levels protect against breast cancer but the verdict is still out on whether this protective effect is the same for women who currently have breast cancer. Women taking DHEA should also be taking Melatonin, Vitamin E, Indole 3 Carbinol and getting enough soy and vitamin D.

We try to return the DHEA Sulfate serum levels, of our patients, to that of a twenty to thirty year old. Depending on a patient's DHEA Sulfate level, daily doses of DHEA, taken orally, range from 25mg to 150 mg. We monitor DHEA levels closely to ensure that serum levels are maintained in a safe and healthful range. DHEA should not be taken without careful monitoring by a trained and qualified physician, preferably a board certified anti-aging physician or an endocrinologist, well versed on the clinical uses of DHEA. Since hormones are very powerful biological substances in the body and DHEA is one of the most plentiful hormones in the body, it is of little wonder that adequate levels of DHEA are critical in maintaining good health and well being.

Melatonin:

Melatonin is a powerful antioxidant as well as the hormone that regulates our sleep patterns. Melatonin is produced in the brain, in the pineal gland. As we age, our melatonin levels decrease. That is why older people sleep less, even though they need to sleep the same amount of time as they did when they were younger adults. It is a falsehood to think we need less sleep as we age. When we get a good night's sleep, we are able to function better during the day. A good night sleep, because melatonin levels are adequate, may decrease nighttime visits to the bathroom. Also, because of a good night's sleep, a person's mood may improve or it may be that increased levels of melatonin also mean increased levels of serotonin, which we know enhances mood. Sleep deprivation is a significant concern because it can lead to many serious illnesses.

Our sleep cycle is controlled by our "inner clock" known as the circadian rhythm. Melatonin manages the circadian rhythm by telling the body to slow down metabolism and decrease body temperature when there is less light. Melatonin levels are higher at night because melatonin production is suppressed by bright light. The higher your melatonin level, the sleepier you may feel.

Although melatonin is produced naturally in the pineal gland, we need the amino acid tryptophan, which is found in many of the foods we eat, to produce melatonin. Tryptophan is converted into serotonin, which is then converted into melatonin. You can see why eating a healthy diet with the proper ratios of favorable proteins, favorable carbohydrates and favorable fats, is essential for proper hormonal activity in the body.

At sometime in our forties, our melatonin levels decrease drastically because the pineal gland runs out of gas. The pineal gland is important, not only for producing melatonin but it also helps in restoring the thymus gland, which begins to shrink drastically after about the age of twelve. More on the thymus gland and the thymic hormones later. Most likely, however, because of the pineal gland's direct effect on the thymus gland, where many of our T- "natural killer" cells are produced, adequate melatonin levels will improve our immunity.

As you may remember, in Chapter Seven, we discussed the role of the hormone cholecystokinin (CCK), which tells the brain you have had enough to eat. Melatonin works with CCK, in the digestive tract to decrease the incidence and severity of many symptoms associated with colitis and gastric ulcers.

There have been impressive studies done in animals that showed the administration of melatonin after a stroke decreased brain damage. Melatonin has a neuro protective effect on the brain. Melatonin may also help fight against cancer because, once again, of its protective effect on cells. As a result of this protective effect, melatonin may make chemotherapy more effective because it protects healthy cells and helps them to more effectively combat the cancer in the body. In Europe, some physicians are using Melatonin, in doses up to 50 mg per night to treat cancer since it has proven so effective in the prevention of various cancers, including breast cancer. Patients with leukemia or lymphoma should consult their physician before taking Melatonin because we do not know enough at this time about the effects of Melatonin on these types of cancers.

It is also interesting to note, that a study done on rats with cataracts were treated with melatonin and the incidence of cataracts decreased in the group of rats that were given melatonin. There are other studies currently being conducted to see if there is any correlation between melatonin levels and the incidence of migraine headaches.

As mentioned earlier, melatonin is a powerful antioxidant because it enhances the activity of the body's natural antioxidant glutathione. Low glutathione levels have been found in many patients with heart and lung diseases.

Did you know that Melatonin has been used for birth control in Europe for years? The benefits of melatonin are far reaching and we have, most likely, only touched on this hormone's many benefits.

One last word about melatonin. You may or may not know that melatonin is helpful for treating jet lag. If you are planning a trip where you will cross several time zones, try taking some melatonin. Take the lowest dose possible that will induce sleep. As an example, if you were flying to London from Los Angeles, you know that there is an eight-hour time difference between Los Angeles and London. If you leave Los Angeles at 4 p.m., it will be midnight in London. Try taking your melatonin shortly after leaving Los Angles because you want to tell your body to go to sleep since it is midnight in

London and your body needs to adjust to London time. In summary, when flying any significant distance, take your melatonin when you know it is bedtime at your final location. You will be surprised how the effects of jet lag will significantly decrease.

In regards to melatonin administration, we usually start our patients on 500 mcg of melatonin orally, to be taken one hour before bedtime and increase the dose to 1 mg in about two to three weeks. One milligram of melatonin is the minimum dose that should be taken for any patient over the age of forty. Occasionally, some patients my feel a bit drowsy for one or two days, after starting melatonin but this usually passes. If drowsiness persists, or depression occurs, we discontinue the melatonin. We have also had one or two patients, out of hundreds of patients, who cannot take melatonin because it keeps them awake. This response is quite unusual but it is possible. Doses of melatonin vary for each patient. Doses may range of 500 mcg to 45 mg per night. For patients that have great difficulty getting to sleep we may recommend 3 to 6 mg of sublingual melatonin, taken about 15 minutes before bedtime, combined with 3 to 6 mg of timed-release melatonin taken at bedtime.

Thymic Hormones:
Behind your breastbone, known as the sternum, lies the thymus gland. The thymus gland produces thymic peptides known as killer T-cells. T-cells, when they mature become either CD4 or CD8 cells. CD4 cells are part of the immune system response because they help the body recognize foreign substances while CD8 cells, are the actual "killer" cells since they destroy the foreign substances recognized by the CD4 cells. The activity of the CD4 and CD8 cells, literally control the body's immune system.

Patients with AIDS have few, if any, T-cells. Enhancing T-cell production can keep a patient who is HIV positive, from converting to full-blown AIDS. The thymus gland also assists in the development of brain cells because it helps maintain the central nervous system. A healthy and functioning thymus gland helps maintain healthy adrenal glands, a healthy pituitary gland, healthy ovaries and a healthy thyroid gland. The thymus gland also helps our lymphocytes fight viral and bacterial infections.

We know that human growth hormone has been shown to increase the size and activity of the thymus gland, which is virtually non-existent in older adults. There is also a thymic peptide known as Thymic Protein-A, which is commercially available and given sub-lingually, which supposedly replaces many of the missing thymic proteins. At this time, we rely on the administration of HGH to enhance thymic activity and do not prescribe Thymic Protein-A to our patients.

In conjunction with a proper diet and exercise, natural hormone replacement therapy, which includes human growth hormone, testosterone, estrogen, progesterone, thyroid, DHEA, pregnenolone and melatonin will do a great deal in improving your health. Returning hormones, naturally and gently to the youthful range of a twenty-thirty year old will not make you twenty-five or thirty in chronological years but in biological terms, you will be much younger than you are now. Returning hormones to a youthful range just might make you feel ten to twenty years younger with the zest for life that you once had. Isn't it worth your time to see if you are a candidate for natural hormone replacement therapy? What better gift to give yourself than the gift of good health and vitality.

REMEMBER THIS

- "We age because our hormones decline, our hormones do not decline because we age"

- Hormones are chemical substances in our bodies that are released to have an effect on tissues somewhere else in the body

- Hormones control our response to illness by controlling our immune system, our response to stress, our sexual development, our growth and our metabolism

- When hormone levels are balanced in our bodies, we are more likely to enjoy good health provided our lifestyle choices are also healthful

- Most people in their twenties have optimal hormonal levels

- Usually, estrogen levels in women decline drastically, over a one to three year period at the time of menopause

- In men, testosterone levels decline slowly over a thirty-year period

- The secretion of human growth hormone in both sexes decreases steadily between the ages of forty and ninety

- DHEA decreases to very low levels in both men and women after the age of forty

- Insulin sensitivity becomes much less as we age or we are affected by obesity

- We usually do not feel the effects of declining hormone levels until our late thirties, early forties or occasionally, late forties or early fifties

- We now know that natural (bioidential) hormone replacement therapy, when clinically indicated, can improve a person's physical and mental status to that of a person ten to twenty years younger

- Your hormone levels affect the incidence of osteoporosis

- Osteoporosis is preventable

- Osteoporosis is more common in women than men

- Osteoporosis causes bones to become more brittle and less dense, which increases the chance for fractures

- Osteoporosis is the leading cause of hip fractures in the U.S

- Osteoporosis is an imbalance in new bone formation and bone resorption

- Low estrogen levels in women, low testosterone levels in both men and women, low growth hormone levels in both sexes, calcium and vitamin D deficiencies, lack of exercise, alcohol consumption, tobacco, caffeine, beverages containing phosphate and certain medications such as some anti-seizure and some cortisone drugs can all be contributing factors to the incidence of osteoporosis

- People with osteoporosis may experience bone deformities

- Currently more than 5 million men in the United States suffer from the effects of hyopgonadism or low testosterone levels

- Testosterone, primarily a male sex hormone, is also found in females

- Testosterone, produced in the testes and adrenal glands in males, is needed for male sexual development and plays a primary role in libido, cardiovascular health, lung function, improved bone mass, brain health (memory enhancer) erectile function of the penis, mood enhancement and a person's overall energy level

- As a person ages, his/her testosterone levels decline

- In men, the "free" testosterone level (the testosterone that is available for use in the body and not bound) begins to decline gradually in a person's thirties. This decline in available testosterone in males is known as andropause or male menopause

- In addition to aging, stress can also lower testosterone levels

- Low levels of testosterone are associated with increased body fat (especially abdominal fat) decreased energy levels, depression, sexual dysfunction, wasting of bones and muscles, increased blood pressure and increased incidence of heart disease

- A man in his eighties has about one-fifth the amount of testosterone in his body as he had in his youth

- Testosterone, in women, is produced primarily in the ovaries and is known to improve clitoral and nipple sensitivity, increase libido, improve the quality of orgasm and can increase muscle strength and bone density

- Testosterone may also improve various symptoms of menopause including "hot flashes," weight gain, fatigue, lethargy and may decrease the risk of breast cancer

- When testosterone levels decline, a man's prostate gland will enlarge

- An enlarged prostate gland has been associated with a greater risk for cancer of the prostate

- Natural testosterone replacement therapy has been shown to improve prostate health

- Saw palmetto has been known to improve the symptoms associated with an enlarged prostate such as frequent nighttime urination and decreased flow of urine

- Proscar (finasteride) a prescription medication has been used successfully in decreasing serum levels of dihyrotestosterone (DHT) which, when too high have typically been associated with enlargement of the prostate gland

- Other herbal supplements that improve prostate health include

Pygeum and Urtica. Indole 3 Carbinol, a dietary supplement made from cruciferous vegetables like broccoli and cauliflower, also has a protective effect on the prostate because of its anti-cancer properties

- Zinc is a mineral that is needed, in proper amounts, for optimal prostate health

- Natural testosterone replacement therapy can improve energy levels, increase bone density, decrease blood pressure, increase sexual drive and performance, decrease heart disease, lower LDL cholesterol levels, raise HDL cholesterol levels, enhance blood glucose levels, improve muscle strength, improve brain function and decrease body fat

- For male and female patients, we prescribe natural testosterone transdermal creams or gels, which are easily absorbed and are quite efficient at returning serum testosterone levels to youthful levels

- The dose of testosterone transdermal creams or gels for every patient is different depending on a person's serum testosterone levels. Women require a much smaller dose of testosterone than men do

- Estrogen, in females, is made primarily in the ovaries

- For approximately thirty-five years of a woman's life, estrogen, progesterone and testosterone usually maintain a healthy equilibrium throughout the reproductive years

- "Estrogens" are the primary female sex hormones. The three major estrogens found in the female are estradiol, estriol and estrone

- Estradiol is the most active estrogen in the body but may not be well absorbed

- Estrone, known to relieve some of the symptoms of menopause has been associated with some forms of cancer and is selectively used in natural (bioidentical) hormone replacement therapy

- Estriol has been shown to have anti-cancer effects and inhibits breast cancers

- Adequate levels of natural estrogens can prevent heart disease, decrease cholesterol levels, control carbohydrate metabolism, assist with blood clotting, improve memory, prevent osteoporosis and prevent or decrease the incidence of Alzheimer's Disease, will help decrease the symptoms associated with menopause (hot flashes, vaginal dryness, mood swings, increased urination at night, incontinence) and prevent strokes

- Low estrogen levels can cause a women to have symptoms of anxiety, migraine headaches, decreased memory, decreased skin thickness, hot flashes and depression while estrogen levels that are too high can cause symptoms of irritability, fluid retention, food cravings, hot flashes, urinary frequency, fatigue, breast tenderness and anxiety

- In women, hot flashes can occur when estrogen levels are either too high or too low

- Almost all, postmenopausal women need natural hormone replacement therapy which includes estrogen, progesterone, testosterone and thyroid

- Many soy products contain natural plant estrogens and may be beneficial for all women because of their anti-cancer effects

- When clinically indicated, we prescribe natural (bioidentical) estrogen transdermal creams for our female patients that are comprised of estradiol and estriol made from plant estrogens known as phytoestrogens

- Some of the side effects of natural estrogen replacement therapy may be fluid retention, increased body fat (usually 5-10 pounds) and increased risk of breast and uterine cancer if not given in conjunction with natural progesterone

- We always prescribe natural progesterone to all of our female patients on estrogen replacement therapy

- The dosage for the estrogen cream is dependent upon a woman's serum estradiol level

- We do not recommend oral estrogens because they interfere with insulin/glucose metabolism in the body and with human growth hormone metabolism

- Progesterone is primarily a female hormone but is also found in males

- Progesterone helps estrogen levels stay in a therapeutic range

- Progesterone protects against osteoporosis, protects against breast cancer, decreases fluid retention, normalizes blood clotting, helps maintain normal blood sugar levels, assists in lowering LDL cholesterol levels, improves libido and has a sedative effect on the central nervous system

- Progesterone levels decline as we age

- Synthetic progestins (i.e., Provera) produce unwanted side effects such as fluid retention, weight gain, depression and breast tenderness

- We prescribe oral micronized natural (bioidentical) progesterone (made from the wild yam) lozenges or pills for our female patients

- The dosage of progesterone is different for every patient, depending upon the serum progesterone level

- The thyroid hormones control metabolism

- The thyroid hormones tell the body how fast or slow it should use the fuel we eat, especially carbohydrates and fat

• The thyroid hormones thyroxine (T4) and triiodothyronine (T3) and calcitonin regulate metabolism and the amount of calcium in the body, respectively

• Approximately 80% of the thyroid hormones produced in the body is T4

• Thyroxine (T4) is not readily available and is stored by the body, only to be released when T3 levels are low

• Triiodothyronine (T3) is approximately four times more powerful than T4 and is the active thyroid hormone in the body

• Smoking, a toxic environment, stress, chronic antibiotic therapy, congenital defects, genetic disorders, infection, nutritional disorders, radiation, hormonal imbalances and tumors can all affect thyroid function

• When thyroid levels are too high, it is called hyperthyroidism, which can cause anxiety, fatigue, heart palpitations, weight loss, heat intolerance, diarrhea and sweating

• When thyroid levels are too low, it is called hypothyroidism, which may cause hair loss, fatigue, dry skin, constipation, weight gain and sensitivity to cold

• In children, low thyroid levels can retard normal growth and development

• Hypothyroidism has been found in some children that are hyperactive and in many adults with compromised cardiac function

• Low thyroid levels in some women can cause irregular menstrual cycles or even cessation of menstrual bleeding

• Elevated cholesterol levels, elevated triglyceride levels, fluid retention, sexual disorders, memory problems, depression, recurrent upper respiratory infections, joint stiffness and soreness, severe nighttime muscle cramps, low back pain, osteoporosis and anemia may be caused by hypothyroidism

- Patients with severe cases of hypothyroidism may experience epileptic seizures

- The health of the cells in our body depend on a study supply of nutrients, oxygen and thyroid hormones

- Adequate levels of the thyroid hormones also enhance night vision because thyroid hormones assist in the production of retinine, which is needed for nighttime visual acuity

- Many synthetic thyroid replacement medications only replace T4 and not T3

- Adequate amounts of T3 and T4 are needed for proper thyroid function

- We prescribe Amour Desiccated Thyroid (a combination of T3 and T4) or Thyrolar to our patients who need thyroid supplementation

- Armour Desiccated Thyroid is a natural substance derived from the thyroid glands of pigs

- Thyrolar is an effective and safe synthetic mixture of T3 and T4

- The dose prescribed for thyroid replacement is dependent upon the serum TSH, free T4 and free T3 levels

- Pregnenolone is produced in the mitochondria (our energy producing cells) in the brain and in the adrenal glands

- Pregnenolone levels decline by as much as 60% by the time we are 75 years old

- Pregnenolone is known as the "grandmother" hormone in the body because it is a precursor to progesterone and to DHEA (dehydroepiandrosterone)
- Pregnenolone is derived from cholesterol, as are all other steroidal

hormones

- Our steroidal hormones are the body's best source of defense against stress

- Pregnenolone is important in neutralizing cellular toxins

- Large concentrations of pregnenolone are found in the brain and are known to improve all of our mental functions

- Pregnenolone has been used successfully to treat many of the symptoms of arthritis including muscle and joint pain, decreased energy levels, decreased strength and decreased mobility without any of the unwanted side effects associated with the current standard cortisone treatments

- Pregnenolone has a protective action against the unwanted effects of elevated cortisol levels

- Pregnenolone improves mood, decreases fatigue, enhances memory and improves a person's ability to cope with stress

- Pregnenolone is an important component in repairing the fatty layer that protects nerves, known as the myelin sheath

- When clinically indicated, we prescribe Pregnenolone to our patients. Dosage usually ranges from 100 mg to 200 mg per day and should be taken in the morning

- All people over the age of forty (40) years of age are deficient in DHEA

- DHEA levels can decline as much as 90% by the time we are seventy (70) years of age

- DHEA is one of the most plentiful hormones in the body

- DHEA makes androstenedione, which turns into estrone and testosterone
- Adequate levels of DHEA can improve sexual function (in

women, adequate levels of DHEA can increase testosterone levels) increase muscle mass, decrease body fat (by speeding up the metabolism and decreasing muscle insulin resistance) improve memory, improve mental acuity, decrease depression and improve the immune system response (by controlling cortisol levels and adrenaline levels)

- When DHEA levels are in an optimal range, you have less risk of developing: arteriosclerosis because DHEA lowers cholesterol levels

- DHEA lowers insulin levels, decreasing the risk for developing adult onset diabetes

- DHEA decreases the risk of malignant tumors or cancers because it enhances the immune system response

- DHEA can help prevent the decrease in mental functioning, which can be a precursor to Parkinson or Alzheimer's disease, since it protects the neurons in the brain

- Due to DHEA's protective benefit in so many areas of the body, it assists in improving symptoms associated with learning disabilities, impaired memory, HIV infection, obesity and autoimmune diseases such as chronic fatigue syndrome, arthritis, lupus, herpes and Epstein-Barr

- DHEA may also play a role in treating and/or preventing osteoporosis

- DHEA, like estrogen, may also inhibit bone resorption

- Like testosterone, DHEA may help on bone formation

- DHEA may assist in slowing the aging process

- DHEA should never be given to male patients with existing prostate disease
- The use of DHEA can be of great benefit in preventing prostate

cancer in healthy male patients without prostate disease

- DHEA supplementation in female patients can sometimes raise testosterone levels

- DHEA may also raise estrogen levels enough, so that estrogen replacement therapy may not be needed

- Women with breast cancer should consult their physician before taking DHEA

- Women taking DHEA, should also be taking Melatonin, Vitamin E, Indole 3 Carbinol and getting enough soy and vitamin D

- We try to return the DHEA Sulfate serum levels, of our patients, to that of a twenty to thirty year old

- Depending on a patient's DHEA Sulfate level, daily doses of DHEA, taken orally, range from 25mg to 150 mg

- We monitor DHEA levels closely to ensure that serum levels are maintained in a safe and healthful range

- DHEA should not be taken without careful monitoring by a trained and qualified physician, preferably a board certified anti-aging physician or an endocrinologist, well versed on the clinical uses of DHEA

- Melatonin is a powerful antioxidant as well as the hormone that regulates our sleep patterns

- Melatonin is produced in the brain, in the pineal gland.

- As we age, our melatonin levels decrease

- Adequate levels of melatonin also mean increased levels of sero-tonin, which we know enhances mood
- Melatonin manages the circadian rhythm by telling the body to

slow down metabolism and decrease body temperature when
there is less light

- Although melatonin is produced naturally in the pineal gland, we
  need the amino acid tryptophan, which is found in many of the
  foods we eat, to produce melatonin

- Tryptophan is converted into serotonin, which is then converted
  into melatonin

- At sometime in our forties, our melatonin levels decrease drastically because the pineal gland runs out of gas

- The pineal gland is important, not only for producing melatonin
  but it also helps in restoring the thymus gland, which begins to
  shrink drastically after about the age of twelve

- Because of the pineal gland's direct effect on the thymus gland,
  where many of our T- "natural killer" cells are produced, adequate melatonin levels will improve our immunity

- Melatonin works with cholecystokinin (CCK) to decrease the incidence and severity of many symptoms associated with colitis and
  gastric ulcers

- Melatonin has a neuro protective effect on the brain

- Melatonin may also help fight against cancer because of its protective effect on cells

- Patients with leukemia or lymphoma should consult their physician before taking Melatonin because we do not know enough at
  this time about the effects of Melatonin on these types of cancer

- Melatonin is a powerful antioxidant because it enhances the activity of the body's natural antioxidant glutathione. Low glutathione
  levels have been found in many patients with heart and lung diseases
- The benefits of melatonin are far reaching and we have, most like-

ly, only touched on this hormone's many benefits

• Melatonin is also helpful for treating jet lag

• We usually start our patients on 500 mcg of melatonin orally, to be taken one hour before bedtime and increase the dose to 1 mg in about two to three weeks

• One milligram of melatonin is the minimum dose that should be taken for any patient over the age of forty

• Occasionally, some patients my feel a bit drowsy for one or two days, after starting melatonin but this usually passes. If drowsiness persists, or depression occurs, discontinue the melatonin

• We have also had one or two patients, out of hundreds of patients that cannot take melatonin because it keeps them awake. This response is quite unusual but it is possible

• Doses of melatonin vary for each patient. Doses may range of 500 mcg to 45 mg per night

• For patients that have great difficulty getting to sleep we may recommend 3 to 6 mg of sublingual melatonin, taken about 15 minutes before bedtime, combined with 3 to 6 mg of timed-release melatonin taken at bedtime

• Behind your breastbone, known as the sternum, lies the thymus gland

• The thymus gland produces thymic peptides known as killer T-cells

• Patients with AIDS have few, if any T-cells

• Enhancing T-cell production can keep a patient who is HIV positive, from converting to full-blown AIDS

• The thymus gland assists in the development of brain cells because it helps maintain the central nervous system

• A healthy and functioning thymus gland helps maintain healthy adrenal glands, a healthy pituitary gland, healthy ovaries and a healthy thyroid gland

• The thymus gland also helps our lymphocytes fight viral and bacterial infections

• Human growth hormone has been shown to increase the size and activity of the thymus gland, which is virtually non-existent in older adults

• We rely on the administration of HGH to enhance thymic activity

• In conjunction with a proper diet and exercise, natural hormone replacement therapy, which includes human growth hormone, testosterone, estrogen, progesterone, thyroid, DHEA, pregnenolone and melatonin will do a great deal in improving your health

• Returning hormones to a youthful range just might make you feel ten to twenty years younger with the zest for life that you once had

CHAPTER THIRTEEN

BRAIN HEALTH

We have explained the three major building blocks for good health; proper diet, appropriate exercise and natural hormone replacement therapy. If you eat the correct diet (remember, you must eat a hormonally correct diet) exercise at least three to five times per week and find a well-trained and qualified anti-aging physician to assist you with naturally returning your hormones to a youthful range, chances are you will experience increased health and well being. Isn't that what we all want? By doing the aforementioned, your brain health will also improve because your brain, like other parts of your body, is an organ that is made out of flesh and blood. Ensuring that your brain will continue to function properly, even as you age chronologically, is the most important thing you can do for yourself. Without a healthy brain that functions properly, what type of life will you have?

Alzheimer's Disease:
Not all cognitive decline is caused by Alzheimer's disease. Many things can cause age related cognitive decline (ARCD) including elevated cortisol levels (found in people with chronic stress) decreased blood flow to the brain and decreased hormonal levels throughout the body. Dementia, in any form, is generally defined as a loss of circuitry in the brain. The incidence of Alzheimer's disease, however, is on rise. Did you know that it is predicted that by the year 2050, 14 million people in the United States will have Alzheimer's disease? Knowing that, we think it prudent for individuals to begin taking an active roll in preventing disease and illness in their life. The exact cause of Alzheimer's disease is unknown at this time. There may not even be an exact cause but a combination of things that contribute to the manifestation of the disease and the contributing factors may be different for every individual inflicted with the disease. Very simply stated, Alzheimer's disease causes brain cells to die. When brain cells die in significant numbers, the

brain can shrink and change shape. In your lifetime, approximately 20% of your brain cells will die but in patients with Alzheimer's disease, brain cell death is so extensive that over time, death will occur because the brain can no longer function adequately to direct the rest of your bodily activities.

The chances of acquiring Alzheimer's disease increase with age. After age sixty-five (65) two to six percent of the population in America are diagnosed with Alzheimer's disease. Approximately half of the population over eighty-five (85) years old have Alzheimer's disease and about half the nursing home admissions in the United States are due to Alzheimer's disease. The increasing incidence of Alzheimer's disease is very frightening to us, both from a health perspective and from an economic perspective. We hope the statistics alarm you enough to take action and improve your brain health.

Alzheimer's is more common in women and also more common if someone in your family has the disease. If a family member has Alzheimer's your chances of getting it are four times greater than someone who does not have a family member diagnosed with Alzheimer's disease. To explain further, you inherit one set of genes from your mother and one set of genes from your father. Researchers have found the Apo E (apolipoprotein E) gene is somehow connected to the incidence of Alzheimer's disease. There are three kinds of Apo E genes. Apo E-2 protects individuals from Alzheimer's, Apo E-3 increases the risk factor for the possible occurrence of Alzheimer's and Apo E-4 almost certainly increases the odds of getting Alzheimer's. Therefore, if you received an Apo E-2 gene from both your mother and your father, it would seem that your chances of getting Alzheimer's are quite low. However, worst-case scenario, if you inherited an Apo E-4 gene from both your mother and your father, your chances of getting Alzheimer's are quite high. The good news is that most people have one or two Apo E-3 genes and their risk of developing Alzheimer's is somewhere in the middle.

The onset of Alzheimer's can take from one to ten years. Some of the characteristics of Alzheimer's are a severe and continual decline in cognitive abilities for which no other known cause can be identified. More often than not, patients in the early stages of Alzheimer's become increasingly forgetful and find it difficult to carry out complex thought processes. Presently, medical science has suggested that some of the contributing factors to the disease may be the following:

- Genetic predisposition to the disease (explained earlier)
- Abnormal calcium regulation in the nerve cells in the brain
- Toxic levels of aluminum, lead, iron or some other heavy metal in the body
- Malnutrition
- Decreased blood flow to the brain
- Extensive free radical damage
- Environmental toxins
- Hormonal imbalances in the brain
- Some type of slow acting virus that has yet to be identified
- Immune system malfunction
- Excessive levels of cortisol in the body

One major contributing factor to Alzheimer's disease and overall brain deterioration, we believe, is too much cortisol in the body. We need cortisol in our bodies but not too much. When we are in stressful situations, the adrenal glands, which sit on top of your kidneys, release cortisol, which assists in controlling the body's use of fats, proteins and carbohydrates and helps us respond efficiently to stress. However, if we are chronically stressed, cortisol levels will remain abnormally high and rob the brain of the glucose it needs to thrive. As you can guess, too much cortisol for long periods of time will destroy not millions but billions of brain cells because all the neurotransmitters in the brain need glucose to function. Too much cortisol in your brain damages the proper functioning of the neuroendocrine system, which is the connection between your mind and your body.

What we currently know on autopsy, about the brains of Alzheimer's patients is that there are abnormal fibers surrounding the brain cells and eventually those fibers become so ensnarled that brain cells die. Alzheimer's patients also have a lot of dead cellular waste products in their brains, which are known as senile plaques. Since the area in the brain that controls movement (the cerebellum) does not seem to be as susceptible to senile plaques as other areas of the brain, it explains why Alzheimer's patients are able to move until the disease finally overwhelms the cerebellum.

Because Alzheimer's patients have a significantly decreased amount of acetylcholine (the memory transporter) in their brains, memory in these patients can be decreased by as much as ninety (90) percent.

How Your Brain Works:
Did you know that your brain is the most important organ in the body? In most humans, the brain usually weighs a little less than three pounds and no, brain size does not determine intelligence. Do not confuse your brain with your mind. Your brain is an organ in the body and your mind is the enigma that makes each of us all that we are. Your brain controls everything in your body. There is an old saying about the body that states, "trouble goes from north to south." If you are having trouble in one part of your body, the chances are that it can be traced to some malfunction in your brain. If your brain is the conductor of the orchestra, then the conductor needs to be in optimal form to ensure that all members of the orchestra are performing to their fullest capacity. Your brain needs fuel, in the form of glucose, to function and it needs about twenty-five percent of the circulating blood in your body.

Your brain has three major regions known as the brain stem, the cerebellum and the cerebrum. Your brain stem or primary brain was the first part of your brain to be developed. It rests on top of your spinal column and controls your breathing and heartbeat. It also is a relay center for all of your senses. The cerebellum, which sits behind your brain stem, controls your movement and muscle action. The cerebellum is the memory center for all forms of movement. The more movements you master, the more developed the cerebellum will be. The cerebrum sits on top of your brain stem and your cerebellum. The cerebrum controls your thoughts, your memory and your emotions. A thin beige layer known as the neocortex covers the cerebrum. The neocortex makes you the person you are and is known as the "thinking" part of the brain. The neocortex has a surface area of about 2 1/2 square feet but due to all the "nooks and crannies" in the brain, very little of the neocortex is visible. The more nooks and crannies you have, supposedly, the more intelligent you are. Actually, the number of connections between the neurons in the brain determines intelligence. Just below the neocortex is a thick white material that performs much of the biochemical work that keeps us alive.

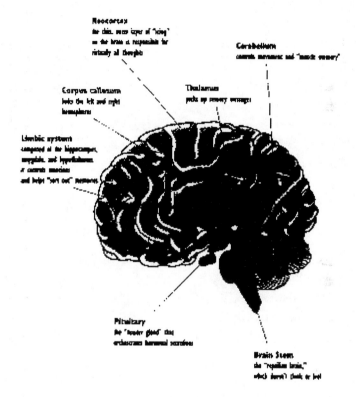

The cerebrum is comprised of four lobes. The frontal lobe, located on the forward part of the cerebrum, is where your abstract problem solving takes place, the parietal lobe, which is right behind the frontal lobe, processes the information from your senses, the occipital lobe, which is positioned at the base of your brain, controls your vision and the temporal lobe, located on the right and left side of the cerebrum, close to your temples, governs your hearing, your language capabilities and your memory. The right side of the cerebrum (your emotion center) is predominately dedicated to creative processes while the left side of the cerebrum (the logic center) focuses more on analytical thinking. Generally speaking, females have a more developed right brain and males a more developed left-brain. The right and left side of the brain is joined by a sophisticated system of nerve fibers known as the corpus callosum. Usually, this band of nerve fibers is denser in females and may explain why females may have better communication between the right and the left brain and why males may have more compartmentalized capabilities, such as increased aptitudes in the areas of engineering and mathematics.

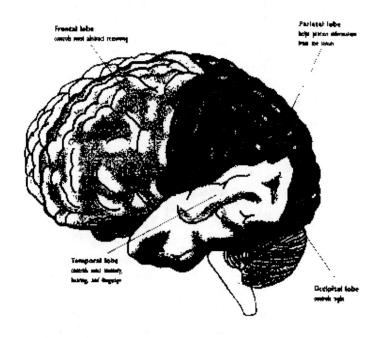

Located in the cerebrum, just below the corpus collusum and sitting on top of the brain stem, are the hypothalmus, the hippocampus, the amygdala, the thalamus and the pituitary gland, which comprise the limbic system in the brain or the emotion center of the brain. The hippocampus is your brain's memory center and stores your short term as well as a few long-term memories. Most long-term memories are sent to the neocortex by the hippocampus. The hippocampus is very vulnerable to the effects of Alzheimer's disease and this may explain why Alzheimer's patients lose their short-term memory before they lose their long-term memory.

When you are in trouble, the hypothalmus tells your body to increase the production of adrenaline. The hypothalmus controls sexual function, body temperature, thirst and hunger. It sends messages to the pituitary gland, which in turn sends messages to the body through its own set of hormones. The hypothalmus tells the body how to respond to different stimuli after the neocortex, amygdala and the hippocampus have determined the importance of the stimuli.

At the center of the emotional processing center is the amygdala. Working with the hippocampus and the neocortex, the amygdala determines the degree of emotion in each of your thoughts. If you did not have an amygdala in your brain, you would not have any emotion. The thalamus processes all incoming messages (with the exception of smell) and sends them to the correct processing center in the brain. The pituitary gland, which is only the size of a pea, is the master endocrine gland. It tells all of your other endocrine glands what to do by releasing hormones or sending releasing factors that affect hormones in other parts of the body. The limbic system is where thought and emotion converge and mind and body unite. If the limbic system is overloaded with too much emotion, in the form of anxiety and fear, it can be damaging.

Your endocrine system starts with the limbic system. The endocrine system controls your body. The endocrine system is a group of glands throughout your body that secrete hormones. Remember, as stated in previous chapters, that hormones are the chemicals that travel throughout the body to activate other organs in the body by triggering target cells in each organ. In your brain, hormones are responsible for triggering emotions.

The glands in the endocrine system are the hypothalamus and the pituitary gland, which we have already discussed, the pineal gland, which secretes melatonin, the parathyroid glands, which control the level of calcium in the blood, the thyroid gland, which controls your immune system and metabolism, the thymus gland, which produces "T" cells that help fight disease and infection, the liver, which regulates most of the bodies chemicals and clears the blood of harmful substances, the pancreas, which secretes necessary digestive juices and insulin and glucagon, the adrenal glands, which secrete aldosterone, cortisol and various androgen hormones into the body, the kidneys, which regulate blood and electrolytes and eliminate waste products, the ovaries in females, which secrete the female sex hormones and the testes in males, which secrete the male sex hormones. The liver and kidneys are not glands but they secrete hormones and we thought they should be mentioned in this section because of their vital importance.

Your sex hormones, testosterone, DHEA, estrogen and progesterone effect how well you think, how much you remember, how good you feel emotionally and how well you perform physically. We know that females with therapeutic levels of natural estrogen seem to have a slower progression of memory loss than those females who do not have enough natural estrogen circulating in their bodies. Further, low DHEA levels can also impact memory and returning DHEA levels to a therapeutic level can enhance memory. Although we did not mention all of the hormones in the body, in this section, we stress, once again; hormonal levels that are not kept in a youthful therapeutic range will have detrimental effects on the body, including your brain.

Your Thoughts:
Your brain runs on electricity. Don't worry; you do not have to plug yourself into the wall socket to be able to think. There is enough electricity in your brain to light a 25-watt light bulb. Your thoughts travel along an electrical current that is created by chemical processes in your body. Remember that your brain is part of your body. The electrical currents in your brain are known as memory chains or memory traces. The memory chains resemble a tree, with a root system and many branches. These little brain cell trees are so small that approximately 20,000 of them would fit in the head of a pin. These trees are more commonly called neurons. The root system of the neuron is called the axons and the branches of the neuron are called dendrites. When you have a thought, information flows into the axons to the center or nucleus of the neuron and out to the dendrites. The thought, driven by an electrical charge and converted into a neurotransmitter then passes to the next neuron via a synapse. The synapse is the gap between neurons. Brain cells never touch but are connected by chemicals known as neurotransmitters, which help the thought travel or swim across the synapse to the

next neuron. There are hundreds of known neurotransmitters and each one has a different function that expresses different feelings or emotions.

The most important transmitter for memory and thought is acetylcholine. Acetylcoline is the most plentiful of all the neurotransmitters. Acetylcoline also helps generate muscle movement. Acetylcoline is necessary for helping males achieve erection and orgasm. It also controls the blood flow to the genitals in both females and males. People with age associated memory loss most likely have low levels of acetylcholine. Estrogen, lecithin, the B vitamins, vitamin C and certain minerals enhance the production of acetylcoline.

Norepinephrine, another important neurotransmitter, helps the brain to be more alert in times of stress. Norepinephrine is necessary for transporting short-term memories from the hippocampus to long-term storage in the neocortex. Because of norepinephrine we are able to remember, quite well, exciting or stressful events in or lives. Norepinephrine assists in regulating your sexual drive, helps stimulate your metabolism and helps you maintain a positive mood. Too much norepinephrine, however, can keep you awake at night or decrease your appetite.

The neurotransmitter dopamine primarily controls physical movement. Patients with Parkinson's disease have low dopamine levels, which explains their involuntary muscle movements and tremors. As we age, our dopamine levels decrease and that is why it is said that if you live long enough, you will eventually develop Parkinson's disease. Dopamine enhances immune system function, improves your libido, improves your mood and improves your ability to remember. Dopamine also stimulates the pituitary gland to secrete human growth hormone. A medication that we will discuss later, called Deprenyl, is noted for increasing levels of dopamine in the body.

Serotonin is the neurotransmitter that induces sleep and controls pain. Serotonin is known as the "feel good" neurotransmitter. Serotonin is second in importance of all the neurotransmitters. The medication Prozac increases the amount of serotonin in your brain. When indicated, we prefer to give our patients more natural substances to induce the production of serotonin.

L-glutamate is the neurotransmitter that helps you create new memories and recall old memories. L-glutamate helps neutralize the chronic stress response and therefore, the over-production of cortisol. Cognitive function can be impaired when levels of L-glutamate are low.

The neurotransmitter that has a calming effect on your brain and keeps it from being over stimulated is gamma-aminobutyric acid, more commonly known as GABA. GABA is essential for relaxation and sleep. Alcoholics tend to have low levels of GABA.

Endorphins, although not really a neurotransmitter, have many of the same effects as neurotransmitters. Endorphins relieve anxiety and pain and are released by the body in response to any type of major emotional or physical stress. When you exercise you increase endorphin production. Endorphins help you focus, concentrate and keep interested in what you are doing. When you are hurt, endorphins flood your brain, so that you initially may not feel any pain from your injury. Endorphins, actually neuropeptides, are also the connection between the mind and the immune system.

We have only discussed the major neurotransmitters in your body. Neurotransmitters are critical for life and from the few that we have discussed; it is obvious how profoundly neurotransmitters impact your health and well being.

Your Memory:

Every brain cell has a small portion of a complete memory. Your thoughts or your senses create pieces of memory. In each brain cell, ribonucleic acid (RNA) is the brain cell memory bank. Memories are stored in the RNA in the form of "coded" proteins. When information enters the brain through hearing, seeing or doing, brain cells encode it as a memory.

There are three types of memory. Your hearing or auditory memory is stored in the neocortex on the left side of the brain. Visual memories are stored in the neocortex on the right side of the brain and your doing or kinesthetic memory is stored in the cerebellum. Kinesthetic memory is usually the memory the lasts the longest but visual and auditory memories can reside in long-term memory in people with healthy brains.

Memories are sent to long-term storage via the limbic system. If a fact or an event stimulates you, the neurotransmitter norepinephrine imprints memories on your brain. Another way memories are transported to long-term storage is by repeating the fact or thought over and over. The more you think about a piece of information, the more familiar it becomes. This is known as long-term potentiation. The more a memory is repeated, the easier it is for the thought or memory to be processed by the brain. A simple analogy is a road you travel frequently becomes more familiar and easier to travel than a road that you have never traveled on before. As people age, their long-term potentiation abilities decline. Therefore, it is crucial to maintain a healthy brain and to continually utilize this ability to learn by repetition.

Brain cells can only survive for two to four minutes without oxygen and glucose, which is supplied by your blood. As stated earlier, the brain utilizes about twenty-five (25) percent of the circulating blood in the body. When someone suffers a stroke, some part or parts of their brain is robbed of the oxygen and glucose it needs and brain cells die. Older people are more susceptible to minor or major strokes. Strokes can cause dementia if too many brain cells die.

Another way that memory can decline is by the lifestyle choices we make. Poor nutrition, certain pharmaceutical medications, recreational drugs, alcohol, cigarette smoking, environmental toxins and allergic substances can cause irreparable harm to the brain. When you drink alcohol, the protective blood brain barrier that keeps harmful substances from entering the brain is deactivated by the alcohol, leaving the brain exposed to toxic substances. Chronic use of alcohol can shrink various areas of the brain and destroy the protective myelin sheath that surrounds nerve fibers.

Certain sedatives, painkillers and some antidepressants can severely impact your brain's capabilities. Valium, Darvon, Percodan and Elavil are just a few of the medications that can contribute to cognitive decline. For any medication you may be taking find out what the side effects are, especially what the potential effects can be on your cognitive abilities.

Recreational drug use is very hazardous to your health. Stimulants such as amphetamines and cocaine cause an over production of neurotransmitters. When the supply of neurotransmitters has been depleted, new memories cannot be formed. That is what happens when drug users "blackout." They are physically incapable of remembering. Marijuana, although less harmful than some other drugs, can also rob the brain of the neurotransmitters it needs to function properly.

Poor nutrition is harmful to the brain. For example, inadequate levels of vitamin C can decrease brain function. Also, the B vitamins are very important for brain function. Vitamin B1 (thiamine) and vitamin B12 are needed to produce acetylcoline. Vitamin B12 also helps build the protective myelin sheath and prevents pernicious anemia, which can deplete oxygen levels in the brain. Niacin (Vitamin B3) prevents a form of psychosis and helps people relax because it is essential in the formation of the neurotransmitter GABA. A poor diet and a diet that is too restricted in calories can cause neuronal death. The brain also needs adequate levels of copper, zinc, magnesium, iron, iodine and other minerals to function. Most vitamins and minerals necessary for brain health can be obtained from a proper diet and nutritional supplementation.

As you know, smoking is hazardous to your health and to your brain's health. If you smoke, you are not only damaging your lungs but also constricting your blood vessels. The same vessels that carry oxygen to your brain.

Exposure to environmental toxins and heavy metals can impair your brain. Aluminum, lead and mercury are all harmful to your brain. Lead poisoning can cause brain swelling. Many industrial waste products and pesticides contain arsenic and other substances that threaten brain health.

Food allergies and certain other allergic responses can damage your brain. Some people with food allergies may not know that they have them. Food allergies can cause forgetfulness, migraine headaches, anxiety, depression and hyperactivity. When patients participate in a food elimination process, the allergen can be identified and the patient can avoid the particular food(s) that is causing the allergic reaction.

In regards to memory loss, we know that auditory memory capabilities decline faster than visual memory capabilities until about age 80. We also know that as memory declines, so does someone's creativity because creativity is interwoven to memory.

Memory loss can cause depression and/or depression can cause memory loss. As people lose their vitality and purpose in life, due to illness, cognitive decline or some other set of circumstances, they can become depressed. More than thirty percent of the population over sixty-five years of age suffers from some form of clinical depression. You have a choice. You can take action to improve your memory or you can do nothing. If you do nothing to improve your brain health, you know what the results will be. Your brain, like the rest of your body deteriorates with age but you have the capability to improve your brain health. We know that the decline in the level of neurotransmitters in the brain can be halted and even improved with proper diet, exercise (including brain exercises) medications and supplementation.

Poor circulation also damages your brain. Again proper diet, exercise, medications and supplementation can improve your circulation. Elevated cortisol levels damage your brain. Too much cortisol in the brain is toxic because it allows too much calcium into the brain, which creates more free radicals. The brain oxidizes faster than any other part of the body because it is primarily composed of fat and fat oxidizes quickly. Keeping the brain free of unnecessary free radicals is important. A free radical is an unpaired electron looking for a partner. When the free radical finds a partner, a cell is destroyed. Taking antioxidants such as vitamin C, vitamin E, the nutrient CoEnzyme 10, and the minerals selenium and zinc help prevent unnecessary free radical damage in the brain and throughout the body.

Summary:

Cognitive decline can be prevented. Even if you or someone you know or love has some form of cognitive decline, the situation is not hopeless. Because memories are stored in many parts of the brain, you can actually rebuild some of the circuitry in your brain and improve your memory if you eat wisely, take the appropriate vitamins, minerals and smart drugs, exercise your mind and body, balance your hormone levels and control your response to the stress in your life. You have heard the term, "Use it or lose it." This applies to your brain as well as other skills or attributes you may have. As you age, it is important to keep learning new things. Every time you learn something new, more dendrites form in the brain. The more we learn, hopefully, the more wisdom we gain. Read, write, draw, play a musical instrument, engage in stimulating conversations, pursue interesting hobbies and keep busy. Your brain also needs time to relax so try to decrease the stress levels in your life. In the next chapter we will discuss some brain relaxing therapies that you should consider. Before concluding this chapter, we wanted to mention some of the "brain boosting" medications we recommend to our patients.

Smart Drugs:

There are certain prescription medications as well as nutritional supplements, which have the ability to enhance your cognitive ability. In the following paragraphs, we will discuss the medications and supplements, we recommend for many of our patients.

Deprenyl, a prescription medication, has been studied since the 1950's. Deprenyl increases libido, improves memory, enhances attention and language abilities and most importantly it slows the progression of Parkinson's disease. Deprenyl improves a person's reaction time and it increases energy and vitality. Deprenyl is a selective MAO inhibitor. MAO is an enzyme that breaks down neurotransmitters. Deprenyl stimulates the substantia nigra region in the brain where the neurotransmitter, dopamine regulates sex drive and motor control. Deprenyl protects the substantia nigra from the degenerative effects of disease and aging. After the age of 40, dopamine levels in the brain can decrease by as much as thirteen (13) percent per decade. When dopamine levels are only 30% of the youthful range, Parkinson's disease appears. When people with

Parkinson's disease have only have about 10% of the dopamine levels they had in their youth, they die. Deprenyl increases the lifespan of dopamine neurons and is now also being used for patients with Alzheimer's disease. Because of its incredible effect on enhancing dopamine levels, we recommend 5 mg daily of Deprenyl (also known as Selegeline or Eldepryl) to many our patients over 45 years of age and 5 mg every other day to patients under 45 years of age, who show signs of mental decline.

Piracetam, is known as an intelligence booster. It enhances memory with no side effects. Piracetam is known as a Nootropic medication, which means it acts on the mind. Piracetam increases the communication between the right and the left-brain and has been used successfully to treat dyslexia. Piracetam increases creativity because it increases the use of the neurotransmitter acetylcholine. Because Piracetam increases the use of acetylcoline, we recommend taking the supplement choline when taking Piracetam. Piracetam, when combined with Hydergine is five times more effective. The dose for Piracetam can range from 1600 mg to 2400 mg per day.

Oxiracetam works in the same manner as Piracetam but it seems better at improving psychosomatic and neurological symptoms. Oxiracetam also decreases clot formation. It is being studied for use with Alzheimer's patients.

Pyroglutamate (PCA) is an amino acid that is used to improve memory. The standard dose is 500 - 1000 mg daily.

Vinpocetine is a memory enhancer. It comes from the periwinkle plant. Vinpocetine increases cerebral blood flow by increasing red blood cells and decreasing the thickness of the blood. It has anticonvulsant properties and increases the production of the brain cell energy molecule known as ATP. Vinpocetine improves cerebral metabolism overall. The standard dose of Vinpocetine is 5 to 45 mg daily but we have found that three 30 mg tabs daily, two in the morning and one in the afternoon, provide maximum benefit from this supplement.

Acetyl L Carnitine, which is found naturally in milk, transports fats into the mitochondria. The mitochondria are the energy power-houses in every cell. Because of its direct involvement with the mitochondria, Acetyl L Carnitine can improve depression because it maintains a constant supply of energy to the brain. Acetyl L Carnitine has a neuro-protective effect as well as a brain nourishing effect. It increases attention span and prevents fatty deposit build-up in the brain. The standard dose is 500 mg - 2000 mg daily.

Lucidryl is an intelligence booster and a powerful free radical scavenger. It decreases fat deposit build-up in the brain and repairs synapses. Since Lucidryl can have a stimulating effect, it is best to take it in the morning. The standard dose is 1000 to 3000 mg per day.

Choline is a precursor to the neurotransmitter acetylcholine, which is important for memory. Choline improves memory by increasing the amount of acetylcholine. The standard dose of choline is 250 mg daily. Too much choline can cause diarrhea.

Lecithin contains phosphatidyl choline. Lecithin repairs nerve and brain cells and helps metabolize fats. It also regulates cholesterol levels and nourishes the myelin sheath around nerve fibers. It should not be used in patients with manic depression because it can cause more depression. The standard dose is 3 GM daily.

DHEA (dehydroepiandrosterone) is a steroidal hormone produced in the adrenal glands. It has anti-obesity, anti-tumor, anti-aging and anti-cancer properties. DHEA protects brain cells. There is 6.5 more DHEA in the brain cells than other cells in the body. DHEA enhances memory and immune system function. It is important to keep serum DHEA Sulfate levels in the range of a 25-year old. The standard dose for DHEA is between 25 mg and 150 mg daily, depending on serum DHEA Sulfate levels.

DMAE (dimethylaminoethanol) is found in the brain in small amounts. DMAE is a brain enhancer. It increases mood, increases memory, increases learning capabilities, increases intelligence and promotes sound sleep. DMAE increases the production of the neurotransmitter acetylcholine. The standard dose is 500 mg - 1000 mg daily.

Ginkgo Biloba is an herb that comes from the ginkgo biloba tree. It has been around for 300 years. Ginkgo Biloba improves cerebral circulation, mental alertness and overall brain functioning. It improves brain metabolism and decreases blood clotting. It also improves nerve cell transmission and is a powerful antioxidant. The standard dose is 120 mg to 240 mg daily.

Ginseng increases resistance to stress. It improves brain function, improves concentration, enhances memory, and improves learning capabilities. Ginseng can normalize heart rhythm, normalize blood sugar levels, normalize cholesterol levels and increase metabolic functions. Ginseng quenches free radicals and generally normalizes activities in the body. Additionally, Ginseng regulates energy in the body and the brain. The standard dose is 500 mg - 3000 mg daily.

Hydergine is an extract of Ergot, which is a fungus that grows on rye. Hydergine has anti-hypertensive properties and it improves cognition. Hydergine increases blow flow and oxygen levels in the brain. It enhances brain cell metabolism, protects the brain from free radical damage, prevents increased cortisol levels in the brain and eliminates age spots (lipofuscin) on the brain. Lipofuscin are the brown spots found on the skin and on the nerve cells of older people. They are the waste products of free radical damage done to proteins and fats in the body. Hydergine increases intelligence, improves memory, enhances learning capabilities and recall, lowers cholesterol, reduces tiredness, decreases symptoms of dizziness and decreases symptoms of tinnitus (ringing in the ears). Hydergine mimics the effects of nerve growth factor (NGF), which stimulates the growth of dendrites in the brain. The average dose is 5mg —15 mg daily.

B Vitamins, as mentioned earlier, are important for proper brain function. Overall, the B vitamins improve the health of the nervous system and improve brain function. The B vitamins also have a profound effect on motor control. Vitamin B1 (thiamine) is an antioxidant that protects nerve cells. Vitamin B3 (niacin) is a memory enhancer and can lower cholesterol. Niacin should be used with caution in patients with high blood pressure. Because niacin is very acidic it is used cautiously in patients with ulcers or patients who have diabetes. Vitamin B5 (Pantothenic acid) is an antioxidant and a stamina enhancer. It is essential for the formation of steroidal hormones and is needed for making the neurotransmitter acetylcoline. Vitamin B6 helps in the production of the neurotransmitters dopamine, norepinephrine and serotonin. Vitamin B12 enhances brain function and increases learning capabilities. The recommended doses for the B vitamins are:

- Vitamin B1 (Thiamin) 100 mg daily
- Vitamin B2 100 mg daily
- Vitamin B3 (Niacin) 50 mg of niacin and 150 mg of niacinamide daily
- Vitamin B5 400-mg daily
- Vitamin B6 100 mg daily
- Vitamin B12 400 mcg daily
- Biotin 600 mcg daily

Vitamin C discussed earlier, is a powerful antioxidant and assists in the manufacture of neurotransmitters and nerve cell structures. The recommended daily therapeutic dose for vitamin C is 2000 mg daily.

Vitamin E is a fat-soluble antioxidant. It protects brain cells from free radical damage. Vitamin E is one of the most important antioxidants you can take to prevent brain cell damage. The recommend daily dose of vitamin E is between 400 and 800 mg every morning.

Melatonin is a neuropeptide secreted by the pineal gland in the brain. Melatonin inhibits atherosclerosis; decreases triglyceride levels and improves cellular immunity. Melatonin is a powerful antioxidant and also regulates our sleep patterns. As people age, melatonin levels decrease, which can cause sleep disturbances, memory disorders and decreased thinking ability. When melatonin is taken about 30 minutes before bedtime, it can improve sleep and enhance mental performance during waking hours. Melatonin also inhibits tumor growth. The average dose is between 1 mg and 10 mg per night. The minimum dose of Melatonin for any patient over the age of forty is one milligram every night before bedtime.

<u>Phosphatidylserine</u> is found in all cells but more predominately in brain cells. It keeps brain cells "cleaned-out" and it also enhances brain glucose metabolism and increases neuro receptor sites. Phosphatidylserine encourages nerve growth of damaged nerve networks. Phosphatidylserine has been used successfully in treating depression in older patients. It may cause slight nausea and should not be used with patients who are on anticoagulants. The standard dose is 100 mg daily.

<u>Pregnenolone</u> is a steroidal hormone precursor and is made from cholesterol. It is a memory enhancer and has also been used for years to treat the symptoms of arthritis. The standard dose of Pregnenolone is 100 mg daily.

Brain Exercise:
One of the mandatory screening tests we include as part of our comprehensive Evaluation Day is a cognitive assessment test developed by the Cognitive Care System Corporation in Irvine, California. The Cognitive Care System is an Internet based measurement program that has been designed to evaluate, monitor and improve cognitive health. It is much more accurate and sensitive than many current psychometric tests and can more readily detect early signs of cognitive impairment such as memory loss, slow reaction times and depression.

This testing system can assess your brain's efficiency and information processing speed. The tests included in the system help the physician detect and treat subtle changes in memory, thinking and attention before they become big problems.

Patients 40 years of age and older, patients with a family history of Alzheimer's disease, patients diagnosed with Attention Deficit Disorder and patients taking medications that may be impairing memory should take this test. It has been our experience that most patients score within the normal range but we have had a small percentage of patients that have scored outside the normal range. When this occurs, treatment, including brain exercises, can be implemented. The brain exercises recommended are really a form of anaerobic exercises specifically designed to improve cognitive abilities. Your brain needs specific and effective exercise, just like the rest of your body.

Just as we recommend a comprehensive exercise program for all of our patients, we also recommend brain exercises for all of our patients. The Cognitive Care System provides an at-home interactive set of brain exercises called ThinkFast! ThinkFast! is a series of six fun and stimulating memory challenges. Patients who exercise their brains regularly by using ThinkFast! have shown improvement in awareness, alertness, reaction time, decision-making, memory and concentration. Once a baseline test has been done, we encourage our patients to be tested annually, to measure their improvement. We will also test patients, at any time, if they notice any abnormalities in their cognitive abilities.

Your cognitive health, as stated at the beginning of this chapter, is vital to your overall health and well-being. We can offer our professional recommendations but it will be up to you, on a daily basis, to implement those recommendations. The choice is yours.

REMEMBER THIS

- If you eat a hormonally correct diet, exercise at least three to five times per week and find a well-trained and qualified anti-aging physician to assist you with naturally returning your hormones to a youthful range, your brain health will also improve because your brain, like other parts of your body, is an organ that is made out of flesh and blood

- Ensuring that your brain will continue to function properly, even as you age chronologically, is the most important thing you can do for yourself

- Not all cognitive decline is caused by Alzheimer's disease

- Many things can cause age related cognitive decline (ARCD) including elevated cortisol levels (found in people with chronic stress) decreased blood flow to the brain and decreased hormonal levels throughout the body

- Dementia, in any form, is generally defined as a loss of circuitry in the brain

- By the year 2050, 14 million people in the United States will have Alzheimer's Disease

- The exact cause of Alzheimer's disease is unknown at this time. There may not even be an exact cause but a combination of things that contribute to the manifestation of the disease and the contributing factors may be different for every individual inflicted with the disease

- Alzheimer's disease causes brain cells to die

- When brain cells die in significant numbers, the brain can shrink and change shape

- In your lifetime, approximately 20% of your brain cells will die

- The chances of acquiring Alzheimer's disease increase with age

- Alzheimer's is more common in women and also more common if someone in your family has the disease

- If a family member has Alzheimer's your chances of getting it are four times greater than someone who does not have a family member diagnosed with Alzheimer's disease

- You inherit one set of genes from your mother and one set of genes from your father. Researchers have found the Apo E (apolipoprotein E) gene is somehow connected to the incidence of Alzheimer's disease. There are three kinds of Apo E genes. Apo E-2 protects individuals from Alzheimer's, Apo E-3 increases the risk factor for the possible occurrence of Alzheimer's and Apo E-4 almost certainly increases the odds of getting Alzheimer's. If you received an Apo E-2 gene from both your mother and your father, it would seem that your chances of getting Alzheimer's are quite low. However, worst-case scenario, if you inherited an Apo E-4 gene from both your mother and your father, your chances of getting Alzheimer's are quite high. The good news is that most people have one or two Apo E-3 genes and their risk of developing Alzheimer's is somewhere in the middle

- The onset of Alzheimer's can take from one to ten years

- Some of the characteristics of Alzheimer's are a severe and continual decline in cognitive abilities for which no other known cause can be identified

- Patients in the early stages of Alzheimer's become increasingly forgetful and find it difficult to carry out complex thought processes

- Presently, medical science has suggested that some of the contributing factors to the disease may be the following:

  - Genetic predisposition to the disease (explained earlier)
  - Abnormal calcium regulation in the nerve cells in the brain

- Toxic levels of aluminum, lead, iron or some other heavy metal in the body
- Malnutrition
- Decreased blood flow to the brain
- Extensive free radical damage
- Environmental toxins
- Hormonal imbalances in the brain
- Some type of slow acting virus that has yet to be identified
- Immune system malfunction
- Excessive levels of cortisol in the body

- One major contributing factor to Alzheimer's Disease and overall brain deterioration, we believe, is too much cortisol in the body

- We need cortisol in our bodies but not too much. When we are in stressful situations, the adrenal glands, which sit on top of your kidneys, release cortisol, which assists in controlling the body's use of fats, proteins and carbohydrates and helps us respond efficiently to stress

- If we are chronically stressed, cortisol levels will remain abnormally high and rob the brain of the glucose it needs to thrive

- Too much cortisol for long periods of time will destroy not millions but billions of brain cells

- Alzheimer's patients have a significantly decreased amount of acetylcholine (the memory transporter) in their brains; memory in these patients can be decreased by as much as ninety (90) percent

- Your brain is the most important organ in the body

- In most humans, the brain usually weighs a little less than three pounds

- Brain size does not determine intelligence

- Do not confuse your brain with your mind. Your brain is an organ in the body and your mind is the enigma that makes each of us all that we are

- Your brain controls everything in your body

- If your brain is the conductor of the orchestra, then the conductor needs to be in optimal form to ensure that all members of the orchestra are performing to their fullest capacity

- Your brain needs fuel, in the form of glucose, to function and it needs about twenty-five percent of the circulating blood in your body

- Your brain has three major regions known as the brain stem, the cerebellum and the cerebrum

- Your brain stem or primary brain was the first part of your brain to be developed. It rests on top of your spinal column and controls your breathing and heartbeat. It also is a relay center for all of your senses

- The cerebellum, which sits behind your brain stem, controls your movement and muscle action. The cerebellum is the memory center for all forms of movement. The more movements you master, the more developed the cerebellum will be

- The cerebrum sits on top of your brain stem and your cerebellum. The cerebrum controls your thoughts, your memory and your emotions

- A thin beige layer known as the neocortex covers the cerebrum. The neocortex makes you the person you are and is known as the "thinking" part of the brain. The neocortex has a surface area of about 2 1/2 square feet but due to all the "nooks and crannies" in the brain, very little of the neocortex is visible

- The more nooks and crannies you have, supposedly the more intelligent you are. Actually, the number of connections between the neurons in the brain determines intelligence

- The cerebrum is comprised of four lobes. The frontal lobe, located on the forward part of the cerebrum, is where your abstract problem solving takes place, the parietal lobe, which is right behind the frontal lobe, processes the information from your senses, the occipital lobe, which is positioned at the base of your brain, controls your vision and the temporal lobe, located on the right and left side of the cerebrum, close to your temples, governs your hearing, your language capabilities and your memory

- The right side of the cerebrum (your emotion center) is predominately dedicated to creative processes while the left side of the cerebrum (the logic center) focuses more on analytical thinking. Generally speaking, females have a more developed right brain and males a more developed left-brain. The right and left side of the brain is joined by a sophisticated system of nerve fibers known as the corpus callosum. Usually, this band of nerve fibers is denser in females and may explain why females may have better communication between the right and the left brain and why males may have more compartmentalized capabilities, such as increased aptitudes in the areas of engineering and mathematics

- Located in the cerebrum, just below the corpus collusum and sitting on top of the brain stem, are the hypothalmus, the hippocampus, the amygdala, the thalamus and the pituitary gland, which comprise the limbic system in the brain or the emotion center of the brain. The hippocampus is your brain's memory center and stores your short term as well as a few long-term memories. Most long-term memories are sent to the neocortex by the hippocampus

- The hippocampus is very vulnerable to the effects of Alzheimer's disease and this may explain why Alzheimer's patients lose their short-term memory before they lose their long-term memory

- When you are in trouble, the hypothalmus tells your body to increase the production of adrenaline. The hypothalmus controls sexual function, body temperature, thirst and hunger. It sends messages to the pituitary gland, which in turn sends messages to the body through its own set of hormones. The hypothalmus tells the body how to respond to different stimuli after the neocortex, amygdala and the hippocampus have determined the importance of the stimuli

- At the center of the emotional processing center is the amygdala. Working with the hippocampus and the neocortex, the amygdala determines the degree of emotion in each of your thoughts. If you did not have an amygdala in your brain, you would not have any emotion

- The thalamus processes all incoming messages (with the exception of smell) and sends them to the correct processing center in the brain

- The pituitary gland, which is only the size of a pea, is the master endocrine gland. It tells all of your other endocrine glands what to do by releasing hormones or sending releasing factors that affect hormones in other parts of the body

- The limbic system is where thought and emotion converge and mind and body unite. If the limbic system is overloaded with too much emotion, in the form of anxiety and fear, it can be damaging

- Your endocrine system starts with the limbic system. The endocrine system controls your body. The endocrine system is a group of glands throughout your body that secrete hormones

- Hormones are the chemicals that travel throughout the body to activate other organs in the body by triggering target cells in each organ. In your brain, hormones are responsible for triggering emotions

- The glands in the endocrine system are the hypothalamus and the pituitary gland, the pineal gland, which secretes melatonin, the parathyroid glands, which control the level of calcium in the blood, the thyroid gland, which controls your immune system and metabolism, the thymus gland, which produces "T" cells that help fight disease and infection, the liver, which regulates most of the bodies chemicals and clears the blood of harmful substances, the pancreas, which secretes necessary digestive juices and insulin and glucagon, the adrenal glands, which secrete aldosterone, cortisol and various androgen hormones into the body, the kidneys, which regulate blood and electrolytes and eliminate waste products, the ovaries in females, which secrete the female sex hormones and the testes in males, which secrete the male sex hormones

- The liver and kidneys are not glands but they secrete hormones

- Your sex hormones, testosterone, DHEA, estrogen and progesterone effect how well you think, how much you remember, how good you feel emotionally and how well you perform physically

- Females with therapeutic levels of natural estrogen seem to have a slower progression of memory loss

- Low DHEA levels can impact memory

- Returning DHEA levels to a therapeutic level can enhance memory

- Your brain runs on electricity

- There is enough electricity in your brain to light a 25-watt light bulb

- Your thoughts travel along an electrical current that is created by chemical processes in your body

- The electrical currents in your brain are known as memory chains or memory traces

- The memory chains resemble a tree, with a root system and many branches. These little brain cell trees are so small that approximately 20,000 of them would fit in the head of a pin

- These trees are more commonly called neurons

- The root system of the neuron is called the axons and the branches of the neuron are called dendrites

- When you have a thought, information flows into the axons to the center or nucleus of the neuron and out to the dendrites. The thought, driven by an electrical charge and converted into a neu-

rotransmitter then passes to the next neuron via a synapse
- The synapse is the gap between neurons

- Brain cells never touch but are connected by chemicals known as neurotransmitters, which help the thought travel or swim across the synapse to the next neuron. There are hundreds of known neurotransmitters and each one has a different function that express different feelings or emotions

- The most important transmitter for memory and thought is acetylcholine. Acetylcoline is the most plentiful of all the neuro-transmitters. Acetylcoline also helps generate muscle movement. Acetylcoline is necessary for helping males achieve erection and orgasm. It also controls the blood flow to the genitals in both females and males

- People with age associated memory loss most likely have low levels of acetylcholine

- Estrogen, lecithin, the B vitamins, vitamin C and certain minerals enhance the production of acetylcoline

- Norepinephrine, another important neurotransmitter, helps the brain to be more alert in times of stress

- Norepinephrine is necessary for transporting short-term memories from the hippocampus to long-term storage in the neocortex. Because of norepinephrine we are able to remember, quite well, exciting or stressful events in or lives. Norepinephrine assists in regulating your sexual drive, helps stimulate your metabolism and helps you maintain a positive mood. Too much norepineph-rine can keep you awake at night or decrease your appetite

- The neurotransmitter dopamine primarily controls physical movement

- Patients with Parkinson's disease have low dopamine levels

- As we age, our dopamine levels decrease and that is why it is said that if you live long enough, you will eventually develop

Parkinson's disease

- Dopamine enhances immune system function, improves your libido, improves your mood and improves your ability to remember

- Dopamine also stimulates the pituitary gland to secrete human growth hormone

- A medication called Deprenyl is noted for increasing levels of dopamine in the body

- Serotonin is the neurotransmitter that induces sleep and controls pain

- Serotonin is known as the "feel good" neurotransmitter

- Serotonin is second in importance of all the neurotransmitters

- L-glutamate is the neurotransmitter that helps you create new memories and recall old memories. L-glutamate helps neutralize the chronic stress response and therefore, the over-production of cortisol

- Cognitive function can be impaired when levels of L-glutamate are low

- The neurotransmitter that has a calming effect on your brain and keeps it from being over stimulated is gamma-aminobutyric acid, more commonly known as GABA. GABA is essential for relaxation and sleep

- Endorphins, although not really a neurotransmitter, have many of the same effects as neurotransmitters. Endorphins relieve anxiety and pain and are released by the body in response to any type of major emotional or physical stress

- When you exercise you increase endorphin production

- Endorphins help you focus, concentrate and keep interested in what you are doing

- Endorphins are the connection between the mind and the immune system

- Neurotransmitters are critical for life

- Every brain cell has a small portion of a complete memory

- Your thoughts or your senses create pieces of memory

- In each brain cell, ribonucleic acid (RNA) is the brain cell memory bank

- Memories are stored in the RNA in the form of "coded" proteins. When information enters the brain through hearing, seeing or doing, it is encoded by brain cells as a memory

- There are three types of memory. Your hearing or auditory memory is stored in the neocortex on the left side of the brain. Visual memories are stored in the neocortex on the right side of the brain and your doing or kinesthetic memory is stored in the cerebellum

- Kinesthetic memory is usually the memory the lasts the longest but visual and auditory memories can reside in long term memory in people with healthy brains

- Memories are sent to long-term storage via the limbic system

- If a fact or an event stimulates you, the neurotransmitter norepinephrine imprints memories on your brain

- Another way memories are transported to long-term storage is by repeating the fact or thought over and over

- The more you think about a piece of information, the more familiar it becomes. This is known as long-term potentiation

- The more a memory is repeated, the easier it is for the thought or memory to be processed by the brain

- Brain cells can only survive for two to four minutes without oxygen and glucose, which is supplied by your blood

- The brain utilizes about twenty-five (25) percent of the circulating blood in the body

- Strokes can cause dementia if too many brain cells die

- Poor nutrition, certain pharmaceutical medications, recreational drugs, alcohol, cigarette smoking, environmental toxins and allergic substances can cause irreparable harm to the brain

- Chronic use of alcohol can shrink various areas of the brain and destroy the protective myelin sheath that surrounds nerve fibers

- Certain sedatives, painkillers and some antidepressants can severely impact your brain's capabilities. Valium, Darvon, Percodan and Elavil are just a few of the medications that can contribute to cognitive decline

- Inadequate levels of vitamin C can decrease brain function

- The B vitamins are very important for brain function. Vitamin B1 (thiamine) and vitamin B12 are needed to produce acetylcoline. Vitamin B12 also helps build the protective myelin sheath and prevents pernicious anemia, which can deplete oxygen levels in the brain. Niacin (Vitamin B3) prevents a form of psychosis and helps people relax because it is essential in the formation of the neurotransmitter GABA

- The brain needs adequate levels of copper, zinc, magnesium, iron, iodine and other minerals to function

- Smoking is hazardous to your health and to your brain's health. If you smoke, you are not only damaging your lungs but also constricting your blood vessels. The same vessels that carry oxygen to your brain

- Exposure to environmental toxins and heavy metals can impair your brain. Aluminum, lead and mercury are all harmful to your brain. Lead poisoning can cause brain swelling

- Many industrial waste products and pesticides contain arsenic and other substances that threaten brain health

- Food allergies and certain other allergic responses can damage your brain

- Auditory memory capabilities decline faster than visual memory capabilities until about age 80

- As memory declines, so does someone's creativity because creativity is interwoven to memory

- Memory loss can cause depression and/or depression can cause memory loss

- Poor circulation also damages your brain

- Elevated cortisol levels damage your brain

- The brain oxidizes faster than any other part of the body because it is primarily composed of fat and fat oxidizes quickly

- Taking antioxidants such as vitamin C, vitamin E, the nutrient CoEnzyme 10, and the minerals selenium and zinc help prevent unnecessary free radical damage in the brain and throughout the body

- Cognitive decline can be prevented

- Memories are stored in many parts of the brain and you can actually rebuild some of the circuitry in your brain and improve your memory if you eat wisely, take the appropriate vitamins, minerals and smart drugs, exercise your mind and body, balance your hormone levels and control your response to the stress in your life

- As you age, it is important to keep learning new things

- Every time you learn something new, more dendrites form in the brain

- There are certain prescription medications as well as nutritional supplements, which have the ability to enhance your cognitive ability

- Deprenyl, a prescription medication, increases libido, improves memory, enhances attention and language abilities and most importantly it slows the progression of Parkinson's disease

- We recommend 5 mg daily of Deprenyl (also known as Selegeline or Eldepryl) to many our patients over 45 years of age and 5 mg every other day to patients under 45 years of age, who show signs of mental decline

- Piracetam is an intelligence booster. It enhances memory with no side effects. Piracetam increases the communication between the right and the left-brain and has been used successfully to treat dyslexia. Piracetam increases creativity

- The dose for Piracetam can range from 1600 mg to 2400 mg per day

- Oxiracetam works in the same manner as Piracetam but it seems better at improving psychosomatic and neurological symptoms. Oxiracetam decreases clot formation

- Pyroglutamate (PCA) is an amino acid that is used to improve memory. The standard dose is 500 - 1000 mg daily

- Vinpocetine is a memory enhancer. Vinpocetine increases cerebral blood flow by increasing red blood cells and decreasing the thickness of the blood. Vinpocetine improves cerebral metabolism overall

- The standard dose of Vinpocetine is 5 to 45 mg daily but we have found that three 30 mg tabs daily, two in the morning and one in the afternoon, provide maximum benefit from this supplement

- Acetyl L Carnitine transports fats into the mitochondria. The mitochondria are the energy powerhouses in every cell. Because of its direct involvement with the mitochondria, Acetyl L Carnitine can improve depression because it maintains a constant supply of energy to the brain. Acetyl L Carnitine has a neuro-protective effect as well as a brain nourishing effect. It increases attention span and prevents fatty deposit build-up in the brain

- The standard dose of Acetyl L Carnitine is 500 mg - 2000 mg daily

- Lucidryl is an intelligence booster and a powerful free radical scavenger

- The standard dose for Lucidryl is 1000 to 3000 mg per day

- Choline improves memory by increasing the amount of acetyl-choline

- The standard dose of choline is 250 mg daily

- Lecithin repairs nerve and brain cells and helps metabolize fats. It also regulates cholesterol levels and nourishes the myelin sheath around nerve fibers. It should not be used in patients with manic depression because it can cause more depression

- The standard dose for Lecithin is 3 GM daily

- DHEA protects brain cells. There is 6.5 more DHEA in the brain cells than other cells in the body

- The standard dose for DHEA is between 25 mg and 150 mg daily, depending on serum DHEA Sulfate levels

- DMAE increases mood, increases memory, increases learning

capabilities, increases intelligence, and promotes sound sleep. DMAE increases the production of the neurotransmitter acetylcholine

• The standard dose of DMAE is 500 mg - 1000 mg daily

• Ginkgo Biloba improves cerebral circulation, mental alertness and overall brain functioning. It improves brain metabolism and decreases blood clotting. It also improves nerve cell transmission and is a powerful antioxidant

• The standard dose of Ginkgo Biloba is 120 mg to 240 mg daily

• Ginseng increases resistance to stress. It improves brain function, improves concentration, enhances memory, and improves learning capabilities. Ginseng can normalize heart rhythm, normalize blood sugar levels, normalize cholesterol levels and increase metabolic functions. Ginseng quenches free radicals and generally normalizes activities in the body. Additionally, Ginseng regulates energy in the body and the brain

• The standard dose of Ginseng is 500 mg - 3000 mg daily

• Hydergine has anti-hypertensive properties and it improves cognition. Hydergine increases blow flow and oxygen levels in the brain. It enhances brain cell metabolism, protects the brain from free radical damage, prevents increased cortisol levels in the brain and eliminates age spots (lipofuscin) on the brain

• Hydergine increases intelligence, improves memory, enhances learning capabilities and recall, lowers cholesterol, reduces tiredness, decreases symptoms of dizziness and decreases symptoms of tinnitus (ringing in the ears). Hydergine mimics the effects of nerve growth factor (NGF) which stimulates the growth of dendrites in the brain

• The average dose of Hydergine is 5mg —15 mg daily

- The B vitamins improve the health of the nervous system and improve brain function

- The B vitamins also have a profound effect on motor control

- Vitamin B1 (thiamine) is an antioxidant that protects nerve cells

- Vitamin B3 (niacin) is a memory enhancer and can lower cholesterol

- Vitamin B5 (Pantothenic acid) is an antioxidant and a stamina enhancer. It is essential for the formation of steroidal hormones and is needed for making the neurotransmitter acetylcoline

- Vitamin B6 helps in the production of the neurotransmitters dopamine, norepinephrine and serotonin

- Vitamin B12 enhances brain function and increases learning capabilities

The recommended doses for the B vitamins are:
  - Vitamin B1 (Thiamin) 100 mg daily
  - Vitamin B2 100 mg daily
  - Vitamin B3 (Niacin) 50 mg of niacin and 150 mg of niacinamide daily
  - Vitamin B5 400-mg daily
  - Vitamin B6 100 mg daily
  - Vitamin B12 400 mcg daily
  - Biotin 600 mcg daily

- Vitamin C is a powerful antioxidant and assists in the manufacture of neurotransmitters and nerve cell structures

- The recommended daily therapeutic dose for vitamin C is 2000 mg daily

- Vitamin E is a fat-soluble antioxidant. It protects brain cells from free radical damage

- Vitamin E is one of the most important antioxidants you can take

to prevent brain cell damage
- The recommend daily dose of vitamin E is between 400 and 800 mg every morning

- Melatonin is a powerful antioxidant and also regulates our sleep patterns

- Melatonin also inhibits tumor growth

- The average dose for Melatonin is between 1 mg and 10 mg per night

- The minimum dose of Melatonin for any patient over the age of forty is one milligram every night before bedtime

- Phosphatidylserine keeps brain cells "cleaned-out" and it also enhances brain glucose metabolism and increases neuro receptor sites. Phosphatidylserine encourages nerve growth of damaged nerve networks

- The standard dose for Phosphatidylserine is 100 mg daily

- Pregnenolone is a memory enhancer

- The standard dose of Pregnenolone is 100 mg daily

- Your brain needs specific and effective exercise, just like the rest of your body

- Just as we recommend a comprehensive exercise program for all of our patients, we also recommend brain exercises for all of our patients. The Cognitive Care System provides an at-home interactive set of brain exercises call ThinkFast!

- ThinkFast! is a series of six fun and stimulating memory challenges. Patients who exercise their brains regularly by using ThinkFast! have shown improvement in awareness, alertness, reaction time, decision-making, memory and concentration
- Your cognitive health is vital to your overall health and well-being

CHAPTER FOURTEEN

STRESS REDUCTION

By this time in the book, we assume that you are well on your way to becoming more healthy and vibrant and that you have a better understanding that anti-aging medicine is based upon sound and effective scientific principles. As we tell our patients, "We can recommend specific treatments that will improve your health and well-being but to be truly effective, you must be willing to make some lifestyle changes and a daily commitment to improving the quality of your life. We can show you what needs to be done but it is up to you to do it." If you are eating correctly, exercising appropriately, replacing hormone levels naturally (under the guidance of your anti-aging physician) and you are doing everything possible to maintain and/or improve your health, you will see the results. If however, you are doing all of these things and still have not managed the stress in your life, you may be sabotaging your efforts.

Stress is a fact of life. How we manage the stress in our lives is what is important. Stress is defined as "any stimulus that disturbs or interferes with the normal equilibrium of an organism." Those of us who have been in the medical field for some time know that the only real crisis in life is when someone stops breathing. When we stop breathing it is all over. So, let us each pay attention to our breathing, as you will learn later, and begin to accept what we cannot change and change what we can with intelligence, grace and an abundance of patience.

When we allow ourselves to become unbalanced by circumstances that may be beyond our control, we become stressed. Each of us has a choice in how we choose to respond to all of the ups and downs life presents. What is your choice?

In prehistoric times, our human response to stress seemed appropriate. In order to survive the elements, starvation and various natural predators, our cortisol levels increased when we were faced with danger. The elevated cortisol levels in our brains caused a "fight or flight" response. We now know, however, that elevated cortisol levels in the brain, for any length of time, can destroy brain cells and be very harmful to the body, overall. So, how do we manage this innate stress response in today's modern world? How do we keep our cortisol levels balanced? We do it by effectively managing our responses to the stress in our lives.

We believe that every individual should find some quiet time, each and every day, to reflect upon nothing at all. We need to be silent and notice the world around us. We need to listen to our breathing, in and out, and marvel at how truly miraculous breathing is. When we concentrate on our breathing, it brings each of us right back into the present; right back into this moment in your life. When we think too long and too hard about yesterday and all of the "what ifs" we can become stressed. When we think too hard and too long about the future, we can become stressed. Do you take a few minutes each day to close your eyes and just feel yourself breathe? Do you try to be in this very moment? Our lives are just moments woven together to create the fabric of life. Every moment is a new beginning for each of us.

The only thing certain in life is change. How we respond to change is critical for managing the stress of living. Living is not yesterday and it is not tomorrow. Living is right now. This is your life, this very moment. Yesterday is a memory and tomorrow is only a possibility. What you do right now and how you respond to this moment is important. If you squander the moments of your life by not being truly present in your life, you will miss many great moments.

Some people move through life on autopilot. When we are on autopilot we are waiting for something unpleasant to pass or for something exciting to arrive. When you are present in your every day life, you will find that each moment of your life is quite extraordinary. You will also find that you can begin to manage stress by paying attention to the moments of your life and by focusing on your breathing.

Breathing, just like our heartbeat is something that goes on automatically for the duration of our lives and gives each of us life. Without breathing and without a beating heart, there is no life at all. We breathe to take in oxygen and rid our body of carbon dioxide. All the cells in our body need oxygen. If we stop breathing for more than a few minutes, brain cells begin to die and so will the rest of the cells in the body.

If we pay attention in our daily lives, we can begin to distinguish between what are real limitations and those that are imagined by us or scripted by our culture. In this chapter, we will share some suggestions for effectively managing the stress in your life. This chapter, however, is only an overview of some the stress-reducing techniques, that we have found useful in everyday life. If you are severely stressed, have had a heart attack, are a victim of angry outbursts, live with chronic pain or a debilitating illness, cannot sleep, have memory problems for which there is no other known cause, live and/or work in a stressful environment or have some other situation going on in your life that seems to be overwhelming you, we strongly recommend that you seek a professional to help manage your stress. There are excellent workshops and treatment centers specifically designed to manage stress. We will list some of the resources later in this chapter.

Stress at any age involves our relationship to a particular event or stressor. Our resources may become taxed and we feel overwhelmed. As many of us have experienced, a perceived threat can produce the same response in the mind and body as a real threat. We think it is beneficial to learn how to distinguish between real or imagined threats in life. A transactional view of stress can be helpful because it recognizes that it is our perception of and reaction to an event that creates the stress in our lives. Since we have no hope of controlling what is outside of ourselves, the fact that our response to a particular event can determine the degree of stress experienced (if any) allows for the possibility of modifying our reactions. As one develops more skillful ways of dealing with the events life offers we may find that our reactions to such events do not have to produce stress.

What about threats that are real such as physical limitations, illness or the loss of loved ones? If, as stated earlier, we know that life is about change, these experiences, and we all have them, can allow us to grow in compassion for all that suffer in this world and to increase our empathy for those around us who share our humanity. If we are not present in our own lives and isolate ourselves, these life-altering events can make us fearful, angry, hostile and sometimes full of self-pity. This isolated state can only increase a person's stress. No one can turn away from the unpleasant things in life forever. The more we are willing to face and deal with what life brings us, the more open we are to accepting what life is. The better we are at accepting, the less likely we are to let stress rule our lives.

Effectively dealing with stress takes practice. To be effective, you need to find some form of meditation that works for you. You can begin by paying attention to your life moment by moment and by listening to yourself breathe, when things become overwhelming. If you do not find some form of meditation, whether it is praying, various forms of yoga, body scanning or just closing your eyes and observing your breath, the feeling of being overwhelmed can become a chronic state of mind and body; a constant companion that turns even minor inconveniences into major traumas. The more drama you allow into your life, the more dramatic your life will become. Too much drama causes a person to become immobilized and ineffective. The more you practice just being in the moment, the more serene you will become.

If you are stressed, pay particular attention to what happens to your body. Do you hold your breath, does your jaw become clenched, do you grind your teeth, does your heart rate increase, does your face or neck become flushed, and do you have a knot in your stomach? What is your mind doing when you become stressed? Observe your mental and physical reactions to stress. Continue doing this until you see a pattern emerging. What triggers your stress response? Is your workload too demanding? Can you change your response to the demands of your job? Is your boss a real creep? Can you change your response to your boss? Is he/she really that important in your moment-to-moment life? Are the phone lines constantly ringing? Can you take a deep breath before answering that next phone call?

You do have choices.

You can choose to be stressed all of the time, which is not healthful or you can choose to live moment to moment, realizing that you are important and that taking a few minutes each day to simply reflect and breathe can bring harmony back into your life. Whatever you are experiencing in life that is causing you stress, you need to sit down for a moment and face it. Let whatever is triggering your stress response pass through you and once it does, it is your decision how you choose to respond to the stressor. Sometimes, we do not even know that we are stressed but our body will tell us. Not being able to sleep, feeling anxious, being angry, loss of memory, loss of concentration, being short of breath are just some of the signs of stress; stress that is not being dealt with.

Finding balance and peace in our lives must come from within. Looking outside of ourselves for our happiness and tranquility never works. Each person's journey in life is unique. Why not stop and experience that journey, if even just for a short time each day? With the exception of life and death matters, what is so important that it cannot wait for a few minutes or a few days? What will happen to all of those critical report deadlines that you are supposed to complete at work? Are you working until midnight because there was a lack of planning at the beginning of a particular project? Is your lack of planning or someone else's lack of planning creating undue stress in your life? It seems that so many people are always in a hurry? Where are they going in such a hurry? In the whole scope of things, can't they slow down and observe their life, if only for a few minutes each day? The health rewards for slowing down and taking good care of your body, your mind and your soul will be significant.

Too many times, we become stressed when our expectations about something are not met. We may expect more from a personal relationship. We may expect more from our jobs. We may expect too much of ourselves or maybe we do not think enough of ourselves, which can set the stage for abuse in our lives. Our expectations can get us into all kinds of trouble. What are expectations? What are we expecting in our lives? Are we expecting to be famous, to be rich, to have the perfect relationship? All of this "expecting" can cause stress. We set expectations for ourselves all of the time. Think about it. Maybe every Saturday morning you make a list of your expectations for the day. You may call the list tasks but they are expectations, which you have decided to make for yourself, for the day. The Saturday expectation list may include cleaning the house, doing the wash, taking the kids to their soccer games, grocery shopping, going to the dry cleaners, getting your hair cut, fixing dinner and the list goes on. What if you did not get all of these things done on Saturday? Would that be so terrible? Once again, we remind you that you do have choices, in every moment of your life, about what you can and cannot do.

Set priorities in your life. Priorities can change because life changes moment by moment. What are your priorities? If your first priority is to maintain your health and well-being, then make time in your life to do that. If you are not healthy you are not going to be the best you can be to any member of your family or the best you can be in your professional life.

Unlike expectations, which can cause undue stress, it is good to have aspirations and goals in life. However, we must realize that events in our lives can alter our goals and aspirations, which is okay; it is not the end of the world. We will get to wherever it is we are going when we are supposed to get there. Sometimes life takes us on a detour but as long as we work towards living moment by moment, we know that life will be okay, no matter what is going on. Nothing ever stays the same. As stated before, the only thing certain in life is change.

What about our egos? Our egos can cause us to become too self-important and to lose sight of what is truly valuable in life. Our egos, when not kept in balance, can make our lives or the lives of those around us more stressful then they need to be. When we practice being in the moment of our lives, we find out that our lives are okay and that our egos can be subdued and managed effectively. It is what we do every day, the little things, which make our life what it is. Are we good to ourselves? Do we treat others the way we would like to be treated? Are we present in our every day lives, conscious of our actions and reactions? We want you to be an active participant in your life and sometimes that means that you need to actively or consciously take the time to observe your life and the environment that surrounds you. When you pay attention and observe, you have given yourself the ability to experience better health and well-being. To reduce your stress and improve your quality of life, we think that Mindfulness-Based Stress Reduction Training is one of the most important gifts you can give yourself. Aren't you worth it?

Mindfulness-Based Stress Reduction training, developed by Jon Kabat-Zinn, Ph.D., at the University of Massachusetts Medical Center teaches people to be awake to every moment in their lives. If we are awake in our daily lives, we have the ability to make choices; moment to moment, rather than being on autopilot and continuing habitual patterns that may be destructive to ourselves and to others. When we learn how to calm down and put ourselves into a state of deep relaxation, we can nourish and invigorate our mind and our body. We may also, along the way, learn a great deal about just who we are.

To quote Dr. Kabat-Zinn, "Learning how to stop all your doing and shift over to a "being" mode, learning how to make time for yourself, how to slow down and nurture calmness and self-acceptance in yourself, learning to observe what your own mind is up to from moment to moment, how to watch your thoughts and how to let go of them without getting so caught up and driven by them, how to make room for new ways of seeing old problems and for perceiving the interconnectedness of things, theses are some of the lessons of mindfulness. This kind of learning involves settling into moments of being and cultivating awareness."

You do not have to be a monk to meditate. If you are willing to pay attention in your life, you can meditate. To meditate effectively takes commitment on your part. No one else can meditate for you. The more you meditate, the more relaxed you will become. We can give you some of the basic tools for beginning your meditation practice but it is up to you to daily perform the actions necessary for effective meditation that will, if you keep it up, reduce your levels of stress.

As you practice meditation, be patient and do not judge your efforts. Do not set any expectations for your meditation practice. Just accept what is happening in the moment. There are no goals to your practice. Just do it and you will become more peaceful and more in tune with yourself. As you practice, listen to your body. If you are doing some form of yoga, or some of the flexibility exercises we describe in Chapter Nine, while you meditate, then it may be important not stretch a certain part of your body, if your body is telling you that you cannot do the stretch.

Stress Reduction Exercises:
Take time each day to sit in a chair or on a cushion, in a quiet, undisturbed place and follow your breath. Do not manipulate your breathing; just notice how it is. Follow the breath as you inhale and follow the breath as you exhale. As you follow the breath, you will notice that your mind begins to wander. Close your eyes, if that feels more comfortable for you. When your mind begins to wander, bring it back to the breath. It does not matter how much the mind wanders. What is important in this stress reduction activity is coming back to the breath each time your mind wanders. This concentration on our breath forces us to be present in our lives at this moment. Isn't that all we really have is this moment in time? The more we practice watching or observing our breath, the easier it becomes and we can incorporate it into our daily activities of living. Meditating takes daily commitment, just like eating correctly, exercising, and yes, taking all of those supplements and medications, to balance your hormones; all of which, we hope, will keep your body in tip-top shape.

When you feel stressed, if you remember to concentrate on your breathing, even if just for a few minutes, you will be able to more effectively deal with the stress in your life. You can begin right now, to start managing the stress in your life by trying some of the techniques that Dr. Zinn offers his patients in his comprehensive eight-week stress reduction classes.

Some of the breathing techniques Dr. Zinn offers his students are as follows:

- Sit quietly and follow your breath as it leaves your body and as it enters your body
- Feel each breath as it enters your nostrils and as it leaves your nostrils or follow each breath by feeling your chest or abdomen as it rises and falls
- As you follow your breath, notice what your mind does. Your mind will lead you away from your breathing
- Each time your mind wanders, be aware of it and come back to the point where you are concentrating on your breath as it leaves your body and as it enters your body
- When you begin concentrating on your breathing, try to stay focused on observing your breathing for just three minutes. Notice how you feel at the end of this exercise
- Every day, sit quietly and increase the time you focus on your breathing. Be conscious of yourself observing your breathing. How do you feel?
- Over a three week period, try to increase your conscious-breathing time to thirty minutes, with the goal to reach forty-five minutes daily for meditative practice
- During the day, try to observe your breathing, for several breaths, two times per day. Notice how you felt when you did this activity in the middle of your busy workday. Keep doing this, every day and after three or four weeks, you will be doing it routinely

When we practice these simple breathing techniques, we learn that we can sit still, breathe and face discomfort, restlessness, physical pain, emotional pain or anything else life has to give us. We can become present in our moment-to-moment lives. When we are present, our stress decreases and we are more able to deal with life's challenges from a balanced perspective.

Another formal practice that can help reduce stress is called the Body Scan. Take time each day to lie down on your back, on a mat or on your bed, and spend some time with this body you inhabit; as it is at this moment. As you lie there, begin by feeling your breath as it enters and leaves your body. Notice the belly as it rises and falls. After a few moments, expand your awareness to include the body as a whole, perhaps experiencing breathing with the entire body, allowing it to sink deeper into the bed or the floor each time you exhale.

When you are ready, begin scanning your body with your mind's eye. Remember your breathing throughout the process of scanning your body. Start with the toes of your right foot and then the toes of the left foot. Feel how each toe feels. Continue moving up the body, slowly. Remember you are not trying to elicit a certain feeling or experience, you are just trying to feel what is happening in your body at this very moment. While you continue your body scan, note what you are feeling in each area of your body. Notice where there is heat, dryness, moisture, tingling, numbness or some other sensation. If you feel tightness in any part of your body, send a message to that part of the body to lengthen and release the tightness. The more you use the body scan technique in your daily life, the easier it will be for you to be aware that the sensations your body is experiencing are constantly changing. When you know this, you can effectively use the body scan to reduce the stress in your life Try doing the body scan by following the simple guidelines listed below:

- Close your eyes and concentrate on your breathing
- Begin by slowly feeling your toes, your legs, your torso, your lower back, your upper back, your arms, your shoulders, your chest rising and falling with each breath and finally feel your neck and head. Notice any area of tightness and send messages to the affected area to release the tightness or discomfort
- Notice how your mind wanders. Keep bringing your mind back to your breathing and your body scan. Notice how relaxed you become as you focus on your breathing and the body scan
- Be conscious of how you feel as you scan your body. Can you feel the tensions leaving your body?
- Think of the body scan as a way of cleansing your body and releasing all of the toxins caused by stress. To help heal your body you must be "in" it. The body scan allows you to be "in" your body
- Try doing the body scan at least once each day. You can do it the

first thing in the morning or later in the day when you come home from work. Don't fall asleep when doing the body scan. If you need to, keep your eyes open. The purpose of this exercise is to get in touch with your body, at this very moment and to release negative energy

Various forms of yoga can teach you to become connected to your body. Hatha yoga is a form of yoga that involves gentle stretching exercises, breathing and various postures that allow you to just "be" in your body as you practice this form of meditation. Yoga can bring calmness into your life and amazingly, after a yoga session, you just may feel wonderfully energized. Yoga may not be for everyone but we encourage you to consider taking a hatha yoga class for about eight weeks, and then decide if you want to continue the practice.

Did you know that you can use your meditation practices of just "being" every time you walk, whether for exercise or just in the course of your normal daily activities? Notice how you are walking. Feel every sensation of your walking as you put one foot in front of the other. You can also incorporate your mindfulness breathing into your walking meditation. We take walking for granted until we can no longer walk. Stop, listen and feel as you walk. Walking, when we are conscious of it, is an incredibly wonderful experience. As we become aware of our walking, we may even slow our steps down and thereby, slow down our thoughts and our metabolism.

Life is about perception. How do you see things in your life? Your vision of your life has a lot to do with the quality of your life. How you see things in your life will have a huge impact on how much stress you will allow into your life. Being awake to your every day, every moment life can improve your health and well-being. We hope you will begin incorporating some of the exercise we have mentioned in this chapter into your daily life and/or you will enroll in a stress reduction program.

As we age chronologically, if we have become present in our every day lives, we have the opportunity to be more compassionate, wiser and more open to the world around us. As we age, if we have truly opened ourselves up to life, we realize that the only sure thing in life, as stated earlier, is change. If you are practicing daily at reducing the stress in your life, if you are eating a hormonally correct diet, exercising regularly, ensuring that your hormone levels are in a youthful, therapeutic range and, if you are doing everything possible to keep your brain healthy, you have given yourself the opportunity to live a more vibrant and fulfilling life. Won't you join us on this incredible journey of making your life the best it can possibly be?

If you are interested in participating in a Mindfulness-based Stress Reduction Program, visit their website to find a program in your local area. Some books that are helpful, as you begin working daily on reducing the stress in your life are:

- Everyday Zen: Love and Work by Charlotte Joko Beck
- When Things Fall Apart: Heart Advice for Difficult Times by Pema Chodron
- Full Catastrophe Living: Using the Wisdom of Your Body and Mind to Face Stress, Pain and Illness by Jon Kabat-Zinn
- Wherever You Go There You Are: Mindfulness Meditation In Everyday Life by Jon Kabat-Zinn

REMEMBER THIS

- Stress is a fact of life

- How we manage the stress in our lives is important

- Stress is defined as "any stimulus that disturbs or interferes with the normal equilibrium of an organism"

- The only real crisis in life is when we stop breathing

- When we stop breathing it is all over

- Begin to accept what you cannot change and change what you can with intelligence, grace and an abundance of patience

- When we allow ourselves to become unbalanced by circumstances that may be beyond our control, we become stressed

- Stress causes elevated cortisol levels. Elevated cortisol levels in the brain, for any length of time, can destroy brain cells and be very harmful to the body, overall

- Find some quiet time, each and every day, to reflect upon nothing at all

- We need to be silent and notice the world around us

- Our lives are just moments woven together to create the fabric of life

- Every moment is a new beginning for each of us

- The only thing certain in life is change

- How we respond to change is critical for managing the stress of living

- Living is not yesterday and it is not tomorrow. Living is right now

- Some people move through life on autopilot

- When we are on autopilot we are waiting for something unpleasant to pass or for something exciting to arrive

- Breathing, just like your heartbeat is something that goes on automatically for the duration of your life and gives each of us life

- If we pay attention in our daily lives, we can begin to distinguish between what are real limitations and those that are imagined by us or scripted by our culture

- If you are severely stressed we strongly recommend that you seek professional assistance to help you manage your stress

- Stress at any age involves our relationship to a particular event or stressor

- We think it is beneficial to learn how to distinguish between real or imagined threats in life

- Effectively dealing with stress takes practice

- Find some form of meditation that works for you. You can begin by paying attention to your life moment by moment and by listening to yourself breathe, when things become overwhelming

- If you do not find some form of meditation, whether it is praying, various forms of yoga, body scanning or just closing your eyes and observing your breath, the feeling of being overwhelmed can become a chronic state of mind and body; a constant companion that turns even minor inconveniences into major traumas

- The more drama you allow into your life, the more dramatic your life will become

- The more you practice just being in the moment, the more serene you will become

- If you are stressed, pay particular attention to what happens to your body. Observe your mental and physical reactions to stress

- You can choose to be stressed all of the time, which is not healthful or you can choose to live moment to moment, realizing that you are important and that taking a few minutes each day to simply reflect and breathe can bring harmony back into your life

- Whatever you are experiencing in life that is causing you stress, you need to sit down for a moment and face it

- Finding balance and peace in our lives must come from within

- With the exception of life and death matters, what is so important that it cannot wait for a few minutes or a few days?

- Too many times, we become stressed when our expectations about something are not met. Expectations are only thoughts until we act upon them to make them a reality

- You do have choices, in every moment of your life, about what you can and cannot do

- Set priorities in your life

- It is good to have aspirations and goals in life. However, we must realize that events in our lives can alter our goals and aspirations, which is okay

- In life, we will get to wherever it is we are going when we are supposed to get there

- Our egos, when not kept in balance, can make our lives or the lives of those around us more stressful then they need to be

- It is what we do every day, the little things, which make our life what it is

- Are you present in your every day life, conscious of your actions and reactions?

- To reduce your stress and improve your quality of life, we think that Mindfulness-Based Stress Reduction Training is one of the most important gifts you can give yourself

- Mindfulness-Based Stress Reduction training, developed by Jon Kabat-Zinn, Ph.D., at the University of Massachusetts Medical Center teaches people to be awake to every moment in their lives

- You do not have to be a monk to meditate. If you are willing to pay attention in your life, you can meditate

- To meditate effectively takes commitment on your part

- No one else can meditate for you

- The more you meditate, the more relaxed you will become

- It is up to you to daily perform the actions necessary for effective meditation that will, if you keep it up, reduce your levels of stress

- As you practice meditation, be patient and do not judge your efforts. Do not set any expectations for your meditation practice. Just accept what is happening in the moment. There are no goals to your practice. Just do it and you will become more peaceful and more in tune with yourself

Stress Reduction Exercises:

BREATHING:
- Sit quietly and follow your breath as it leaves your body and as it enters your body

- Feel each breath as it enters your nostrils and as it leaves your nostrils or follow each breath by feeling your chest or abdomen as it rises and falls

- As you follow your breath, notice what your mind does. Your mind will lead you away from your breathing

- Each time your mind wanders, be aware of it and come back to the point where you are concentrating on your breath as it leaves your body and as it enters your body

- When you begin concentrating on your breathing, try to stay focused on observing your breathing for just three minutes. Notice how you feel at the end of this exercise

- Every day, sit quietly and increase the time you focus on your breathing. Be conscious of yourself observing your breathing. How do you feel?

- Over a three week period, try to increase your conscious-breathing time to thirty minutes, with the goal to reach forty-five minutes daily for meditative practice

- During the day, try to observe your breathing, for several breaths, two times per day. Notice how you felt when you did this activity in the middle of your busy workday. Keep doing this, every day and after three or four weeks, you will be doing it routinely

BODY SCAN:
- Close your eyes and concentrate on your breathing

- Begin by slowly feeling your toes, your legs, your torso, your lower back, your upper back, your arms, your shoulders, your chest rising and falling with each breath and finally feel your neck and head. Notice any area of tightness and send messages to the affected area to release the tightness or discomfort

- Notice how your mind wanders. Keep bringing your mind back to your breathing and your body scan. Notice how relaxed you become as you focus on your breathing and the body scan

- Be conscious of how you feel as you scan your body. Can you feel the tensions leaving your body?

- Think of the body scan as a way of cleansing your body and releasing all of the toxins caused by stress. To help heal your body you must be "in" it. The body scan allows you to be "in" your body

- Try doing the body scan at least once each day. You can do it the first thing in the morning or later in the day when you come home from work. Don't fall asleep when doing the body scan. If you need to, keep your eyes open. The purpose of this exercise is to get in touch with your body, at this very moment and to release negative energy

- Hatha yoga is a form of yoga that involves gentle stretching exercises, breathing and various postures that allow you to just "be" in your body as you practice this form of meditation

- Yoga can bring calmness into your life and amazingly, after a yoga session, you just may feel wonderfully energized

- Did you know that you can use your meditation practices of just "being" every time you walk, whether for exercise or just in the course of your normal daily activities?

- Being awake to your every day, every moment life can improve your health and well-being

- As we age chronologically, if we have become present in our every day lives, we have the opportunity to be more compassionate, wiser and more open to the world around us

- If you are interested in participating in a Mindfulness-based Stress Reduction Program, visit their website to find a program in your local area

- Some books that are helpful, as you begin working daily on reducing the stress in your life are:

  - Everyday Zen: Love and Work by Charlotte Joko Beck
  - When Things Fall Apart: Heart Advice for Difficult Times by Pema Chodron
  - Full Catastrophe Living: Using the Wisdom of Your Body and Mind to Face Stress, Pain and Illness by Jon Kabat-Zinn
  - Wherever You Go There You Are: Mindfulness Meditation In Everyday Life by Jon Kabat-Zinn

PART FOUR

THE "FOREVER AGELESS" PROGRAM

AND

FUTURE ANTI-AGING MEDICAL POSSIBILITIES

PUTTING IT ALL TOGETHER

THE TOMORROW OF ANTI-AGING MEDICINE

CHAPTER FIFTEEN

PUTTING IT ALL TOGETHER

All too soon or maybe not soon enough for some, we have come to the end of this book. We have tried to educate you about anti-aging medicine, to share with you what we do at CHI and also to give you some tools, which will help you take ownership of your health and well-being. There are no guarantees in life but for as long as you live; we hope that you will incorporate what you have learned in this book into your every day life. You can reinvent yourself and improve your health. We encourage you to share this book with your physician because we know that a hormonally correct diet, various vitamins, minerals and other supplements in therapeutic doses, exercise, bio-identical hormone replacement, brain boosting and stress reduction all lead to improved health and well-being.

This is a dynamic book that will not become outdated. Scientific breakthroughs are occurring at a rapid pace today and we want you to know about them and, as appropriate, apply the technology to your activities of daily living. Ownership of this book entitles you to access our website for quarterly updates in anti-aging medicine. We want to keep you informed about the latest trends and technologies in anti-aging medicine so you will continue to improve your health and well-being.

We hope you will find a qualified anti-aging physician soon and begin your own anti-aging program. If you cannot afford a formal anti-aging program at this time, you can learn about the Zone diet and begin eating the proper amounts and types of proteins, carbohydrates and fats. We want you to depend on proven scientific knowledge for improving the quality of your life. For optimal results with the Zone diet, it is best to calculate your daily protein requirements (see Appendix A) but if you are not willing to do that, just look at the palm of your hand. Eat favorable proteins five times per day in the amount that is the size and thickness of the palm of your hand. No one else's palm will do. Fill the rest of your plate with lots of favorable fruits and vegetables and there you have it, you are basically eating in the "Zone." If you are an athlete, your protein requirements may be higher than for the average person, therefore, we strongly recommend that you calculate your daily protein requirements based on your increased activity level.

You must also begin to drink at least eight 8-ounce glasses of purified water daily. The more water you drink the better it is for you. The body needs to be hydrated with purified water to stay healthy. Slowly begin to cutback on other types of beverages you may be consuming and replace them with water.

Once you get into the habit of eating in the Zone, you will feel better and guess what, your cholesterol, triglycerides, fasting insulin and blood glucose levels may also improve dramatically. Adult onset diabetes and cardiovascular disease have both been linked to elevated insulin levels and the Zone diet keeps insulin levels in a therapeutic range.

We do not think that you should deprive yourself of your favorite dessert or pasta dish completely. We certainly do not deprive ourselves but we just eat less of that fancy dessert or delicious pasta dish and we do not eat it too often. The more you eat in the Zone, the better you feel and you will find that you will want to maintain that feeling. So, over a period of time, eating a hormonally correct diet becomes a way of life.

When we eat out of the Zone, we know it right away because we do not think as clearly and we feel sluggish. When we eat in the Zone five times per day, our brains work better, we have more energy and our moods remain quite optimistic all day long. It is a very good feeling. When you eat fruits and vegetables, try to avoid fruits and vegetables with a high sugar content, which means a high glycemic index. Some fruits and vegetables to avoid are bananas, mangos, pineapples and potatoes. In Appendix B we have listed some foods to avoid and some foods that are good for you.

If you are eating a hormonally correct diet, the next thing you need to do is find a good "supra vitamin" that will give you the antioxidant protection you need and also supply you with other necessary supplements for good health. You also need to take at least one gram of omega three fish oil daily. Added to that, we believe that the antioxidants CoQ10 and Carnosine are very important to take every day. If you are female, unless contraindicated, we strongly recommend a calcium, magnesium and boron supplement daily.

We each take approximately fifty pills per day because it is the best thing we have right now to fight the terminal disease we have which is called aging. Do we get sick and tired of all those pills? The answer is yes, of course we do but we practice what we preach and we know all those pills are part of the program to keep us healthy, strong and vigorous, even as we move through our fifties and beyond.

In Chapter Eight, we listed the types and amounts of supplements you should take for health improvement effects. The basic supplements and amounts are listed again in Appendix C for easy reference. Please note that if you are on anti-coagulant medication, you should check with your physician before taking aspirin, ginkgo biloba or vitamin E. If you are currently on any type of medication or have any type of health concern, please check with your physician before taking any of the supplements recommended in Chapter Eight and listed in Appendix C.

The next thing you can do for yourself is to begin some form of exercise. Use the exercises discussed in Chapter Nine or at least begin walking or doing some other form of physical exercise that you enjoy. Start slowly with your exercise program and increase the intensity and duration of your exercise routine as you progress. Set aside time, at least thirty to forty-five minutes, three or four days per week to exercise. If you are like us, you will find that eventually you will want to exercise every day because it really feels good and at the end of your workout, you feel empowered and also quite pleased with yourself. Exercising is contagious, the more you do, the better you feel. Of course, don't overdue it either.

Next, have your blood work done. Take the list of lab tests, discussed in Chapter Three, to your physician and requests that the lab work be done. If your physician refuses to order the necessary lab tests, find a qualified physician who will order the tests. Your improved health depends on knowing what your key hormone levels are and finding a qualified physician who will safely and effectively recommend bio-identical hormone replacement therapy to return your hormone levels to a youthful therapeutic range. If you are on hormone replacement therapy, your blood work should be done at least quarterly because it is essential to monitor hormone levels closely and for your physician to make the necessary modifications in your hormone doses.

What about that brain of yours? You need your brain to work well for a better quality of life. A hormonally correct diet, exercise, taking the appropriate vitamins, minerals and other supplements and returning your hormone levels to a therapeutic youthful range will improve your cognitive ability. In addition to doing all of the aforementioned, we each personally take Deprenyl 5 mg daily to increase levels of the important neurotransmitter dopamine. Additionally, we take Acetyl L Carnitine 500-mg daily, Phosphatidyl Serine 100-mg daily, Pregnenolone 100-mg daily, Vinpocetine 90-mg daily and Vitamin E 400 to 800 mg daily to improve brain function. At CHI, we may recommend other brain booster medications or supplements to patients, depending on their symptoms but the brain boosters we currently take have certainly improved our mental capabilities and the mental capabilities of our patients.

In regards to stress reduction, we try to balance our lives by assessing our priorities constantly. We try to stop and "smell the roses" and we each have the philosophy that our families are precious and need our attention and caring first and foremost. Secondly, we try to take time each day to simply reflect and be in the moment. This daily practice puts life's events in perspective and it also helps to keep our cortisol levels in a therapeutic range.

We are passionate about what we do at CHI and we believe that with our combined sixty plus years in the medical field, we have the best jobs we have ever had. To be able to help people stay healthy and to help them improve their quality of life is a wonderful feeling. We are forever grateful to our incredible patients and for their belief and trust in what we are doing at CHI. We wish for all of you reading this book; a long and healthy life and we hope that tomorrow you will begin on your own anti-aging journey.

THE FUTURE OF ANTI-AGING MEDICINE

We are no longer prisoners of our genetic destiny. We have the capability to alter how our genes express themselves. Anti-aging medicine's primary focus is to treat and even prevent diseases associated with aging. Anti-aging medicine seeks to prevent and repair DNA damage, control glucose and insulin levels, control the production of free radicals, lower homocysteine levels, lower C-reactive protein levels and prevent inflammation overall, control advanced glycation end products (AGE) which occurs when proteins react with sugars during metabolism and to prevent the decline of the neuro-endocrine-immune system.

Living longer and healthier lives will positively impact society. Instead of billions of dollars being spent on coping with the loss of physical and mental functioning, money can be diverted into keeping people healthy until the end of their lives. As we stated at the beginning of this book, we all want to remain healthy until it is our time to go. It makes a lot more sense to keep people healthy from a social, economic and health standpoint. If you know that you may live a longer, healthier life, it will cause you to think about your future and your future needs in, hopefully, a more responsible manner. What you do today will impact all of your tomorrows and the tomorrows of this world we inhabit.

Stem cell research and application, the Human Genome Project, genetic engineering and revolutionary biotechnology will all impact our longevity and quality of life. Stem cells, those basic and fundamental cells that are present at the beginning of our development have the capability of forming into any type of cell. Through genetic engineering, stem cells will eventually have the potential to develop into cells, tissues and organs that can be used for human transplantation.

Nuclear reprogramming or the cloning of cells has already occurred when, in 1997, Dr. Ian Wilmut created the sheep, Dolly, by taking the nucleus of an adult cell and transferring it to an enucleated egg, which resulted in the cloned offspring Dolly. Cloning could be used for the creation of proteins, organs and tissues that would have beneficial biomedical use in humans. In January 2001, injecting an unfertilized egg of a normal Rhesus monkey with the jellyfish gene for green fluorescence created ANDi, a genetically modified Rhesus monkey. The jellyfish DNA joined with the monkey DNA and the egg was fertilized with sperm from a normal male monkey, which resulted in ANDi. Nuclear reprogramming has much potential.

There is current research being conducted that transfers telomerase (the material at the end of the DNA molecule that holds the DNA together) from healthy cells into cells with shortened telomeres, causing the aged cells to increase the amount of telomerase in the cell. The result of this action increases the lifespan of the cell. Pretty amazing, we think.

Nanotechnology is not science fiction. Nanodevices are tiny mechanical devices that contain biological materials that have the potential, in possibly eight to ten years, to deliver healthy cells to a part of the body where non-functioning or diseased cells are present and replacing the affected cells with new healthy cells. Imagine microscopic robots in your body fighting disease at its very core.

Artificial organs are just around the corner. Through tissue engineering, scientists will be able to combine living cells to create various organs in the body. It is proposed that within the next year or two, an artificial vision brain implant will allow many blind people to visualize images in their brains. Imagine checking-into your hospital for replacement of a defective organ part and coming out with a new organ part where you do not have to worry about rejection or taking toxic anti-rejection medications.

It is projected that within the next fifty years, brain implants will be possible. Brain implants will allow enhancement of a person's various skills, where defects may be present. Suppose your motor coordination was less than optimal, enhancing the reflex and coordination centers of the brain just might improve your motor capabilities. The possibilities for this type of digital cerebral communication are amazing. Maybe this technology will greatly improve the quality of life for paraplegics and quadriplegics; let's hope so.

Today, there is a great deal of research being conducted on mice concerning an Alzheimer's vaccine that, when injected decreases beta amyloid plague deposits in the brain of Alzheimer's mice. The results, thus far, have shown a marked improvement in cognitive function after immunization.

Finally, the Human Genome Project has shown us that we have much in common, genetically, with the roundworm and the fruit fly. As we continue to unravel the genetic miracles of life, we find that we are all connected in this great big gene pool. The more we realize how similar we are genetically, wouldn't it be nice if all this incredible scientific research resulted in a better world? In the meantime, as we wait for more and more scientific breakthroughs, we hope you will begin improving your health, so you will be around to benefit from the amazing biomedical technologies we have briefly discussed.

APPENDIX A

CALCULATING YOUR
DAILY PROTEIN REQUIREMENTS

With permission, we have borrowed Dr. Sears' method of calculating your daily protein requirements from his book, <u>The Soy Zone</u>. Following the steps listed below will result in the accurate calculation of your daily protein requirements.

FEMALES:

1. Measure your hips at the widest point (do this three times and use the average measurement)
2. Measure your waist at the belly button (do this three times and use the average measurement)
3. Measure your height in inches in stocking feet or barefoot
4. Record your hip, waist and height measurements
5. Refer to the table Conversion Constants for Prediction of Percentage of Body Fat in Females on the following pages
6. Find your hip measurement on the conversion table and look at Constant A for your particular hip measurement. Write down the appropriate Constant A
7. Find your waist (abdomen) measurement on the conversion table and look at Constant B for your particular waist (abdomen) measurement. Write down the appropriate Constant B
8. Find your height (in inches) measurement on the conversion table and look at Constant C for your particular height measurement. Write down the appropriate Constant C
9. Add Constants A and B
10. Subtract Constant C from the sum of Constants A and B and round to the nearest whole number
11. This number will reflect your percentage of body fat
12. Multiply your weight by your percentage of body fat (remember to use the decimal point because your body fat is a percentage, i.e., if your body fat percentage is 18 percent, it will be written 0.18)
13. You have now calculated your total body fat weight
14. Subtract your total body fat weight from your total weight
15. The result will equal your lean body mass (your lean body mass

is the weight of all body tissue that is not fat tissue)
16. Remember, your lean body mass = your total weight minus your total body fat weight
17. Multiply your lean body mass (in pounds) by your activity factor listed in the Activity Factor table on the following pages and this will give you Your Daily Protein Requirements. The table will also provide representative daily protein requirements based on lean body mass and activity factors to further assist you

EXAMPLE:

Hip measurement = 38 inches = 44.65 (Constant A from table)
Waist (abdomen) measurement = 30 inches = 21.33
  (Constant B from table)
Height (in inches) = 68 inches = 41.45 (Constant C from table)
44.65 (Constant A) + 21.33 (Constant B) = 65.98
65.98 - 41.45 (Constant C) = 24.53 or 25
  (rounded to the nearest whole number)
25 represents the percentage of body fat in this female example, thus the body fat is 25% or 0.25

Weight X body fat percentage = total body fat weight
150 pounds x 0.25 = 37.5 pounds (total body fat weight)
150 pounds - 37.5 pounds = 112.50 pounds (lean body mass)
112.50 (lean body mass) x 0.8 (activity factor) = 90 grams of protein
(DAILY PROTEIN REQUIREMENT)

MALES:

1. Measure your waist at the belly button (do this three times and use the average measurement)
2. Measure the wrist of your dominant hand where the wrist bends
3. Subtract the wrist measurement from your waist measurement
4. Refer to the table Male Percentage Body Fat Calculations and find your weight in pounds and your wrist measurement in inches
5. Where the two columns intersect you will find your approximate percentage body fat
6. Multiply your weight by your percentage of body fat (remember

to use the decimal point because your body fat is a percentage, i.e., if your body fat percentage is 18 percent, it will be written 0.18)

7. You have now calculated your total body fat weight
8. Subtract your total body fat weight from your total weight
9. The result will equal your lean body mass (your lean body mass is the weight of all body tissue that is not fat tissue)
10. Remember, your lean body mass = your total weight minus your total body fat weight
11. Multiply your lean body mass (in pounds) by your activity factor listed in the Activity Factor table on the following pages and this will give you Your Daily Protein Requirements. The table will also provide representative daily protein requirements based on lean body mass and activity factors to further assist you

EXAMPLE:

Waist (abdomen) measurement = 38 inches
Right wrist measurement = 8 inches
38 inches (waist measurement) - 8 inches (wrist measurement) = 30 inches
Weight = 200
Referring to table, 200 pounds (total body weight) and a 30 inch waist/wrist measurement = 19% (0.19) body fat

Weight x body fat percentage = total body fat weight
200 pounds x 0.19 = 38 pounds (total body fat weight)
200 pounds - 38 pounds = 162 pounds (lean body mass)
162 (lean body mass) x 0.7 (activity factor) = 113.4 grams of protein (DAILY PROTEIN REQUIREMENT)

APPENDIX B

Conversion Constants for Prediction of Percentage of Body Fat in Females

HIPS		ABDOMEN		HEIGHT	
INCHES	CONSTANT A	INCHES	CONSTANT B	INCHES	CONSTANT C
30	33.48	20	14.22	55	33.52
30.5	33.83	20.5	14.40	55.5	33.67
31	34.87	21	14.93	56	34.13
31.5	35.22	21.5	15.11	56.5	34.28
32	36.27	22	15.64	57	34.74
32.5	36.62	22.5	15.82	57.5	34.89
33	37.67	23	16.35	58	35.35
33.5	38.02	23.5	16.53	58.5	35.50
34	39.06	24	17.06	59	35.96
34.5	39.41	24.5	17.24	59.5	36.11
35	40.46	25	17.78	60	36.57
35.5	40.81	25.5	17.96	60.5	36.72
36	41.86	26	18.49	61	37.18
36.5	42.21	26.5	18.67	61.5	37.33
37	43.25	27	19.20	62	37.79
37.5	43.60	27.5	19.38	62.5	37.94
38	44.65	28	19.91	63	38.40
38.5	45.32	28.5	20.27	63.5	38.70
39	46.05	29	20.62	64	39.01
39.5	46.40	29.5	20.80	64.5	39.16
40	47.44	30	21.33	65	39.62
40.5	47.79	30.5	21.51	65.5	39.77
41	48.84	31	22.04	66	40.23
41.5	49.19	31.5	22.22	66.5	40.38
42	50.24	32	22.75	67	40.84
42.5	50.59	32.5	22.93	67.5	40.99
43	51.64	33	23.46	68	41.45
43.5	51.99	33.5	23.64	68.5	41.60
44	53.03	34	24.18	69	42.06
44.5	53.41	34.5	24.36	69.5	42.21

FOREVER AGELESS / Rothenberg and Becker

Conversion Constants for Prediction of Percentage of
Body Fat in Females

HIPS		ABDOMEN		HEIGHT	
INCHES	CONSTANT A	INCHES	CONSTANT B	INCHES	CONSTANT C
45	54.53	35	24.89	70	42.67
45.5	54.86	35.5	25.07	70.5	42.82
46	55.83	36	25.60	71	43.28
46.5	56.18	36.5	25.78	71.5	43.43
47	57.22	37	26.31	72	43.89
47.5	57.57	37.5	26.49	72.5	44.04
48	58.62	38	27.02	73	44.50
48.5	58.97	38.5	27.20	73.5	44.65
49	60.02	39	27.73	74	45.11
49.5	60.37	39.5	27.91	74.5	45.26
50	61.42	40	28.44	75	45.72
50.5	61.77	40.5	28.62	75.5	45.87
51	62.81	41	29.15	76	46.32
51.5	63.16	41.5	29.33		
52	64.21	42	29.87		
52.5	64.56	42.5	30.05		
53	65.61	43	30.58		
53.5	65.96	43.5	30.76		
54	67.00	44	31.29		
54.5	67.35	44.5	31.47		
55	68.40	45	32.00		
55.5	68.75	45.5	32.18		
56	69.80	46	32.71		
56.5	70.15	46.5	32.89		
57	71.19	47	33.42		
57.5	71.54	47.5	33.60		
58	72.59	48	34.13		
58.5	72.94	48.5	34.31		
59	73.99	49	34.84		
59.5	74.34	49.5	35.02		
60	75.39	50	35.56		

Male Percentage Body Fat Calculations

Waist-Wrist (in inches)	22	22.5	23	23.5	24	24.5	25
Weight (in lbs.)							
120	4	6	8	10	12	14	16
125	4	6	7	9	11	13	15
130	3	5	7	9	11	12	14
135	3	5	7	8	10	12	13
140	3	5	6	8	10	11	13
145		4	6	7	9	11	12
150		4	6	7	9	10	12
155		4	5	6	8	10	11
160		4	5	6	8	9	11
165		3	5	6	8	9	10
170		3	4	6	7	9	10
175			4	6	7	8	10
180			4	5	7	8	10
185			4	5	6	8	9
190			4	5	6	7	9
195			3	5	6	7	8
200			3	4	6	7	8
205				4	5	6	8
210				4	5	6	8
215				4	5	6	7
220				4	5	6	7
225				3	4	6	7
230				3	4	5	7
235				3	4	5	6
240					4	5	6
245					4	5	6
250					4	5	6
255					3	4	6
260					3	4	5
265						4	5
270						4	5
275						4	5
280						4	5
285						4	4
290						3	4
295						3	4
300						3	4

FOREVER AGELESS / Rothenberg and Becker

Male Percentage Body Fat Calculations

Waist-Wrist (in inches)	25.5	26	26.5	27	27.5	28	28.5
Weight (in lbs.)							
120	18	20	21	23	25	27	29
125	17	19	20	22	24	26	28
130	16	18	20	21	23	25	27
135	15	17	19	20	22	24	26
140	15	16	18	19	21	23	24
145	14	15	17	19	20	22	23
150	13	15	16	18	19	21	23
155	13	14	16	17	19	20	22
160	12	14	15	17	18	19	21
165	12	13	15	16	17	19	20
170	11	13	14	15	17	18	19
175	11	12	12	15	16	17	19
180	11	12	13	14	16	17	18
185	10	11	13	14	15	16	18
190	10	11	12	13	15	16	17
195	10	11	12	13	14	15	16
200	9	10	11	12	14	15	16
205	9	10	11	12	13	14	15
210	9	9	11	12	13	14	15
215	8	9	10	11	12	13	15
220	8	9	10	11	12	13	14
225	8	9	10	11	12	13	14
230	8	8	9	10	11	12	13
235	7	8	9	10	11	12	13
240	7	8	9	10	11	12	13
245	7	8	9	9	10	11	12
250	7	7	8	9	10	11	12
255	6	7	8	9	10	11	12
260	6	7	8	9	10	10	11
265	6	7	8	8	9	10	11
270	6	7	7	8	9	10	11
275	6	6	7	8	9	10	11
280	5	6	7	8	9	9	10
285	5	6	7	8	8	9	10
290	5	6	7	7	8	9	10
295	5	6	6	7	8	9	10
300	5	5	6	7	8	9	9

Male Percentage Body Fat Calculations

Waist-Wrist (in inches)	29	29.5	30	30.5	31	31.5	32
Weight (in lbs.)							
120	31	33	35	37	39	41	43
125	30	32	33	35	37	39	41
130	28	30	32	34	36	37	39
135	27	29	31	32	34	36	38
140	26	28	29	31	33	34	36
145	25	27	28	30	31	33	35
150	24	26	27	29	30	32	33
155	23	25	26	28	29	31	32
160	22	24	25	27	28	30	31
165	22	23	24	26	27	29	30
170	21	22	24	25	26	28	29
175	20	21	23	24	25	27	28
180	19	21	22	23	25	26	27
185	19	20	21	23	24	25	26
190	18	19	21	22	23	24	26
195	18	19	20	21	22	24	25
200	17	18	19	21	22	23	24
205	17	18	19	20	21	22	23
210	16	17	18	19	21	22	23
215	16	17	18	19	20	21	22
220	15	16	17	18	19	20	22
225	15	16	17	18	19	20	21
230	14	15	16	17	18	19	20
235	14	15	16	17	18	19	20
240	14	15	16	17	17	18	19
245	13	14	15	16	17	18	19
250	13	14	15	16	17	18	18
255	13	14	14	15	16	17	18
260	12	13	14	15	16	17	18
265	12	13	14	15	15	16	17
270	12	13	13	14	15	16	17
275	11	12	13	14	15	16	16
280	11	12	13	14	14	15	16
285	11	12	12	13	14	15	16
290	11	11	12	13	14	15	15
295	10	11	12	13	14	14	15
300	10	11	12	12	13	14	15

Male Percentage Body Fat Calculations

Waist-Wrist (in inches)	32.5	33	33.5	34	34.5	35	35.5
Weight (in lbs.)							
120	45	47	49	50	52	54	
125	43	45	46	48	50	52	54
130	41	43	44	46	48	50	52
135	39	41	43	44	46	48	50
140	38	39	41	43	44	46	48
145	36	38	39	41	43	44	46
150	35	36	38	40	41	43	44
155	34	35	37	38	40	41	43
160	33	34	35	37	38	40	41
165	31	33	34	36	37	38	40
170	30	32	33	34	36	37	39
175	29	31	32	33	35	36	37
180	28	30	31	32	34	35	36
185	28	29	30	31	33	34	35
190	27	28	29	30	32	33	34
195	26	27	28	30	31	32	33
200	25	26	28	29	30	31	32
205	25	26	27	28	29	30	31
210	24	25	26	27	28	29	30
215	23	24	25	26	28	29	30
220	23	24	25	26	27	28	29
225	22	23	24	25	26	27	28
230	21	22	23	24	25	26	27
235	21	22	23	24	25	26	27
240	20	21	22	23	24	25	26
245	20	21	22	23	24	25	26
250	19	20	21	22	23	24	25
255	19	20	21	22	23	24	24
260	19	19	20	21	22	23	24
265	18	19	20	21	22	22	23
270	18	19	19	20	21	22	23
275	17	18	19	20	21	22	22
280	17	18	19	19	20	21	22
285	17	17	18	19	20	21	21
290	16	17	18	19	19	20	21
295	16	17	17	18	19	20	21
300	16	16	17	18	19	19	20

Male Percentage Body Fat Calculations

Waist-Wrist (in inches)	36	36.5	37	37.5	38	38.5	39
Weight (in lbs.)							
120							
125							
130	53	55					
135	51	53	55				
140	49	51	53	54			
145	47	49	51	52	54	55	
150	46	47	49	50	52	53	55
155	44	46	47	49	50	52	53
160	43	44	46	47	48	50	51
165	41	43	44	45	47	48	50
170	40	41	43	44	45	47	48
175	39	40	41	43	44	45	47
180	37	39	40	41	43	44	45
185	36	38	39	40	41	43	44
190	35	37	38	39	40	41	43
195	34	35	37	38	39	40	41
200	33	35	36	37	38	39	40
205	32	34	35	36	37	38	39
210	32	33	34	35	36	37	38
215	31	32	33	34	35	36	37
220	30	31	32	33	34	35	36
225	29	30	31	32	33	34	35
230	28	30	31	32	33	34	35
235	28	29	30	31	32	33	34
240	27	28	29	30	31	32	33
245	27	27	28	29	30	31	32
250	26	27	28	29	30	31	31
255	25	26	27	28	29	30	31
260	25	26	27	27	28	29	30
265	24	25	26	27	28	29	29
270	24	25	25	26	27	28	29
275	23	24	25	26	27	27	28
280	23	24	24	25	26	27	28
285	22	23	24	25	26	26	27
290	22	23	23	24	25	26	27
295	21	22	23	24	25	25	26
300	21	22	22	23	24	25	26

FOREVER AGELESS / Rothenberg and Becker

Male Percentage Body Fat Calculations

Waist-Wrist (in inches)	39.5	40	40.5	41	41.5	42	42.5
Weight (in lbs.)							
120							
125							
130							
135							
140							
145							
150							
155	55						
160	53	54					
165	51	52	54	55			
170	49	51	52	54	55		
175	48	49	51	52	53	55	
180	47	48	49	50	52	53	54
185	45	46	48	49	50	51	53
190	44	45	46	48	49	50	51
195	43	44	45	46	47	49	50
200	41	43	44	45	46	47	48
205	40	41	43	44	45	46	47
210	39	40	42	43	44	45	46
215	38	39	40	42	43	44	45
220	37	38	39	41	42	43	44
225	36	37	38	40	41	42	43
230	36	37	38	39	40	41	42
235	35	36	37	38	39	40	41
240	34	35	36	37	38	39	40
245	33	34	35	36	37	38	39
250	32	33	34	35	36	37	38
255	32	33	34	34	35	36	37
260	31	32	33	34	35	35	36
265	30	31	32	33	34	35	36
270	30	31	31	32	33	34	35
275	29	30	31	32	32	33	34
280	29	29	30	31	32	33	33
285	28	29	30	30	31	32	33
290	27	28	29	30	31	31	32
295	27	28	28	29	30	31	32
300	26	27	28	29	29	30	31

Male Percentage Body Fat Calculations

Waist-Wrist (in inches)	43	43.5	44	44.5	45	45.5	46
Weight (in lbs.)							
120							
125							
130							
135							
140							
145							
150							
155							
160							
165							
170							
175							
180							
185	54	55					
190	52	54	55				
195	51	52	53	55			
200	50	51	52	53	54	55	
205	48	49	51	52	53	54	55
210	47	48	49	50	51	53	54
215	46	47	48	49	50	51	52
220	45	46	47	48	49	50	51
225	44	45	46	47	48	49	50
230	44	44	45	46	47	48	49
235	42	43	44	45	46	47	48
240	41	42	43	44	45	46	46
245	40	41	42	43	44	44	45
250	39	40	41	42	43	44	44
255	38	39	40	41	42	43	44
260	37	38	39	40	41	42	43
265	36	37	38	39	40	41	42
270	36	37	37	38	39	40	41
275	35	36	37	38	38	39	40
280	34	35	36	37	38	38	39
285	34	34	35	36	37	38	39
290	33	34	35	35	36	37	38
295	32	33	34	35	36	36	37
300	32	33	33	34	35	36	36

FOREVER AGELESS / Rothenberg and Becker

Male Percentage Body Fat Calculations

Waist-Wrist (in inches)	46.5	47	47.5	48	48.5	49	49.5
Weight (in lbs.)							
120							
125							
130							
135							
140							
145							
150							
155							
160							
165							
170							
175							
180							
185							
190							
195							
200							
205							
210	55						
215	53	54	55				
220	52	53	54	55			
225	51	52	53	54	55		
230	50	51	52	53	54	55	
235	49	50	51	51	52	53	54
240	47	48	49	50	51	52	53
245	46	47	48	49	50	51	52
250	45	46	47	48	49	50	51
255	44	45	46	47	48	49	50
260	43	44	45	46	47	48	49
265	43	43	44	45	46	47	48
270	42	43	43	44	45	46	47
275	41	42	43	43	44	45	46
280	40	41	42	43	43	44	45
285	39	40	41	42	43	43	44
290	39	39	40	41	42	43	43
295	38	39	39	40	41	42	43
300	37	38	39	39	40	41	42

ACTIVITY FACTOR
(GRAMS OF PROTEIN PER POUND OF LEAN MUSCLE MASS)

LEAN BODY MASS (IN LBS.)	0.5	0.6	0.7	0.8	0.9	1.0
90	45	54	63	72	81	90
100	50	60	70	80	90	100
110	55	66	77	88	99	110
120	60	72	84	96	108	120
130	65	78	91	104	117	130
140	70	84	98	112	126	140
150	75	90	105	120	135	150
160	80	96	112	128	144	160
170	85	102	119	136	153	170
180	90	108	1265	144	162	180
190	95	114	133	152	171	190
200	100	120	140	160	180	200
210	105	126	147	168	189	210
220	110	132	154	176	198	220
230	115	138	161	184	207	230
240	120	144	168	192	216	240

ACTIVITY FACTOR:

0.5 = Sedentary (no formal sports activity or training)
0.6 = Light fitness training such as walking
0.7 = **Moderate training (three times per week) or sports participation**
0.8 = Daily aerobic training or daily moderate weight training
0.9 = Heavy daily weight training
1.0 = Heavy daily weight training coupled with intense sports training or twice per day intense sports training

FOOD TO EAT AND FOODS TO AVOID

Foods to Eat:

Proteins:

Skinless turkey breast	Shellfish
Skinless chicken breast	Lowfat cottage cheese
Lean cuts of beef	Eggs
Lean cuts of pork	Natural soy products
Fish	Whey and/or Soy Protein
Powder	

Carbohydrates:

High fiber grains	Lentils
High fiber cereals	Butter beans
Slow-cooking oatmeal	Plain natural yogurt
Wild rice	Oats
Legumes	Pearl Barley
Black beans	Rye

Soy beans (also a good protein source)
High fiber breads (no added sugar)
Oatbran

Favorable fresh vegetables:

(alfalfa sprouts, artichokes, asparagus, bamboo shoots, bean sprouts, bell peppers, bok choy, broccoli, brussel sprouts, cabbage, cauliflower, celery, chickpeas, cucumbers, eggplant, endive, escarole, green beans, jalapeno peppers, kale, kidney beans, leeks, lettuce, mushrooms, onions, okra, radishes, sauerkraut, scallions, snow peas, squash, spinach, swiss chard, tomatoes, turnips, water chestnuts, watercress zucchini)

Favorable fresh fruits:
(apples and unsweetened applesauce, apricots, blackberries, blue-berries, boysenberries, cherries, grapes, grapefruit, kiwi, nectarine, oranges, peaches, pears, plums raspberries, strawberries)

Fats: (monounsaturated fats)

Almonds   Medium black olives
Almond butter   Olive oil
Almond oil   Peanuts
Avocado   Peanut oil
Canola oil   Peanut butter
Cashews   Pistachios
Guacamole   Sesame oil
Macadamia nuts

FOODS TO AVOID:

Proteins:

Bacon
Beef liver
Chicken liver
Hard cheeses
High fat beef
High fat poultry
Processed meats with preservatives and added sugars (salami, pep-peroni, etc.)
Smoked meats

Carbohydrates:

Alcohol (all types)
Mangos
All products with white flour
Most breakfast cereals (too much sugar)
Bagels
Papayas

Baked beans
Pasta
Bananas
Peas
Cakes, cookies and other similar desserts
Pretzels
Candy bars
Pineapple
Canned fruits packed in syrup
Popcorn
Canned soups (sugar added)
Potatoes
Carrots
Potato chips and other types of chips
Crackers
Pumpkin
Corn and corn products
Refried beans
Dried beans
Rice cakes
Dried fruit (all of it)
Sports beverages (with > 10 grams of carbohydrates per 12 ounces)
Energy bars (with > 22 grams of carbohydrates)
Sugar
Flour tortillas
Watermelon
Ice cream
White bread
Jams and jellies
White rice
Fruit juices (they have added sugar)
Yams
Honey

Fats:

Animal fat
Fractionated oils
Heated oils
Margarine (all types)
Palm kernel oil
Partially hydrogenated oils (found in most processed foods, read the label)

APPENDIX C

Important Basic Vitamins, Minerals & Other Supplements

(Always consult your physician before taking any medications or supplements)

- Vitamin C 2000 mg daily
- Beta Carotene 20,000 IU daily
- Vitamin E 400 to 800 IU daily
- Vitamin A 8000 IU daily
- Vitamin B1 (Thiamin) 100 mg daily
- Vitamin B2 (Riboflavin) 100 mg daily
- Vitamin B3 (Niacin) 50 - 150 mg daily
- Vitamin B5 400 mg daily
- Vitamin B6 100 mg daily
- Vitamin B12 400 mcg daily
- Biotin 600 mcg daily
- Vitamin D 400 IU daily
- Vitamin K 60 mcg daily
- Folic Acid 400 - 800 mcg daily
- Lecithin 700 mg daily
- Inositol 200 mg daily
- Lycopene 10 mg daily
- PABA 500 mg daily
- Boron 2 mg daily
- Calcium Citrate 1500 mg daily (men) and 3000 mg daily (women)
- Chromium 400 mcg daily
- Copper 2 mg daily
- Iodine 150 mcg daily
- Magnesium 400 mg daily
- Manganese 10 mg daily
- Molybdenum 200 mcg daily
- Potassium Aspartate 200 mg daily
- Selenium 200 mcg daily
- Vanadium 200 mcg daily
- Zinc 30 mg daily
- Alpha Lipoic Acid 250 mg 2x/ day (If diabetic 250 mg 3-4 times/day)
- Baby aspirin 81 mg daily

- Bifobactgerium bifidum 2 billion parts daily
- Bilberry 100 mg daily
- Carnosine 500 mg 3x/day
- Citrus Bioflavinoids 400 mg daily
- CoQ10 60 mg daily (Solanova brand)
- Garlic 500 mg daily
- Ginger 200 mg daily
- Ginkgo Biloba 120 - 240 mg daily
- Ginseng 300 mg three times per day
- Glucosamine 750 mg daily (more if joint pain)
- Glutamine 1000 mg daily
- Glutathione 50 mg daily
- Grape Seed Extract 50 mg daily
- Green Tea Extract 400 mg daily
- Indole 3 Carbinol (I3C) 200 mg 2x/day (weight 120 pounds or less) 200 mg 3x/day (weight 120-180 pounds) 200 mg 4x/day (weight > 180spounds
- Lactobacillus acidophilus 2 billion parts daily
- Milk Thistle 200 mg daily
- NAC 250 mg daily
- Red Grape Skin Extract 400 mg daily
- MEN ONLY (prostate health):
  Saw palmetto 160 mg 2x/day
  Pygeum 50 mg 2x/day
  Urtica 120 mg 2x/day
- Tumeric 300 mg daily

RESOURCE LIST

American Academy of Anti-Aging Medicine:
1341 West Fullerton Street, Suite 111
Chicago, Illinois 60614
773-528-4333

Laboratories:
Labcorp: 1-800-859-6046
Quest Diagnositcs: 1-800-8484225
Pinnacle Lab: 1-888-556-5567
Pantox Laboratories: 1-888-726-8698 (Vitamin and Lipid Screens)
Berkeley HeartLab: 1-877-454-7437

Compounding Pharmacies:
International Association of Compounding Pharmacists:
1-800-927-4227
University Compounding Pharmacy: 1-800-985-8065
Medquest Pharmacy: 1-888-222-2956

Life Extension Foundation:
P.O. Box 229120
Hollywood, Florida 33022-9120
1-800-841-5433

Zone Nutrition
Barry Sears, Ph.D.
Sears Laboratories
21 Tioga Way
Marblehead, MA 01945
www.drsears.com

BIBLIOGRAPHY

Alexander, F.M., Swerrdloff, R.S., Wang, C. et. al. (1998). Androgen-behavior correlations in hypogonadal men and eugonadal men. II. Cognitive Abilities. P. 85-94.

Almada, A., et. al. (1996). Impact of Chronic Creatine Supplementation on Serum Enzyme Concentration. FASEB Journal. P. 791.

Almada, A., et. al. (1997). Effects of Calcium B-HMB Supplementation With or Without Creatine During Training on Strength & Sprint Capacity. FASEB Journal. P. 374.

Annewieke, W., et al. (2000) Measures of Bioavailable Serum Testosterone and Estradiol and Their Relationship with Muscle Strength, Gone Density, and Body Composition in Elderly Men. The Journal of ClinicaL Endocrinology & Metabolism. Volume 85, No. 9. P. 3276-3282.

Arver, S., Dobs, A.S., Meikle, A.W., Allen, R.P., Sanders, S.W. & Mazer, N.A. (1996, May). Improvement of sexual function in testosterone deficient men treated for 1 year with a permeation enhanced testosterone transdermal system. P. 1604-1608. (On-line) PMID: 88627833.

Asbell, S.O., et. al. (2000, September). Prostate-specific antigen and androgens in African-American and white normal subjects and prostate cancer patients. Journal of the National Medical Association. P. 445-9

Balch, James F., M.D. & Balch, Phyllis A., C.N.C. (1997). Prescription For Nutritional Healing. Avery Publishing Group, Garden City Park, New York.

Barlow-Walden, L.R., Reiter, R.J., Abe, M., Pablos, M., Menendez-Pelaez, A., Chen, L.D. & Poeggeler, B. (1995, May). Melatonin stimulates brain glutathione peroxidase activity. Neurochemical Int. P. 497-502. (On-line) PMID: 7492947.

Barrett-Conner, E., et. al. ((1999). Endogenous sex hormones and cognitive function in older men. Journal of Clinical Endocrinology Metabolism. P. 3681-5.

Baum, H.B., Biller, B.M., Finkelstein, J.S., Cannistraro, K.B., Oppenhein, D.S., Schoenfeld,, D.A., Michel, T.H., Wittink, H. & Klibanski, A. (1996, December) Effects of physiologic growth hormone therapy on bone density and body composition in patients with adult-onset growth hormone deficiency. A randomized, placebo-controlled trial. Annals of Internal Medicine. P. 883-890.

Baum, H.B., Katznelson, L., Sherman, J.C., Biller, B.M., Hayden, D.L., Schoenfeld, D.A., Cannistraro, K.E. & Kilbanski, A. (1998, September) Effects of physiological growth hormone (GH) therapy on cognition and quality of life in patients with adult-onset GH deficiency. Journal of Clinical Endocrinology Metabolism. P. 3184-3189. (On-line) PMID: 9745423.

Beck, Charlotte Joko. (1989). Everyday Zen, Love and Work. HarperCollins Publisher, New York, New York.

Beck, Charlotte Joko. (1993). Nothing Special, Living Zen. HarperCollins Publisher, New York, New York.

Bhasin, S., et. al. (1997, February). Testosterone replacement increases fat-free mass and muscle size in hypogonadal men. Journal of Clinical Endocrinology Metabolism. P. 407-13.

Bhasin, S. (2000, January). The dose-dependent effects of testosterone on sexual function and on muscle mass and function. Mayo Clinic Proc. P. Supplement S70-5.

Binnerts, a., Swart, G.R., Wilson, J.H., Hoogerbrugge, N., Pois, H.A., Birkenhager, J.C. & Lamberts, S.W. (1992, July) The effect of growth hormone administration in growth hormone deficient adults on bone, protein, carbohydrate and lipid home-ostasis, as well as on body composition. Clinical Endocrinology. (On-line) PMID: 1424196.

Bland, Jeffrey, Ph.D. (1997). The 20-Day Rejuvenation Diet Program. Keats Publishing, Inc., New Canaan, Connecticut.

Blanka, Rogina, et. al. (2000, December). Extended Lifespan Conferred by Cotransporter Gene Mutations in Drosophila. Science. P. 2137-2140.

Brown, G.A., (2000, November). Endocrine responses to chronic androstenedione intake in 30- to 56-year-old men. Journal of Clinical Endocrinology Metabolism. P. 4074-80.

Bubenik, G.A., Blask, D.E., Brown, G.M., Maestroni, G.J., Pang, S.F., Reiter, R.J., Viswanathan, M. & Zisapel, N. (1998, July-August). Prospects of the clinical uti-lization of melatonin. Biological Signals Recept. P. 195-219. (On-line) PMID: 9730580.

Bunvicius, Robertas, M.D., Ph.D., Kazanavicius, Gintautas, M.D., Ph.D., Zaukevicius, Rimas, M.D. & Prange, Arthur J., Jr., M.D. (February, 1999) Effects of Thyroxine as Compared with Thyroxine plus Triiodothyronine in Patients with Hypothyroidism. The New England Journal of Medicine. P. 424-429.

Bunevicius, Robertas, M.D., Ph.D., Kazanavicius,Gintautas, M.D., Ph.D., Zzaukevicius, Rimas, M.D., & Prange, Arthur, J., Jr., M.D. (1999, February). Effects of Thyroxine as Compared with Thyroxine Plus Triiodothyronine in Patients with Hypothyroidism. The New England Journal of Medicine. P. 424-429.

Burman, P., Johansson, A.G., Siegbahn, A., Vessby, B. & Karlsson, F.A. (1997, February) Growth hormone (GH)-deficient men are more responsive to GH replacement therapy than women. Journal of Clinical Endocrinology Metabolism. P. 550-555.

Burris, A., et. al. (1992, August). A long-term, prospective study of the physiologic and behavioral effects of hormone replacement in untreated hypogonadal men. Journal of Andrology. P. 297-304.

(no author). (1999, July). Serum testosterone and sex hormone-binding globulin concentrations and the risk of prostate carcinoma: a longitudinal study. Cancer. Pl. 312-315.

Carroll, Linda (1997, October 9). Estrogen therapy becoming option for cancer survivors. Medical Tribune (Oncology). P. 21.

Cheng, W., et. al. (1997). B-Hydroxy B-Methylbutyrate Increases Fatty Acid Oxidation by Muscle Cells. FASEB Journal. P. 381.

Cheng, W., et. al. (1998). Effect of HMB on Fuel Utilization, Membrane Stability, and Creatine Kinase Content of Cultured Muscle Cells. FASEB Journal. P. 950.

Clarkson (1996, October). The effects of hormone replacement therapy on carbohydrate metabolism and cardiovascular risk factors in surgically postmenopausal cynomolgus monkeys. Metabolism. P. 1254-1262.

Clayman, Charles, M.D. (1989). The American Medical Association Encyclopedia of Medicine. Random House, Inc., New York.

Christ, E.R., Carroll, P.V., Russell-Jones, D.L. & Sonksen, P.H. (1997, August) The consequences of growth hormone deficiency in adulthood, and the effects of growth hormone replacement. (On-line) PMID 9297747.

Coleman, Brenda C. (1997, April 16). Company allegedly hid thyroid research. The Register (Associated Press). P. 11 & 14.

Cooper, C.S., et. al. (1998, February). Effect of exogenous testosterone on prostate volume, serum and semen prostate specific antigen levels in healthy young men. Journal of Urology. P. 441-3.

Dean, Ward, M.D. & Morgenthaler John. (1991) Smart Drugs. Smart Publications, Petaluma, California

Dean, Ward, M.D., Morgenthaler, John & Fowkes, Steven Wm. (1993) Smart Drugs II, The Next Generation. Smart Publications, Petaluma, California

de la Torre, J.C. (1997). Cerebromicrovascular pathology in Alzheimer's disease compared to normal aging. Gerontology. P. 26-43.

DeLuca, H.F. & Ostrem, V. (1986). The relationship between the vitamin D system and cancer. Adv. Exp. Med. Biology. (?). P. 413-429.

Dobie, A. (1999). The role of excitotoxicity in neurodegenerative disease: implications for therapy. Pharmacology Therapeutics. P. 163-221.

Donnelly, P. & White, C. (2000, February). Testicular dysfunction in men with primary hypothyroidism; reversal of hypogonadotrophic hypogonadism with replacement thyroxine. Clinical Endocrinology. P. 197-201.

Eades, Michael R., M.D. & Eades, Mary Dan, M.D. (1999) Protein Power. Bantam Books, New York, New York.

Earnest, C., et. al. (1994). Effect of Creatine Monohydrate Injestion on Peak Anaerrobic Power, Capacity, and Fatigue Index. Medicine & Sscience in Slports & Exercise. P. S39.

Earnest, C., et. al. (1996). Influence of Chronic Creatine Supplementation on Hepatorenal Function. FASEB Journal. P. 790.

English, K.M., et. al. (2000, October). Low-dose transdermal testosterone therapy improves angin threshold in men with chronic stable angina. A randomized, double-blind, placebo-controlled study. Circulation. P. 1906-11.

English, K.M., et. al. (2000, June). Men with coronary artery disease have lower levels of androgens than men with normal coronary angiograms. European Heart Journal. P. 890-4.

Ferreira, M., et. al. (1998). Effects of CLA Supplementation During Resistance Training on Body Composition and Strength. Journal of Strength Conditioning Research. P. 280.

Ferrini, Rebecca L. & Barrett-Connor, Elizabeth. (1998). Sex Hormones and Age: A Cross-sectional Study of Testosterone, Estradiol, and Their Bioavailable Fractions in Community-dwelling Men. American Journal of Epidemiology. P. 750-754.

Flook, J.F., Morley, J.E. & Rroberts, E. (1995, November). Pregnenolone sulfate enhances post-training memory processes when injected in very low doses into limbic system structures: the amygdala is by far the most sensitive. Protocols of the National Academy of Sciences USA. P. 10806-10810. (On-line) PMID: 7479888.

Forster,, M.J., et. al. (1996). Age related losses of cognitive function and motor skills in mice are associated with oxidative protein damage in the brain. Protocols Natural Academy of Science USA. P. 4765-9.

Gaby, Alan R., M.D. (1993, Spring). DHEA: The Hormone that "Does it All". Holistic Medicine. P. 19-23.

Gallant, S. (2000, July). Carnosine as A Potential Anti-senescence Drug. Biochemistry (Moscow). P. 866-868.

Gambrell, R. Don, Jr., M.D. (1997, August). When to Consider Hormone Replacement...With Androgens. Consultant. P. 2006.

Gerhard, M., Walsh, B.W., Tawakol, A., Haley, E.A., Creager, S.J., Seely, E.W., Ganz, P. & Creager, M.A. (1998, September). Estradiol therapy combined with progesterone and endothelium-dependent vasodilatation in post menopausal women. Circulation. P. 1158-1163.

Gill, J.J., et. al. (1991). Effect of antioxidants on hyperoxia-induced chromosomal breakage in Chinese hamster ovary cells: protection by carnosine. Mutagenesis. P. 313-318.

Goldzieher, Joseph W., M.D. (1997, April) Postmenopausal Androgen Therapy. The Female Patient.P. 10-13.

Goth, M., Szaboles, I. & Peter, F. (1995, June) Orv Hetil P 1243-1247. (On-line) PMID: 7784045.

Gouras, G.K., et. al. (2000, February). Testosterone reduces neuronal secretion of Alzheimer's beta-amyloid peptides. P. 1202-1205.

Grodstein, r. & Stampfer, M.J. (1998, September). Estrogen for women at varying risk of coronary disease. Maturitas. P. 19-26. (On-line) PMID: 9819779.

Gulyaeva, N.V., et. al. (1987). Superoxide-scavenging activity of carnosine in the presence of copper and zinc ions. Biochemistry (Moscow). P. 1051-4.

Gulyaevea, N.V., et. al. (1987). Carnosine prevents activation of free-radical lipid oxidation during stress. Bulletin Experimental Biology Medicine. P. 148-152.

Gustafsson, et. al. Dihydrotestosterone and testosterone levels in men screened for prostate cancer: a study of a randomized population. British Journal of Urology. P. 433-40.

Guth, L, Zhang, Z. & Roberts, E. (1994, December). Key role for pregnenolone in combination therapy that promotes recovery after spinal cord injury. Protocols of the National Academy of Sciences USA. P. 12308-12312. (On-line) PMID: 7991623.

Hajjar, R.R., Kaiser, F.E. & Morley, J.E. (1997, November). Outcomes of long-term testosterone replacement in older hypogonadal males: a retrospective analysis. Journal of Clinical Endocrinology Metabolism. P. 3793-3796. (On-line) PMID: 9360543.

Hamilton, Kirk, PA-C, ((1997, March) The Truth About Testosterone. Smart Life News. P. 2-4.

Hamilton, Michele A., M.D. (1998, February). Safety and Hemodynamic Effects of Intravenous Triiodothyronine in Advanced Congestive Heart Failure. The American Journal of Cardiology. P. 443-447.

Hanson, P.A., Han, D.H., Nolte, L.A., Chen, M. & Holloszy, J.O. (1997, November). DHEA protects against visceral obesity and muscle insulin resistance in rats fed a high-fat diet. American Journal of Physiology. P. 1704-1709. (On-line) PMID: 9374813.

Hargrove, Joel T., M.D., & Osteen, Kevin G., Ph.D. (1995, October) An Alternative Method of Hormone Replacement Therapy Using the Natural Sex Steroids. Infertility and Reproductive Medicine Clinics of North America. P. 653-674.

Hayflick, L. (1961). The serial cultivation of human diploid cell strains. Experimental Cell Research. P. 585-621.

Hayflick, L. (1965). The limited in vitro lifetime of human diploid cell strains. Experimental Cell Research. P. 614-36.

Heffner, S.M. (1996). Sex hormone-binding protein, hyperinsulinemia, insulin resistance and noninsulin-dependent diabetes. Hormone Response. P. 233-7.

Heffner, S.M. (2000, June 24). Sex hormones, obesity, fat distribution, type 2 diabetes and insulin resistance: epidemiological and clinical correlation. International Journal Obesity Related Metabolic Disorders. P. Supplement S56-58.

Himmel, Peter, M.D. (1997, October). Pregnenolone: Overview and Original Research Part 1 of a 3 Part Series. Focus. P. 1-3.

Hipkiss, A.R., et. al. (1995). Non-enzymatic glycosylation of the dipeptide L-carnosine, a potential anti protein cross linking agent. FEBS Letter. P. 81-5.

Hipkiss, A.R., et. al. (1995). Strategies for the extension of human life span. Perspectives Human Biology. P. 59-70.

Hipkiss, A.R., et. al. (1997). Protective effects of carnosine against malondialdehyde-induced toxicity towards cultured rat brain endothelial cells. Neuroscience Letter. P. 135-8.

Hipkiss, A.R., et. al. (1998). Ppluripotent protective effects of carnosine, a naturally occurring depeptide. Annals New York Academy of Science. P. 37-53.

Hipkiss, A.R., et. al. (1998). Carnosine protects proteins against methylglyoxal-mediated modifications. Biochemistry Biophysiology Research Communications. P. 28-32.

Hipkiss, A.R., et. al. (2000). A possible new role for the anti-aging peptide carnosine. Cellular Molecular Life Science. P. 747-753.

Hishikawa, K., Nakaki, T., Narumo, T., Susuki, H., Kato, R., and Saruta, T. (NO DATE) Up-regulation of nitric oxide synthase by estradiol in human aortic endothelial cells. NO PUBLICATION LISTED!

Hoffman, M.A. (2000, March). Is low serum free testosterone a marker for high grade prostate cancer? Journal of Urology. P. 624-7.

Horning, M.S., et. al. (2000). Endogenous mechanisms of neuroprotection: role of zinc, copper and carnosine. Brain Research. P. 56-61.

Huang, X., et. al. (1999). Cu(II) potentiation of alzheimer Ab neurotoxicity. Correlation with cell-free hydrogen peroxide production and metal reduction. Journal Biological Chemistry. P. 37111-6.

Ikeda, D., et. al. (1999). Carnosine stimulates vimentin expression in cultured rat fibroblasts. Cell Structure Function. P. 79-87.

Jain, P., et. al. (2000, August). Testosterone Supplementation for Erectile Dysfunction: Results of Meta-Analysis. Journal of Urology. P. 371-375.

Janowsky, J., et al. (2000, May). Sex steroids modify working memory. Journal of Cognitive Neuroscience. P. 407-414.

Janus, C., et. al. (2000, December). A beta peptide immunization reduces behavioral impairment and plaques in a model of Alzheimer's Disease. Nature. P. 979-982.

Kaiser, F.E., Silver, A.J., Morley, J.E. (1991, March). The effect of recombinant human growth hormone on malnourished older individuals. Journal American Geriatric Society. P. 235-240. (On-line) PMID: 2005335.

Kalimi, Mohammed, M.D. & Regelson, William, M.D. (1999) Dehydroepiandrosterone (DHEA) Biochemical, Physiological and Clinical Aspects. Walter de Gruyter, Berlin, New York.
Kantha, S.S., et. al. (1996). Carnosine sustains the retention of cell morphology in continuous fibroblast culture subjected to nutritional insult. Biochemistry Biophysiology Research Communications.P. 278-282.

Kasal, H. (1997). Analysis of a form of oxidative DNA damage, 8-hydroxy-2-deoxyguanosine, as a marker of cellular oxidative stress during carcinogenesis. Mutation Research. P. 147-163.

Khalsa, Dharma Singh, M.D. (1997). Brain Longevity. Warner Books, Inc., New York, New York.

Klatz, Ronald M., D.O., M.D. (1999). Ten Weeks To A Younger You. The American Academy of Anti-Aging, Chicago, Illinois.

Klein, Irwin, M.D. & Ojamaa, Kaie, Ph.D. (1998). Thyroid Hormone Treatment of Congestive Heart Failure. Excerpts Medica, Inc.. P. 490-491.

Knoll, J., et. al. (1989). Striatal dopamine, sexual activity and lifespan. Longevity of rats treated with (-)deprenyl. Life Science. P. 525-31.

Korenman, S.G., Morley, J.E., Mooradian, A.D., et. al. ((1990) Secondary hypogonadism in older men: its relationship to impotence. Journal of Clinical Endocrinology Metabolism. P. 963-969.

Krieder, R., et. al. (1997). Effects of Calcium B-HMB Supplementation With or Without Creatine During Training on Body Composition Alterations. FASEB Journal. P. 374.

Kreider, R., et. al. (1998). Effects of Conjugated Linoleic Acid (CLA) Supplementation During Resistance-Training on Bone Mineral Content, Bone Mineral Density, & Markers of Immune Stress. FASEB Journal. P. 244.

Kreider, R., et. al. (1998). Effects of Creatine Supplementation During Training on the Incidence of Muscle Cramping, Injuries, and GI Disorders. Journal of Strength and Conditioning Research. P. 275.

Krieder, R., et. al. (1998). Hematological & Metabolic Effects of Calcium-HMB Supplementation During Resistance-Training. 26th Annual Southeast American College of Sports Medicine Meeting, Destin, Florida.

Labrie, F., Diamond, P., Cusan, L., Gomez, J.L., Belanger, A. & Candas, B. (1997, October) Effect of 12-month dehydroepiandrosterone replacement therapy on bone, vagina, and endometrium in postmenopausal women. Journal of Clinical Endocrinology Metabolism. P. 498-505. (On-line) PMID: 9329392.

Langer, Stephen, M.D. How Low Thyroid Function Undermines Longevity. Abstract. (8 pages)
Lanza, R., et. al. (2000, April). Telomere restoration and extension of cell lifespan in animals cloned from senescent somatic cells. Science.

Life Extension Foundation. (2000). Life Extension Disease Prevention and Treatment Protocols. Life Extension Media, Hollywood, Florida.

Life Extension Foundation (1999) Female Hormone Modulation Therapy - Disease Therapy. (On-line), http://www.lef.org/protocols/prtcls-txt/t-prtel-133.html

Lissoni, P., Paolorossi, F., Ardizzoia, A., Barni, S., Chilelli, M., Mancusco, M., Tancini, G., Conti, A. & Masestroni, G.J. (1998, August) A randomized study of chemotherapy with cisplantin plus etoposide versus chemoendocrine therapy with cisplatin, etoposide and the pineal hormone melatonin as a first-line treatment of advanced non-small cell lung cancer patients in a poor clinical state. Journal of Pineal Research. P. 15-19.

Lowery, L.M., et. al. (1998). Conjugated Linolei Acid Enhances Muscle Size and Strength Gains in Novice Bodybuilders. Medicine & Science in Sport & Exercise. P. 182.

Margolese, H.C., et. al. (2000, Summer). The male menopause and mood: testosterone decline and depression in the aging male-is there a link? Journal of Geriatric Psychiatry Neurology. P. 93-101.

Marek, j., Spacil, J., Weiss, J., Malik, J. Sperl, M., Petrasek, J. & Haas, T. (1998, June). Treatment of hypopituitarism in adults with growth hormone improves the thickness of the arterial intima). Cas Lek Cesk. (On-line) PMID: 9721471.

Mark, R.J., et. al. (1997). A role for 4-hydroxynonenal, an aldehydic product of lipid peroxidation, in disruption of ion homeostasis and neuronal death induced by amyloid beta-peptide. Journal Neurochemistry. P. 255-264.

(no author). (1999, November). HRT and cancer risk: separating fact from fiction. Maturitas. P. 65-72.

Mayequ, Edward J., Jr., M.D., & Johnson, Cynda, Johnson, M.D. (1996, July). Current Concepts in Postmenopausal Hormone Replacement Therapy. The Journal of Family Practice. P. 60-74.

McFarland, G.A., et. al. (1994). Retardation of the senescence of cultured human diploid fibroblasts by carnosine. Experimental Cell Research. P. 167-175.

McFarland, G.A., et. al. (1999). Further evidence for the rejuvenating effects of the dipeptide L-carnosine on cultured human diploid fibroblasts. Experimental Gerontology. P. 35-45.
McKinney, Merritt. (1998, November). Testosterone may help to restore sex drive during menopause. Medical Tribune, Women's Health. P. 18

Meikle, A.W., Arver, S. Dobs, A.S., Sanders, S.W., Rajaram, L. & Mazer, N.A. (1996, March). Pharmacokinetics and metabolism of a permeation-enhanced testosterone transdermal system in hypogonadal men: influence of application site- -a clinical research center study. P. 1832-1840.

Melov, S., et. al. (2000, September). Extension of Life-Span with Superoxide Dismutase/Catalase Mimetics. Science. P. 1567-9.

Mitchell, T., et. al. (1996). Creatine Reduces Blood Lipid Concentrations in Men and Women. FASEB Journal. P. A521.

Montilla, P.L., Vargas, J.F., Tunez, I.F., Munoz de Agueda, M.C., Valdelvira, M.E. & Cabrera, E.S. (1998, September) Oxidative stress in diabetic rats induced by streptozotocin: protective effects of melatonin. Journal of Pineal Research. P 94-100.

Morley, J.E., Perry, H.M. 3rd, Kaiser, F.E., Kraenzle, D., Jensen, J. Houston, K., Mattammal, M. & Perry, H.M., Jr. (1993, February). Effects of testosterone replacement therapy in old hypogonadal males: a preliminary study. Journal of the American Geriatric Society. P. 149-152. (On-line) PMID: 8426037.

Morley, J.E., Kaiser, F.E., Perry, H.M. 3rd, Patrick, P., Morley, P.M., Stauber, P.M., Vellas, B., Baumgartner, R. N. & Garry, P.J. (1997, April) Longitudinal changes in testosterone, luteinizing hormone, and follicle-stimulating hormone in healthy older men. Metabolism. (On-line) PMID: 9109845.

Morley, J.E., Kaiser, F.E., Sih, R., Hajjar, R. & Perry, H.M. 3rd. (1997, November). Testosterone and frailty. Clinical Geriatric Medicine. P. 685-695. (On-line) PMID: 9354749.

Morley, J.E. (2000, January). Testosterone replacement and the physiologic aspects of aging in men. Mayo Clinic Proc. P. Supplement S83-7.

Munich, G., et. al. (1997). Influence of advanced glycation end-products and AGE-inhibitors on nucleation-dependent polymerization of beta-amyloid peptide. Biochemistry Biophysiology Acta. P. 17-29.

Munich, G., et. al. (1998). Alzheimer's disease-synergistic effects of glucose deficit, oxidative stress and advanced glycation end products. Journal of Neural Transmission. P. 439-461.

Murray, Michael T., N.D. & Pizzorno, Joseph E., Jr., N.D. (1996). A Textbook of Natural Medicine, Volumes I and II. Bastyr University Publications, Bothell, Washington.

Murray, Michael T., N.D. (1996). Saw Palmetto: Nature's answer to enlarged prostate. Health Counselor Magazine. P. 9-12.

Nagal, K., et. al. (1986). Action of carnosine and beta-alanine on wound healing. Surgery. P. 815-21.

Nankin, H.R., et. al. (December 6, 1986). Decreased bioavailable testosterone in aging normal and Impotent men. Journal of Clinical Endocrinology Metabolism. P. 1418-20. (On-line) PMID: 3782425.

Ong, P.J., et. al. (2000, January 15). Testosterone enhances flow-mediated brachial artery reactivity in men with coronary artery disease. American Journal of Cardiology. P. 269-272.

Panzer, A. (1997, June). Melatonin in osteosarcoma: an effective drug? Medical Hypotheses. P. 523-525. (On-line) PMID: 9247897

Parker, D.R., Jr. & Conway-Meyers, B.A. (1998, May). The effects of dehydroepiandrosterone (DHEA) on the thymus, spleen, and adrenals of prepubertal and adult female rats. Endocrinology Research. P. 113-126. (On-line) PMID: 9738691.

Pasquali, R. et. al. (1997, May). Effects of acute hyperinsulinemia on testosterone serum concentrations in adult obese and normal weight men. Metabolism. P. 526-9.

Phillips, G.B. (1994, May). The association of hypotestosteronemia with coronary artery disease in men. Arterioscler Thromb. P. 701-706.
Phillips, G.B., Pinkernell, B.H., & Jing, T.Y. (1996, November). The association of hyperestrogenemia with coronary thrombosis in men. Arterioscler. Thromb. Vascular Biology?. P. 1383-1387.

Preston, J.E., et. al. (1998). Toxic effects of beta-amyloid (25-35) on immortalized rat brain endothelial cell: protection by carnosine, homocysteine and beta-alanine. Neuroscience Letter. P. 1105-8.

The Editors of Prevention Health Books. (1996) Healing With Vitamins. Rodale Press, Inc., Emmaus, Pennsylvania.

Quinn, P.J., et. al. (1992). Carnosine: its properties, functions and potential therapeutic applications. Molecular Aspects of Medicine. P. 379-444.

Rako, S. (1998, September). Testosterone deficiency: a key factor in the increased cardiovascular risk to women following hysterectomy or with natural aging? Journal of Women's Health. P. 825-829. (On-line) PMID: 9785308.

Rako, S. (2000, October). Testosterone supplemental therapy after hysterectomy with or without concomitant oophorectomy: estrogen alone is not enough. Journal of Women's Health. P. 917-23.

Reichman, Judith, M.D., (1999, March) Passion Potion, Gynecologist and author Judith Reichman promotes testosterone as a boost for lack luster libido in women. People Magazine. P. 119-120.

Reiter, R.J. (1995, October). Oxygen radical detoxification processes during aging: the functional importance of melatonin. Aging (Milano). P. 340-351.

Rizza, R.A. (200, January). Androgen effect on insulin action and glucose metabolism. Mayo Clinic Proc. P. Supplement S61-4.

Rosano, G.M., et. al. (1999, April). Acute anti-ischemic effect of testosterone in men with coronary artery disease. Circulation. P. 1666-70.

Rudman, Daniel, M.D., (1990, July). Effects of Human Growth Hormone in Men Over 60 Years Old. The New England Journal of Medicine. P. 1-6.

Russell-Jones, D.L., Weissberger, A.J., Bowes, S.B., Kelly, J.M., Thomason, M. Umpleby, A.M., Jones, R.H. & Sonksen, P.H. (1993, April) The effects of growth hormone on protein metabolism in adult growth hormone deficient patients. Clinical Endocrinology. (On-line) PMID 8319375.

Sadovsky, Richard, M.D. (1997) Plasma Total Testosterone and Cardiovascular Risk Factors. American Family Physician. P. 2284.

Sahelian, Ray, M.D. (1998). 5-HTP Nature's Serotonin Solution. Avery Publishing Group, Garden City Park, New York.

Santen, Richard J., and Petroni, Gina R. (June, 1999) Relative Versus Attributable Risk of Breast Cancer from Estrogen Replacement Therapy. The Journal of Clinical Endocrinology & Metabolism. P. 1875-1881.

Schmidt, A.M., et. al. (1999). Activation of receptor for advanced glycation end products: a mechanism for chronic vascular dysfunction in diabetic vasculopathy and atherosclerosis. Circulation Research. P. 489-97.

Sears, Barry, Ph.D. (1995). Enter The Zone. HarperCollins Publishers, Inc., New York, New York.

Sears, Barry, Ph.D. (1997). Mastering The Zone. HarperCollins Publishers, Inc., New York, New York.

Sears, Barry, Ph.D. (1999). Zone Meals In Minutes. HarperCollins Publishers, Inc. New York, New York.

Sears, Barry, Ph.D. (2000). The Soy Zone. HarperCollins Publishers, Inc., New York, New York.

Sewell, D.A., et. al. (1998). The Effect of Acute Dietary Creatine Supplementation Upon Indices of Renal, Hepatic, and Hematological Function in Humans. Proceedings of the Nutrition Society. P17A.

Sherwin, B.B. (1998). Estrogen and/or androgen replacement therapy and cognitive functioning in surgically menopausal women. Psychoneuroendocrinology. P. 345-357. (On-line) PMID: 3067252.

Shifren, J.L., et. al. (2000, September). Transdermal testosterone treatment in women with impaired sexual function after oophorectomy. New England Journal of Medicine. P. 682-8.

Sih, R., Morley, J.E., Kaiser, F.E., Perry, H.M. 3rd, Patrick, P. & Ross, C. (1997, June). Testosterone replacement in older hypogonadal men: a 12-month randomized controlled trial. Journal of Clinical Endocrinology Metabolism. P. 1661-1667. (On-line) PMID: 9177359.

Skaggs, S.R. & Cris, D.M. (1991) Exogenous human growth hormone reduces body fat in obese women. Hormone Res. P. 19-24. (On-line) PMID: 1916649.

Smith, M.A., et. al. (1998). Cytochemical demonstration of oxidative damage in Alzheimer disease by immunochemical enhancement of the carbonyl reaction with 2,44-dinitrophenylhydrazine. Journal of Histochemistry Cytochemistry. P. 731-5.

Solomon, F., Cuneo, R.C., Hesp, R. & Sonksen, R.H. (1989, December) New England Journal of Medicine. The effects of treatment with recombinant human growth hormone on body composition and metabolism in adults with growth hormone deficiency. P. 1797-1803. (On-line). PMID: 2687691.

Stadtman, E.R. (1992). Protein oxidation and aging. Science. P. 1220-4.

Stadtman, E.R., et. al. (2000). Protein Oxidation. Annals New York Academy of Science. P. 191-208.

Stellato, R.K. (2000, April 23). Testosterone, sex hormone-binding globulin, and the development of type 2 diabetes in middle-aged men: prospective results from the Massachusetts male aging study. Diabetes Care. P. 490-4.

Stiller, M.J., Shupack, J.L., Kenny, C. Jondreau, L., Cohen, D.E. & Soter, N.A. (1994, April). A double-blind, placebo-controlled clinical trial to evaluate the safety and efficacy of thymopentin as an adjunctive treatment in atopic dermatitis. Journal of American Academy of Dermatology. P. 597-602. (On-line) PMID: 8157786.

Stuerenburg, E.R., et. al. (1999). Concentrations of free carnosine (a putative membranne-protective antioxidant) in human muscle biopsies and rat muscles. Archives Gerontology Geriatrics. P. 107-113.

Stvolinsky, S.L., et. al. (1999). Carnosine: an endogenous neuroprotector in the ischaemic brain. Cellular Molecular Neurobiology. P. 45-56.

Tan, Robert, M.D. & Bransgrove, Linda, Ph.D. (1997, September) Andropause: Is There a Place for Hormone Replacement Therapy? Clinical Geriatrics. P. 46-48, 57. Thomas, T., et. al. (1996). B-Amyloid-mediated vasoactivity and vascular endothelial damage. Nature. P. 168-71.

Tricker, R., et. al. (1996, October). The effects of supraphysiological doses of testosterone on angry behavior in healthy eugonadal men-a clinical research center study. The Journal of Clinical Endocrinology Metabolism. P. 3754-8.

Trotto, Nancy E. (1999) Exercise Prescription. (On-line). A4M - World Health Network - Longevity, Life Expectancy & Anti-Aging Medicine.

Tsai, E.C., et. al. (2000, April 24). Low serum testosterone level as a predictor of increased visceral fat in Japanese-American men. International Journal Obesity Related Metabolic Disorders. P. 485-91.

Unimed Pharmaceuticals. (1997, September) Unimed Pharmaceuticals Initiates Phase III Geriatric Hypogonadism Study in Elderly Men, Broad U.S. Patent Covering DHT Delivery for Androgen Therapy is Issued.

Valentine, Gail, D.O. (1997, October). Natural Progesterone. Life Enhancement. P. 11-15.

Vance, Mary Lee, M.D. & Mauras, Nelly, M.D. (1999, October) Growth Hormone Therapy In Adults And Children. The New England Journal of Medicine. P 1206 - 1216.

van den Beld, et. al. (2000, September). Measures of bioavailable serum testosterone and estradiol and their relationship with muscle strength, bone density, and body composition in elderly men. Journal of Clinical Endocrinology Metabolism. P. 3276-82.

van Vollenhoven, R.F., Morabito, L.M. Engleman, E.G. & McGuire, J.L. (1998, February). Treatment of systemic lupus erythematosus with dehydroepiandrosterone: 50 patients treated up to 12 months. Journal of Rheumatology. P. 285-289. (On-line) PMID: 9489820.

Vherhelst, J., Aabs, R., Vandeweghe, M. Mockel, J., Legros, J.J., Copinschi, G., Mahler, C., Velkeniers, A.B., Vanhaelst, L.L., Van Aelst, A., De Rijdt, D. Stevenaert, A. & Beckers, A. (1997, October) Two years of replacement therapy in adults with growth hormone deficiency. Clinical Endocrinology. (On-line) PMID:

Viziiolli, M.R., et. al. (1983). Effects of carnosine on the development of rat sponge induced granulation tissue. II. Histoautoadlographic oberservations on collagen biosynthesis. Cellular Molecular Biology. P. 1-9.

Vukovich, M.D., et. al. (1997). Effect of B-Hydroxy B-Methylbutyrate (HMB) On VO2 Peak and Maximal Llactate in Endurance Trained Cyclists. Medicine & Science in Sports & Exercise. Pp.. 252.

Wagner, J.D., Cefalu, W.T., Anthony, M.S., Litwak, K.N., Zhang, L. & Clarkson, T.B. (NO DATE). Dietary soy protein and estrogen replacement therapy improve cardiovascular risk factors and decrease aortic cholesteryl ester content in over-iectomized cynomolgus monkeys. NO JOURNAL LISTED.

Wang, A.M., et. al. (2000). Use of carnosine as a natural anti-senescence drug for human beings. Biochemistry (Moscow). P. 898-71.

Wang, C., et. al. (2000). Transdermal Testosterone Gel Improves Sexual Function, Mood, Muscle Strength, and Body Composition Parameters in Hypogonadal Men. Journal of Clinical Endocrinology Metabolism. P. 2839-2853.

Warner, Susan L., M.D., MPH. (1995, October). Preventive Health Care for the Menopausal Woman. Infertility and Reproductive Medicine Clinica of North America. P. 675.

Webb, C.M., et. al. (1999, October). Effects of testosterone on coronary vasomotor regulation in men with coronary heart disease. Circulation. P. 1690-6.

Wolkowitz, O.M., Reus, V.I., Roberts, E., Manfredi, F., Chan, T., Raum, W.J., Ormiston, S., Johnson, R., Canick, J., Brizendine, L. & Weingertner, H. (1997, February). Dehydroepiandrsterone (DHEA) treatment of depression. Biological Psychiatry. P. 311-318. (On-line) PMID: 9024954.

Yamano, Y., Sakane, S., Takamatsu, J., Ohsawa. N. (1999, April). Estrogen supplementation for bone dematuration in young epileptic man treated with anticonvulsant therapy; a case report. Endocrinology Journal. (On-line) PMID: 10460015.

Yan, S.D., et. al. (1996). RAGE and amyloid-beta peptide neurotoxicity in Alzheimer's disease. Nature. P. 685-91.

Yuneva, M.O., et. al. (1999). Effect of carnosine on age-induced changes in seneescence-accelerated mice. Journal of Anti-Aging Medicine. P. 337-42.

Zaloga, G.P., et. al. (1997). Carnosine iss a novel peptide modulator of intracellular calcium and contractility in cardiac cells. American Journal of Physiology. P. 462-8.

Zhou, J., et. al. (2000, September). Testosterone inhibits estrogen-induced mammary epithelial proliferation and suppresses estrogen receptor expresssion. FASEB Journal. P. 1725-30.

Zinn, John Kabat, Ph.D. (1990). Full Catastrophe Living. Delacorte Press, New York, New York.

REFERENCES FOR HGH
REPLACEMENT THERAPY

Acid-labile subunit (ALS) measurements in children
http://www.ncbi.nlm.nih.gov/entrez/query.fcgi?cmd=Retrieve&db=PubMed&
list_uids=10890197&dopt=Abstract
Serum ALS levels are regulated by GH, and the measurement of ALS is useful for
the diagnosis of CGHD in children.

Structure and properties of members of the hGH family: a review.
Endocr J. 2000 Mar;47 Suppl:S1-8.
http://www.ncbi.nlm.nih.gov/entrez/query.fcgi?cmd=Retrieve&db=PubMed&
list_uids=10890174&dopt=Abstract
The hGH(44-191), strongly anti-insulin peptide, may be involved in diabetic
retinopathy. It is believed that this peptide is the long sought after diabetogenic
substance of the pituitary gland.

The novel hypothalamic peptide ghrelin stimulates food intake and growth hormone secretion.
Endocrinology. 2000 Nov;141(11):4325-8.
http://www.ncbi.nlm.nih.gov/entrez/query.fcgi?cmd=Retrieve&db=PubMed&
list_uids=11089570&dopt=Abstract
These data suggest a possible role for the newly identified endogenous hypothalamic peptide, ghrelin, in stimulation of feeding and growth hormone secretion.

The effect of four weeks of supraphysiological growth hormone administration
on the insulin-like growth factor axis in women and men. GH-2000 Study Group.
J Clin Endocrinol Metab. 2000 Nov;85(11):4193-200.
http://www.ncbi.nlm.nih.gov/entrez/query.fcgi?cmd=Retrieve&db=PubMed&
list_uids=11095453&dopt=Abstract
males are significantly more responsive than females to exogenous GH; 2) the
increase in IGF-I is more robust compared with those in IGFBP-3 and ALS; 3)
IGFBP-2 changes very little during GH treatment; and 4) among IGF-related substances, IGF-I is the most specific marker of supraphysiological GH exposure.

Effects of human growth hormone in men over 60 years old.
N Engl J Med. 1990 Jul 5;323(1):1-6.
http://www.ncbi.nlm.nih.gov/entrez/query.fcgi?cmd=Retrieve&db=PubMed&
list_uids=2355952&dopt=Abstract
Diminished secretion of growth hormone is responsible in part for the decrease
of lean body mass, the expansion of adipose-tissue mass, and the thinning of the
skin that occur in old age.

Is the somatopause an indication for growth hormone replacement?
J Endocrinol Invest. 1999;22(5 Suppl):142-9. Review.

http://www.ncbi.nlm.nih.gov/entrez/query.fcgi?cmd=Retrieve&db=PubMed&
list_uids=10442584&dopt=Abstract
The long-term safety of GH replacement is clearly a matter for concern but we do
now know that life without GH is poor both in quantity and quality.
Growth hormone - hormone replacement for the somatopause?
Horm Res. 2000;53 Suppl 3:37-41. Review.
http://www.ncbi.nlm.nih.gov/entrez/query.fcgi?cmd=Retrieve&db=PubMed&
list_uids=10971102&dopt=Abstract
Safety issues will require close scrutiny, but the data available so far are suffi-
ciently positive to undertake large multicentre, placebo-controlled trials, particu-
larly looking at endpoints associated with prevention of frailty and loss of inde-
pendence.

Interrelationships between growth hormone and sleep.
Growth Horm IGF Res. 2000 Apr;10 Suppl B:S57-62.
http://www.ncbi.nlm.nih.gov/entrez/query.fcgi?cmd=Retrieve&db=PubMed&
list_uids=10984255&dopt=Abstract
Pharmacological stimulation of SW sleep results in increased GH release, and
compounds that increase SW sleep may therefore represent a novel class of GH
secretagogues.

Age-related changes in slow wave sleep and REM sleep and relationship with
growth hormone and cortisol levels in healthy men.
JAMA. 2000 Aug 16;284(7):861-8.
http://www.ncbi.nlm.nih.gov/entrez/query.fcgi?cmd=Retrieve&db=PubMed&
list_uids=10938176&dopt=Abstract
In men, age-related changes in slow wave sleep and REM sleep occur with
markedly different chronologies and are each associated with specific hormonal
alterations.

Age-related alterations in sleep quality and neuroendocrine function: interrelationships and implications.
JAMA. 2000 Aug 16;284(7):879-81.
http://jama.ama-assn.org/issues/v284n7/ffull/jed00060.html
age-related alterations in sleep quality may contribute to concomitant changes in
body composition and function via their influence on neuroendocrine functions;
some of the "age changes" are firmly in place and therapeutic interventions
should be assessed relatively early in adult life; and measures that augment SW
sleep may potentially serve as useful therapeutic GH secretagogues.

Growth hormone treatment of abdominally obese men reduces abdominal fat
mass, improves glucose and lipoprotein metabolism, and reduces diastolic blood
pressure.
J Clin Endocrinol Metab. 1997 Mar;82(3):727-34.
http://www.ncbi.nlm.nih.gov/entrez/query.fcgi?cmd=Retrieve&db=PubMed&
list_uids=9062473&dopt=Abstract
GH can favorably affect some of the multiple perturbations associated with

abdominal/visceral obesity. This includes a reduction in abdominal/visceral obesity, an improved insulin sensitivity, and favorable effects on lipoprotein metabolism and diastolic blood pressure.

Impact of acute exercise intensity on pulsatile growth hormone release in men.
J Appl Physiol. 1999 Aug;87(2):498-504.
http://www.ncbi.nlm.nih.gov/entrez/query.fcgi?cmd=Retrieve&db=PubMed&list_uids=10444604&dopt=Abstract
The GH secretory response to exercise is related to exercise intensity in a linear dose-response pattern in young men.

Ipamorelin, a new growth-hormone-releasing peptide, induces longitudinal bone growth in rats.
Growth Horm IGF Res. 1999 Apr;9(2):106-13.
http://www.ncbi.nlm.nih.gov/entrez/query.fcgi?cmd=Retrieve&db=PubMed&list_uids=10373343&dopt=Abstract
Whether ipamorelin or other GH secretagogues may have a place in the treatment of children with growth retardation requires demonstration in future clinical studies.

Oral arginine-lysine does not increase growth hormone or insulin-like growth factor-I in old men.
J Gerontol. 1993 Jul;48(4):M128-33.
http://www.ncbi.nlm.nih.gov/entrez/query.fcgi?cmd=Retrieve&db=PubMed&list_uids=8315224&dopt=Abstract
Oral arginine/lysine is not a practical means of chronically enhancing GH secretion in old men.

Endocrine and lipid effects of oral L-arginine treatment in healthy post-menopausal women.
J Lab Clin Med. 2000 Mar;135(3):231-7.
http://www.ncbi.nlm.nih.gov/entrez/query.fcgi?cmd=Retrieve&db=PubMed&list_uids=10711861&dopt=Abstract
The observed lack of effect on major endocrine hormones and lipid profile support the safety of oral L-arginine administration.

Insulin-like growth factor-I and cognitive function in healthy older men.
J Clin Endocrinol Metab. 1999 Feb;84(2):471-5.
http://www.ncbi.nlm.nih.gov/entrez/query.fcgi?cmd=Retrieve&db=PubMed&list_uids=10022403&dopt=Abstract
circulating IGF-I may play a role in the age-related reduction of certain cognitive functions, specifically speed of information processing.

Growth hormone increases connexin-43 expression in the cerebral cortex and hypothalamus.
Endocrinology. 2000 Oct;141(10):3879-86.
http://www.ncbi.nlm.nih.gov/entrez/query.fcgi?cmd=Retrieve&db=PubMed&

list_uids=11014245&dopt=Abstract
The results show that administration of bGH increases the abundance of cx43 in specific brain regions, suggesting that GH may influence gap junction formation and thereby intercellular communication in the brain.

Growth hormone in the brain: characteristics of specific brain targets for the hormone and their functional significance.
Front Neuroendocrinol. 2000 Oct;21(4):330-48.
http://www.ncbi.nlm.nih.gov/entrez/query.fcgi?cmd=Retrieve&db=PubMed&list_uids=11013068&dopt=Abstract
The functions mediated by the GH receptors identified in the hippocampus are not yet known but recently it was speculated that they may be involved in the hormone's action on memory and cognitive functions.

Effects of two years of growth hormone (GH) replacement therapy on bone metabolism and mineral density in childhood and adulthood onset GH deficient patients.
J Endocrinol Invest. 1999 May;22(5):333-9.
http://www.ncbi.nlm.nih.gov/entrez/query.fcgi?cmd=Retrieve&db=PubMed&list_uids=10401706&dopt=Abstract
Patients with childhood or adulthood onset GH deficiency have osteopenia that can be improved by long-term treatment with GH.

Growth hormone and mild exercise in combination markedly enhance cortical bone formation and strength in old rats.
Endocrinology. 1998 Apr;139(4):1899-904.
http://www.ncbi.nlm.nih.gov/entrez/query.fcgi?cmd=Retrieve&db=PubMed&list_uids=9528976&dopt=Abstract
GH injections and mild excercise in combination modulate and increase further the formation and strength of cortical bone in old female rats.

Bone loss is correlated to the severity of growth hormone deficiency in adult patients with hypopituitarism.
J Clin Endocrinol Metab. 1999 Jun;84(6):1919-24.
http://www.ncbi.nlm.nih.gov/entrez/query.fcgi?cmd=Retrieve&db=PubMed&list_uids=10372687&dopt=Abstract
A significant reduction of BMD associated with abnormalities of bone turnover parameters was found only in patients with very severe or severe GHD, whereas normal BMD values were found in non-GHD hypopituitary patients.

Hip fracture patients, a group of frail elderly people with low bone mineral density, muscle mass and IGF-I levels.
Acta Physiol Scand. 1999 Dec;167(4):347-50.
http://www.ncbi.nlm.nih.gov/entrez/query.fcgi?cmd=Retrieve&db=PubMed&list_uids=10632638&dopt=Abstract
A lower IGF-I level and lower bone and lean body mass in hip fracture patients than in an age-matched group of patients have been found.

Effect of recombinant human growth hormone in elderly osteoporotic women.
Clin Endocrinol (Oxf). 1999 Dec;51(6):715-24.
http://www.ncbi.nlm.nih.gov/entrez/query.fcgi?cmd=Retrieve&db=PubMed&
list_uids=10619976&dopt=Abstract
GH attenuates the decrease in muscle strength and bone mass as well as the gain
of abdominal fat with ageing in elderly women.

Effects of physiologic growth hormone therapy on bone density and body composition in patients with adult-onset growth hormone deficiency. A randomized,
placebo-controlled trial.
Ann Intern Med. 1996 Dec 1;125(11):883-90.
http://www.ncbi.nlm.nih.gov/entrez/query.fcgi?cmd=Retrieve&db=PubMed&
list_uids=8967668&dopt=Abstract
Growth hormone administered to men with adult-onset growth hormone deficiency at a dose adjusted according to serum IGF-1 levels increases bone density
and stimulates bone turnover, decreases body fat and increases lean mass, and is
associated with a low incidence of side effects.

Effects of 42 months of GH treatment on bone mineral density and bone turnover
in GH-deficient adults.
Eur J Endocrinol. 1999 Jun;140(6):545-54.
http://www.ncbi.nlm.nih.gov/entrez/query.fcgi?cmd=Retrieve&db=PubMed&
list_uids=10377504&dopt=Abstract
GH treatment in GH-deficient adults increased BMD for up to 30-36 months, with
a plateau thereafter. Concurrently with the plateau in BMD the bone turnover rate
normalized.

Effect of aging on growth hormone-induced insulin-like growth factor-I secretion
from cultured rat chondrocytes.
Growth Horm IGF Res. 1998 Oct;8(5):403-9.
http://www.ncbi.nlm.nih.gov/entrez/query.fcgi?cmd=Retrieve&db=PubMed&
list_uids=10984302&dopt=Abstract
GH availability in the course of aging appears to be a determinant factor in tissue
responsiveness and underscores the hypothesis that GH replacement could present a therapeutic potential against the aging senescent changes.

The effects of 10 years of recombinant human growth hormone (GH) in adult GH-
deficient patients.
J Clin Endocrinol Metab. 1999 Aug;84(8):2596-602.
http://www.ncbi.nlm.nih.gov/entrez/query.fcgi?cmd=Retrieve&db=PubMed&
list_uids=10443645&dopt=Abstract
GH treatment for 10 yr in GHD adults resulted in increased lean body and muscle mass, a less atherogenic lipid profile, reduced carotid intima media thickness,
and improved psychological well-being.

Growth hormone (GH) treatment reverses early atherosclerotic changes in GH-deficient adults.
J Clin Endocrinol Metab. 1999 Feb;84(2):453-7.
http://www.ncbi.nlm.nih.gov/entrez/query.fcgi?cmd=Retrieve&db=PubMed&list_uids=10022400&dopt=Abstract
GH treatment of hypopituitary GHD men reverses early morphological and functional atherosclerotic changes in major arteries and, if maintained, may reduce vascular morbidity and mortality. GH seems to act via IGF-I, which is known to have important effects on endothelial cell function.

Decrease in carotid intima-media thickness after one year growth hormone (GH) treatment in adults with GH deficiency.
J Clin Endocrinol Metab. 1999 Apr;84(4):1329-33.
http://www.ncbi.nlm.nih.gov/entrez/query.fcgi?cmd=Retrieve&db=PubMed&list_uids=10199774&dopt=Abstract
The contrast between the limited metabolic effect of treatment and the importance and precocity of the changes in IMT suggests that the decrease in IMT was not exclusively attributable to a reversal in the atherosclerotic process.

A preliminary study of growth hormone in the treatment of dilated cardiomyopathy.
N Engl J Med. 1996 Mar 28;334(13):809-14.
http://www.ncbi.nlm.nih.gov/entrez/query.fcgi?cmd=Retrieve&db=PubMed&list_uids=8596546&dopt=Abstract
Recombinant human growth hormone administered for three months to patients with idiopathic dilated cardiomyopathy increased myocardial mass and reduced the size of the left ventricular chamber, resulting in improvement in hemodynamics, myocardial energy metabolism, and clinical status.

Growth hormone improves cardiac function in rats with experimental myocardial infarction.
Eur J Clin Invest. 1997 Jun;27(6):517-25.
http://www.ncbi.nlm.nih.gov/entrez/query.fcgi?cmd=Retrieve&db=PubMed&list_uids=9229233&dopt=Abstract
GH in a physiological dose improves systolic function in an experimental model of heart failure without signs of hypertrophy, suggesting a potential role as a therapeutic agent in the treatment of heart failure and merits further investigation.

The growth hormone secretagogue hexarelin improves cardiac function in rats after experimental myocardial infarction.
Endocrinology. 2000 Jan;141(1):60-6.
http://www.ncbi.nlm.nih.gov/entrez/query.fcgi?cmd=Retrieve&db=PubMed&list_uids=10614623&dopt=Abstract
Hex improves cardiac function and decreases peripheral resistance to a similar extent as exogenous GH in rats postmyocardial infarction.

Impaired cardiac performance in elderly patients with growth hormone deficiency.
J Clin Endocrinol Metab. 1999 Nov;84(11):3950-5.
http://www.ncbi.nlm.nih.gov/entrez/query.fcgi?cmd=Retrieve&db=PubMed&list_uids=10566633&dopt=Abstract
Disease duration was significantly correlated with heart rate at peak exercise (r = 0.614; P < 0.05) and with systolic and diastolic blood pressures both at rest (r = 0.745; P < 0.01 and r = 0.650; P < 0.05) and at peak exercise (r = 0.684; P < 0.05 and r =

Growth hormone for optimization of refractory heart failure treatment.
Arq Bras Cardiol. 1999 Oct;73(4):391-8.
http://www.ncbi.nlm.nih.gov/entrez/query.fcgi?cmd=Retrieve&db=PubMed&list_uids=10754593&dopt=Abstract
Growth hormone may benefit selected patients with refractory heart failure

Growth hormone (GH) status is an independent determinant of serum levels of cholesterol and triglycerides in healthy adults.
Clin Endocrinol (Oxf). 1999 Sep;51(3):309-16.
http://www.ncbi.nlm.nih.gov/entrez/query.fcgi?cmd=Retrieve&db=PubMed&list_uids=10469010&dopt=Abstract
GH may exert direct effects on lipid metabolism.

Interrelationships of spontaneous growth hormone axis activity, body fat, and serum lipids in healthy elderly women and men.
Metabolism. 1999 Nov;48(11):1424-31.
http://www.ncbi.nlm.nih.gov/entrez/query.fcgi?cmd=Retrieve&db=PubMed&list_uids=10582552&dopt=Abstract
Endogenous nocturnal GH secretion predicts total, LDL, and HDL cholesterol levels independently of total or abdominal fat, suggesting that it is an independent cardiometabolic risk factor in healthy elderly people.

Effects of growth hormone administration on inflammatory and other cardiovascular risk markers in men with growth hormone deficiency. A randomized, controlled clinical trial.
Ann Intern Med. 2000 Jul 18;133(2):111-22.
http://www.ncbi.nlm.nih.gov/entrez/query.fcgi?cmd=Retrieve&db=PubMed&list_uids=10896637&dopt=Abstract
Long-term growth hormone replacement in men reduces levels of inflammatory cardiovascular risk markers, decreases central fat, and increases lipoprotein(a) and glucose levels without affecting lipid levels.

The somatogenic hormones and insulin-like growth factor-1: stimulators of lymphopoiesis and immune function.
Endocr Rev. 1997 Apr;18(2):157-79. Review. No abstract available.
http://www.ncbi.nlm.nih.gov/entrez/query.fcgi?cmd=Retrieve&db=PubMed&list_uids=9101135&dopt=Abstract

The immune-endocrine loop during aging: role of growth hormone and insulin-like growth factor-I.
Neuroimmunomodulation. 1999 Jan-Apr;6(1-2):56-68. Review.
http://www.ncbi.nlm.nih.gov/entrez/query.fcgi?cmd=Retrieve&db=PubMed&list_uids=9876236&dopt=Abstract
The sharing of common activation molecules, despite vastly different protein structures of their receptors, forms a molecular explanation for the possibility of cross talk between IL-4 and IGF-I in regulating many of the events associated with hematopoietic differentiation, proliferation and survival.

A preliminary study of growth hormone therapy for Crohn's disease.
N Engl J Med. 2000 Jun 1;342(22):1633-7.
Growth hormone and body composition.
J Pediatr Endocrinol Metab. 1996 Jun;9 Suppl 3:365-8. Review
http://www.ncbi.nlm.nih.gov/entrez/query.fcgi?cmd=Retrieve&db=PubMed&list_uids=8887182&dopt=Abstract
Knowledge of the actions of growth hormone (GH) and the clinical consequences of GH deficiency has increased enormously within the last decade.

Growth Hormone and Adipocyte Function in Obesity.
Horm Res. 2000 Jul;53 Suppl S1:87-97.
http://www.ncbi.nlm.nih.gov/entrez/query.fcgi?cmd=Retrieve&db=PubMed&list_uids=10895049&dopt=Abstract
GH treatment has a favorable effect on obesity-associated dyslipidemia, but the effects on insulin sensitivity have been conflicting.

Psychosocial and CNS effects. Growth hormone in adults 1996, Cambridge University Press.
Book. No web address available.

A preliminary study of growth hormone therapy for Crohn's disease.
N Engl J Med. 2000 Jun 1;342(22):1633-7.
http://www.ncbi.nlm.nih.gov/entrez/query.fcgi?cmd=Retrieve&db=PubMed&list_uids=10833209&dopt=Abstract
The preliminary study suggests that growth hormone may be a beneficial treatment for patients with Crohn's disease.

The growth hormone (GH)-releasing hormone-GH-insulin-like growth factor-1 axis in patients with fibromyalgia syndrome.
J Clin Endocrinol Metab. 1999 Sep;84(9):3378-81.
http://www.ncbi.nlm.nih.gov/entrez/query.fcgi?cmd=Retrieve&db=PubMed&list_uids=10487713&dopt=Abstract
Patients with FM exhibited a marked decrease in spontaneous GH secretion, but normal pituitary responsiveness to exogenously administered GHRH, thus suggesting the existence of an alteration at the hypothalamic level in the neuroendocrine control of GH in these patients.

Growth hormone, burns and tissue healing.
Growth Horm IGF Res. 2000 Apr;10 Suppl B:S39-43.
http://www.ncbi.nlm.nih.gov/entrez/query.fcgi?cmd=Retrieve&db=PubMed&
list_uids=10984252&dopt=Abstract
Positive results reported regarding both the efficacy and safety of GH and IGF-I,
therefore warranting continued investigation.

Increased mortality associated with growth hormone treatment in critically ill
adults.
N Engl J Med. 1999 Sep 9;341(11):785-92.
http://www.ncbi.nlm.nih.gov/entrez/query.fcgi?cmd=Retrieve&db=PubMed&
list_uids=10477776&dopt=Abstract
In patients with prolonged critical illness, high doses of growth hormone are
associated with increased morbidity and mortality.

Bengtsson, Bengt-Ake
http://jcem.endojournals.org/cgi/search?volume=84&firstpage=&author1=Ben
gtsson&author2=&titleabstract=&fulltext=&journalcode=jcem&fmonth=Sep&fy
ear=1998&tmonth=Dec&tyear=2000&hits=10&sendit=Search&fdatedef=1+Septe
mber+1965&tdatedef=1+December+2000
Multiple articles written by this author in this issue of the journal. See site above
for more information.

Growth hormone therapy in adults and children.
N Engl J Med. 1999 Oct 14;341(16):1206-16. Review.
http://www.nejm.org/content/1999/0341/0016/1206.asp

Growth hormone therapy and malignancy.
Horm Res. 1997;48 Suppl 4:29-32. Review.
http://www.ncbi.nlm.nih.gov/entrez/query.fcgi?cmd=Retrieve&db=PubMed&
list_uids=9350443&dopt=Abstract
So far the results from single centre studies and from the pharmaceutical industry surveillance programs have shown no evidence of an increased risk of malignancy, recurrent or de novo.

Long-term risk of gastrointestinal tumor recurrence after postoperative treatment
with recombinant human growth hormone.
JPEN J Parenter Enteral Nutr. 2000 May-Jun;24(3):140-4.
http://www.ncbi.nlm.nih.gov/entrez/query.fcgi?cmd=Retrieve&db=PubMed&
list_uids=10850937&dopt=Abstract
The results demonstrate no evidence for an increased risk of tumor recurrence
after rhGH treatment for a short period of time after removal of a gastrointestinal
adenocarcinoma.

Beenties et al. Clinical Endocrinology 2000 Apr ; 52(4): 457-62
No title. No abstract available.

No evidence of tumor growth stimulation in human tumors in vitro following treatment with recombinant human growth hormone.
Anticancer Drugs. 2000 Sep;11(8):659-64.
http://www.ncbi.nlm.nih.gov/entrez/query.fcgi?cmd=Retrieve&db=PubMed&list_uids=11081460&dopt=Abstract
This preclinical study in 20 human tumor models indicated no direct risk for tumor growth enhancement.

Prospective study of colorectal cancer risk in men and plasma levels of insulin-like growth factor (IGF)-I and IGF-binding protein-3.
J Natl Cancer Inst. 1999 Apr 7;91(7):620-5.
http://www.ncbi.nlm.nih.gov/entrez/query.fcgi?cmd=Retrieve&db=PubMed&list_uids=10203281&dopt=Abstract
The findings suggest that circulating IGF-I and IGFBP-3 are related to future risk of colorectal cancer.

Insulin-like growth factor-I and binding protein-3 and risk of cancer.
Horm Res. 1999;51 Suppl 3:34-41. Review.
http://www.ncbi.nlm.nih.gov/entrez/query.fcgi?cmd=Retrieve&db=PubMed&list_uids=10592442&dopt=Abstract
High levels of IGF-I and low levels of IGFBP-3 are associated with an increased risk of at least several types of carcinoma that are common in economically developed countries.

P53 and IGFBP-3: apoptosis and cancer protection.
Mol Genet Metab. 2000 Jun;70(2):85-98. Review.
http://www.ncbi.nlm.nih.gov/entrez/query.fcgi?cmd=Retrieve&db=PubMed&list_uids=10873390&dopt=Abstract
IGFBP-3 induction by p53 constitutes a new means of cross-talk between the p53 and IGF axes, and suggests that the ultimate function of IGFBP-3 may be to serve a protective role against the potentially carcinogenic effects of growth hormone and IGF-I.

The insulin-like growth factor binding protein superfamily: new perspectives.
Pediatrics. 1999 Oct;104(4 Pt 2):1018-21.
http://www.ncbi.nlm.nih.gov/entrez/query.fcgi?cmd=Retrieve&db=PubMed&list_uids=10506255&dopt=Abstract
Low-affinity binders are members of an IGFBP superfamily, capable of regulating cell growth by both IGF-dependent and IGF-independent mechanisms.insulin-like growth factor, insulin-like growth factor binding proteins

Blum W. IGF and IGFBP Growth Hormone in Adults,1996, Cambridge University Press
Book. No web address available.

Plasma and Insulin-like Growth Factor-I and Prostate Cancer Risk: A Prospective Study (Chan)

http://www.sciencemag.org/cgi/content/abstract/279/5350/563
Identification of plasma IGF-I as a predictor of prostate cancer risk may have
implications for risk reduction and treatment.

The significance of serum levels of insulin-like growth factor-1 in patients with
prostate cancer.
BJU Int. 2000 Jan;85(1):125-9.
http://www.ncbi.nlm.nih.gov/entrez/query.fcgi?cmd=Retrieve&db=PubMed&
list_uids=10619960&dopt=Abstract
No significant association between IGF-1 serum levels and prostate cancer. Short-
term androgen withdrawal using LHRH analogues combined with anti-andro-
gens had no effect on the levels of IGF-1.

Racial variation in insulin-like growth factor-1 and binding protein-3 concentrations in middle-aged men.
Cancer Epidemiol Biomarkers Prev. 1999 Dec;8(12):1107-10.
http://www.ncbi.nlm.nih.gov/entrez/query.fcgi?cmd=Retrieve&db=PubMed&
list_uids=10613344&dopt=Abstract
Although differences in circulating IGF-1 do not seem to account for the greater
prostate cancer risk among African-American men, their absolute lower levels of
IGFBP-3 may be contributory.

Effect of growth hormone (GH) and insulin-like growth factor I on prostate diseases: an ultrasonographic and endocrine study in acromegaly, GH deficiency,
and healthy subjects.
J Clin Endocrinol Metab. 1999 Jun;84(6):1986-91.
http://www.ncbi.nlm.nih.gov/entrez/query.fcgi?cmd=Retrieve&db=PubMed&
list_uids=10372698&dopt=Abstract
Chronic excess of GH and IGF-I cause prostate overgrowth and further phenom-
ena of rearrangement, but not prostate cancer.

Insulin-like growth factor I is not a useful marker of prostate cancer in men with
elevated levels of prostate-specific antigen.
J Clin Endocrinol Metab. 2000 Aug;85(8):2744-7.
http://www.ncbi.nlm.nih.gov/entrez/query.fcgi?cmd=Retrieve&db=PubMed&
list_uids=10946875&dopt=Abstract
In screen-positive men with elevated serum PSA, serum IGF-I is not a useful diagnostic test for prostate cancer, but it may be associated with benign prostatic
hyperplasia and enlargement.

Growth Hormone and Prostate Cancer: Guilty by Association? (Grimberg)
http://www.kurtis.it/endoinv2.htm
Clinical state, body composition and IGF-I assessed together remain the best
methods of monitoring GH replacement therapy and that measurements of
IGFBP-3 and ALS do not confer any advantage over IGF-I.

Growth hormone replacement therapy in the elderly with hypothalamic-pituitary

disease: a dose-finding study.
J Clin Endocrinol Metab. 1999 Jan;84(1):131-6.
http://www.ncbi.nlm.nih.gov/entrez/query.fcgi?cmd=Retrieve&db=PubMed&list_uids=9920073&dopt=Abstract
GH replacement dose in elderly subjects is considerably lower than that required by younger adults with GH deficiency.

Optimizing growth hormone replacement therapy by dose titration in hypopituitary adults.
J Clin Endocrinol Metab. 1998 Nov;83(11):3913-9.
http://www.ncbi.nlm.nih.gov/entrez/query.fcgi?cmd=Retrieve&db=PubMed&list_uids=9814468&dopt=Abstract
This is the first report of a uniform titration regimen based on a defined target range of serum IGF-I in a large patient cohort.

Murray et al. Clinical Endocrinology. May 52(5): 537-42
No Title. No abstract available.

Growth hormone therapy in adults and children
341 (16):1206 - Review Article
Vance ML, Mauras N

Laursen ,T. Pharmacological aspects of GH replacement therapy. Growth Hormone in Adults,1996, Cambridge University Press.
Book. No address available.

A switch from oral (2 mg/day) to transdermal (50 microg/day) 17beta-estradiol therapy increases serum insulin-like growth factor-I levels in recombinant human growth hormone (GH)-substituted women with GH deficiency.
J Clin Endocrinol Metab. 2000 Jan;85(1):464-7.
http://www.ncbi.nlm.nih.gov/entrez/query.fcgi?cmd=Retrieve&db=PubMed&list_uids=10634425&dopt=Abstract
Further investigation should be undertaken to answer the question whether the increase in serum IGF-I levels is due to lower serum levels of estradiol or to differences in the mode of administration of estradiol.

Route of estrogen administration helps to determine growth hormone (GH) replacement dose in GH-deficient adults.
J Clin Endocrinol Metab. 1999 Nov;84(11):3956-60.
http://www.ncbi.nlm.nih.gov/entrez/query.fcgi?cmd=Retrieve&db=PubMed&list_uids=10566634&dopt=Abstract
The observations may be useful in anticipating appropriate starting and final doses of GH in adult hypopituitary patients.

Sustained release of human growth hormone from PLGA solution depots.
Pharm Res. 1999 Dec;16(12):1825-9.
http://www.ncbi.nlm.nih.gov/entrez/query.fcgi?cmd=Retrieve&db=PubMed&

list_uids=10644069&dopt=AbstractBy taking advantage of the effects of low aqueous affinity and protein particle densification, a PLGA solution depot was produced with the capability of sustaining hGH levels in normal rats at a serum level of 10 to 200 ng/ml for 28 days.

The stabilization and encapsulation of human growth hormone into biodegradable microspheres.
Pharm Res. 1997 Jun;14(6):730-5.
http://www.ncbi.nlm.nih.gov/entrez/query.fcgi?cmd=Retrieve&db=PubMed&list_uids=9210189&dopt=Abstract
Using a novel process, rhGH can be stabilized and encapsulated in a solid state into PLGA microspheres and released with unaltered properties at different rates.

The effects of treatment and the individual responsiveness to growth hormone (GH) replacement therapy in 665 GH-deficient adults. KIMS Study Group and the KIMS International Board.
J Clin Endocrinol Metab. 1999 Nov;84(11):3929-35.
http://www.ncbi.nlm.nih.gov/entrez/query.fcgi?cmd=Retrieve&db=PubMed&list_uids=10566630&dopt=Abstract
Large longitudinal surveillance databases can serve in defining the optimum dose regimen for GH replacement and indicate that women may need a higher replacement dose of GH than men.

Long-Term Effects of Growth Hormone (GH) Replacement in Men with Childhood-Onset GH Deficiency
J Clin Endocrinol Metab 1999 84: 2373-2380.
http://jcem.endojournals.org/cgi/content/abstract/84/7/2373
Long term GH replacement is safe and beneficial. It improves cardiac performance without inducing left ventricular hypertrophy and progressively increases bone mineral density.